THE DISTANT DRUM

A record of 'old, unhappy, far-off things,
and battles long ago'.

'Oh, the brave music of a *distant* drum.'
Omar Khayyam

The Distant Drum: A Memoir of a Guardsman in the Great War

'Dedicated to my friends in the Household Battalion and the Coldstream Guards.'

This edition published in 2010 by Frontline Books, an imprint of
Pen and Sword Books Ltd., 47 Church Street, Barnsley,
S. Yorkshire, S70 2AS.

Visit us at www.frontline-books.com, email info@frontline-books.com
or write to us at the above address.

ISBN 978-1-84832-563-0

PUBLISHING HISTORY
The Distant Drum: The Personal History of a Guardsman in the Great War was
printed privately by the author in 1952. This edition includes a new introduction
by Peter Simkins and a new foreword by Carole Noakes, the niece of the author.
The Publisher would like to thank Malcolm Brown for his assistance
in bringing this important work to our attention.

CIP data records for this title are available from the British Library.

Printed in Great Britain by MPG Books Limited

THE
DISTANT DRUM

A Memoir of a Guardsman in the Great War

F. E. Noakes

Foreword by Carole Noakes

Introduction by Peter Simkins

Frontline Books, London

CONTENTS

FOREWORD

Frederick Elias Noakes was born on 27 January 1896 in Tunbridge Wells in Kent, above the draper's shop, the family business that he would eventually join. He was the first of four children, my father being the youngest, and as things turned out, my sister and I were to be Fen's only relatives of the next generation. The name 'Fen' was an acronym of his initials, and was used in the family to distinguish him from his father whose name was the same. He spent a chequered childhood being moved from school to school in a fruitless attempt to alleviate his chronic asthma, a condition that was not well understood in those days. He later lamented that he had not really had a choice about his career in the shop, and that he would never know what he might have done and achieved in other circumstances.

I mention the asthma only because it dictated so much of what was to follow. When the Great War came along nobody expected Fen would take part. After all he was still plagued by his 'old enemy' as he called it, and there was little hope of any change. By his own admission a shy and often solitary man, Fen was not on the face of it ideally suited to army life, and he was horror-stricken at the prospect. Even so, he did not want to appear unpatriotic and felt perhaps that he could satisfy his conscience by applying to enlist and being rejected.

Fen had forged a friendship with two of the young men who worked with him at the shop, and, within weeks of the start of the war, when these two decided to enlist, Fen went along with them to the recruiting station. He added a year to his age, as he hadn't reached the required minimum of nineteen, but got no further than the medical, defeated by asthma. The other two, however, were enlisted and sent for training despite one of them also having to falsify his age for the purpose.

For Fen, honour was only partly satisfied. Public opinion was becoming increasingly antagonistic to men who had not joined up, and once more he went to the recruiting station only to fail the medical again, this time on eyesight as well as asthma. At the beginning of 1916 he duly applied for attestation under the Derby Scheme and passed a very perfunctory medical, being rewarded with one day's pay and a khaki armlet. He was called to the Colours a few weeks later, but once again failed the medical and was discharged from attestation.

In July one of his friends was reported missing on the Somme, and Fen tried to enlist yet again. This time the medical board refused him on the grounds of his previous medical history. He began to exercise (something which had always been discouraged by his parents in view of his health) in an effort to toughen himself up. Meanwhile the other of his two friends was reported killed at Vimy Ridge and it was with a curious mixture of relief and trepidation that Fen was summoned to a medical board in May 1917, this time as a conscript. He was fully expecting to be assigned to Home Service or sedentary work, but to his and probably everyone else's surprise he was passed A1, and so his war began. His parents apparently expected him to succumb to his 'old enemy', and be invalided home within three weeks. Instead, the experience cured him permanently.

After his demobilisation, Fen returned home to run the family shop, and never went abroad again. He died on 12 April 1953, when I was not quite six years old, and my first-hand memories of him are necessarily few. I remember him as a quiet, thoughtful man who let me stand in the shop window, the man who had good ideas (he constructed an elaborate system of cords and pulleys so that his sister could draw her bedroom curtains without leaving her bed). He never learnt to drive, leaving this pleasure to his sister who, as one of the two million so-called 'Surplus Women' who were one of the war's legacies, devoted her life to making a home for her brothers. He remained in the family home with his sister, a large library and a succession of dogs until his death. Photographs taken throughout Fen's adult life show a man who one might describe as lanky – the word he used was 'weedy' – sitting on stiles, on beaches and enjoying picnics. Although his asthma had left him, he was never particularly robust and lived a quiet life, which I suspect suited him perfectly. A picture from the cold winter of 1947 shows a man in a posh suit, he was at a wedding, but with a fairisle jumper to keep him warm. He has Arthur Askey glasses and an Arthur Askey haircut. This is the Fen that I remember.

Even though my sister and I had little recollection of our uncle, he was often in our minds after that because my father had a good stock of stories of Fen's war service and how it had affected those still at home. There was an age gap of nearly ten years between them, and Dad was obviously proud of his brother. One of these stories was about Fen's infamous 'Field Punishment Number One' incident, which Fen himself relates in the book. I don't want to spoil it for you later, but briefly: a letter written somewhat unwisely was intercepted by the censor led to the sentence, from which Fen was saved by the removal on the appointed day of the battalion to another place. Although Fen does not mention it, in the version told by my father, Fen and his guard played cards throughout the train journey. As I grew older Dad sometimes told me that I 'took after' Fen, and sure enough, when he first gave me the book to read I found that there was a cog in my brain that meshed beautifully with a cog in Fen's. I don't think you need that much of a common point of contact to enjoy the book though. What struck me very forcibly was the 'everyday' quality of his writing: his inner thoughts even if not actually articulated, seem to push through and the reader can see what he sees, in the way that he sees it. One of the great strengths of the book derives from the fact that when Fen came to write it in the early 1950s he drew not just on his memory but on a large stack of letters that he had written home, which had been carefully preserved by his mother and sister. These letters were of course written without agenda and without any expectation of an audience wider than the military censor and the family, and the freshness that gave them is carried over into the book to a large extent.

This lack of axe to grind is still present in the book, though he does mention that he had often thought that the memoirs of an ordinary soldier would present a truer picture than those of the Generals behind the lines.

Fen's innate shyness perhaps carried him through the War, allowing him to draw on inner resources, and afterwards he remained as self-contained as he had always been. Addressing a large gathering would have been anathema to him, but I have absolutely no doubt that he would be gratified to know that his words will now find a larger audience.

Carole Noakes

INTRODUCTION

Since the end of the Great War, hundreds of memoirs and auto-biographies have been written by officers and men who fought with the British and Dominion forces on the Western Front. However, only a comparatively small number of such works deal primarily with the tumultuous events of 1918 or reflect the experiences of the conscript soldiers who represented a considerable proportion of the British Expeditionary Force (BEF) in the closing months of the conflict. There are several well-known memoirs by Guards officers – including those of Allan Adair, Horace Buckley, Carroll Carstairs, Stuart Cloete, Duff Cooper, Wilfrid Ewart, Oliver Lyttelton and Harold Macmillan – but very few by soldiers who served in the ranks of the Guards Division, arguably one of the most famous formations in the BEF. Indeed, apart from Stephen Graham's *A Private in the Guards*, published in 1919, and Norman Cliff's brief, hundred-page account, *To Hell and Back with the Guards*, which first appeared as late as 1988, one is hard-pressed to think of any that fall into the latter category. Given the fact that, in the final and victorious Allied offensive of 1918, the Guards Division achieved a success rate of over seventy per cent in attacking operations – placing it among the top ten *British* divisions – the relative paucity of first-hand accounts by its non-commissioned officers and men is perhaps all the more surprising. It has certainly not eased the task of historians of the First World War who, in recent years, have sought to examine and explain how the BEF not only survived the attrition of the Somme and Passchendaele and the crises of March to May 1918 but also ended the war as a modern, all-arms force that was at the tactical and technological cutting-edge of the Allied armies in France and Belgium. For a variety of reasons, therefore, this new edition of F.E. Noakes's superb book *The Distant Drum* is both timely and enormously welcome to all those interested in the story of the British Army on the Western Front.

When Fen Noakes was at last called up for military service in June 1917, after his several fruitless attempts to volunteer, he was posted to Combermere Barracks, Windsor, for training in a reserve unit of the Household Battalion, an infantry formation created in September 1916 from surplus personnel of the Life Guards and Royal Horse Guards. Over the next two years or so, Noakes regularly sent letters home to his family, recording his experiences and impressions of military life in remarkable and illuminating detail. He belonged, of course, to a generation that wrote well and understood grammar and punctuation and, even when one allows for the constraints of wartime censorship, his letters provide a fascinating commentary on the progress of the war, containing candid views on wider political questions as well as highly personal reports on his own daily activities. In 1934 he collated and typed these letters – which can now be read at the Imperial War Museum – and in 1952, following another world war, used them as the basis for his privately printed memoir *The Distant*

Drum, adding many previously omitted geographical and military details as well as including mature reflections on the opinions he had advanced earlier as a young man. His aim in the book, he informs us, is to relate his adventures exactly as he remembered them, without exaggeration or striving for dramatic effect, and, above all, 'to avoid any perversion of the truth which might seem to display myself in an unjustifiably good light'. Because of the author's innate honesty and modesty, the letters and book, together or separately, give the reader a valuable insight into the final eighteen months of the war and can be accepted as a reliable guide to the morale and attitudes of British soldiers on the Western Front at that time.

Having completed four-and-a-half months of recruit training – fully covered in the opening chapter – Private Fen Noakes crossed the Channel in late October 1917 and joined the Household Battalion, then part of the 4th Division which was holding the front near Monchy-le-Preux, east of Arras. At this stage, his 'romantic idealism' was largely undimmed and he still regarded the war as 'a holy crusade for the salvation of the world', though he freely admitted that he felt 'windy' during most of the time he spent in the line. His letters home reveal that, after a few weeks in France, his views on the war had begun to change. On 8 January 1918 he criticised the 'spirit of savagery' in the British press. 'Could the fighting men...of both sides come together there can be no doubt that complete unanimity would result', he commented. He was now convinced that national pride or obstinacy 'will prove a great obstacle in the way of a reasonable settlement' and feared that, without 'much greater openness of mind and humanity', Britain might become infected with 'the very spirit of Prussianism we set out to crush'. By 12 February he was wondering when the 'indiscriminate murder' would stop. '*Everyone*, except the people in power', he wrote, 'is heartily sick of it... There is not a man out here who would not make peace in a moment...' With the benefit of hindsight, however, Noakes conceded in his book that much of this was 'schoolboyish nonsense' and that his temporary wave of disillusionment was probably little more than the 'normal habit of grousing for which the British soldier is notorious'.

From late January until early March 1918, Noakes suffered from leg sores and a poisoned finger and in February was hospitalised for three weeks at Le Tréport, on the coast near Dieppe. While he was away from the front, ongoing manpower problems necessitated a large-scale reorganisation of the BEF and the Household Battalion as disbanded. On recovery, Noakes was transferred to the 3rd Coldstream Guards, part of the newly formed 4th Guards Brigade, which had been attached to the 31st Division. Two days after the Germans had launched their major spring offensive on 21 March, Noakes's battalion was in action near Ervillers, north of Bapaume on the British Third Army's front. Fen Noakes paints a vivid picture of the fighting in this sector between 23 and 25 March, recalling how desperately tired he was after three days and nights without sleep. Heavily shelled in error by British artillery, and in danger of being outflanked and encircled, the battalion was ordered to fall back on the evening of 25 March, Noakes having by now descended into a mood of weary fatalism. 'We scrambled out and ignominiously ran for all we were worth', he confessed: '...Then an indescribable feeling of disgust for the whole show swept over me, and I slowed to a deliberate walk, not caring whether I got through or not'. He managed only a few more paces, in fact, before he was wounded in the forearm and briefly rendered unconscious by a bursting shell.

This time, Fen Noakes spent almost three months in hospital and convalescent camps. The German spring offensives and the spectre of defeat had done much to restore his faith 'in the justice of our cause and the righteousness of our aims', even if his patriotism and idealism were never again so unqualified as in the past. By 5 May he was again sufficiently optimistic to note accurately – if a shade prematurely – that 'I think we have got Fritz on the toasting-fork...He has made progress, but it has cost him far more casualties than he expected, and all the result has been is to put him in an impossible position. He is weakened out of all proportion to his gain, but he cannot stay where he is...' Noakes rejoined his battalion towards the end of June 1918 but only two months later, with many of his comrades, he was transferred to the 1st Battalion, Coldstream Guards, to help replace casualties suffered in the opening phase of the British Third Army's offensive between Albert and Arras, which had begun on 21 August. Fen's new battalion was part of the 2nd Guards Brigade in the prestigious Guards Division, commanded until 30 September by Major-General Geoffrey Feilding and subsequently by Major-General Torquhil Matheson. Noakes was quick to appreciate the changed tactical conditions as the Guards Division advanced towards the Canal du Nord and the Hindenburg Line. 'It was an exhilarating experience, after trench warfare, to be moving freely over open ground in pursuit of a retreating enemy', he wrote. On 13 September he recorded that men coming back from forward positions were saying 'We can't find the enemy' or 'We've lost Fritz'.

The Guards Division soon faced a much stiffer task in its important set-piece assault on the Canal du Nord on 27 September, in one of the four massive hammer-blows delivered, over a four-day period, by the Allied armies in France and Belgium. Fen was hugely impressed by the weight and ferocity of the British supporting barrage – which he graphically describes in Chapter VII – and, although he felt 'stark naked' when crossing open ground under heavy fire, he also experienced 'an extraordinary sensation – curiously like relief – that I was no longer personally responsible for my own safety'. The attack was successful and the battalion's No.2 Company, in which Noakes served, became known unofficially as the 'V.C. Company', following the award of the Victoria Cross to Captain Cyril Frisby and (posthumously) to Lance-Corporal Thomas Jackson for their gallantry on 27 September. It is clear from the book that, more than thirty years later, Noakes's profound admiration for Frisby's leadership and personal qualities was undiminished. At the time, however, Fen and his comrades were too tired to celebrate their achievements in the Canal du Nord operations. In the aftermath of the attack, 'our mouths were dry as lime-kilns' he recalled: 'Nerves were on edge and tempers frayed, as always after the intense strain of "going over the top"...'

In the battalion's next action, at Wambaix, southeast of Cambrai, on 9 October, Noakes was wounded in the leg by another badly ranged British shell. 'This was the end of the war, so far as my insignificant personal part in it went', he remarks. While he was convalescing at Cayeux, near the mouth of the Somme, the Armistice was signed, affording Noakes ' a moment of such undiluted happiness and emotion as I had never known', although he was worried that the Allies might impose harsh and vindictive terms upon Germany. 'A lasting peace it must be', he wrote to his father, 'but it must be an absolutely *clean* peace. Otherwise, the war has been in vain'. Proud of his new rank of 'Guardsman' – introduced shortly after the Armistice – Noakes served in the British occupation forces in Cologne before returning to England in March 1919. He was finally demobilised on 9 October that year and went back to work in his family's drapery business.

Fortunately for us, Fen Noakes compiled and produced this admirable account of his experiences before he died, at the relatively young age of 57, in April 1953. His honesty, integrity and modesty shine through every page and combine with his lucid prose style and shrewd and objective judgements to give this record of his service a quality and appeal rare among books of this genre. *The Distant Drum* is not just about battle. It also offers the reader useful and detailed insights into routine trench warfare; daily life and conditions in the front line and in camps, hospitals and billets; recreation and entertainment; soldiers' rations; and relations with civilians in Britain, France and Germany. One fervently hopes that this new edition will bring the book the wider recognition that it has long deserved.

Peter Simkins

PREFACE

In this book I have tried to set down, simply and unpretentiously, an account of the chief events of my life in the Army during the years 1917 to 1919. I did not write it with any idea of publication, but solely for my own satisfaction, because I wanted to put on private record, while the memory is still comparatively undimmed, what I have always regarded as the most memorable period of my personal life. The part I played in the Great War was, of course, entirely insignificant, but (like many other ex-servicemen) I could not resist the urge to talk about my experiences-even though it might be no more than "talking to myself!"

Recently, however, some friends to whom I showed the manuscript encouraged me to make it more widely available. I could not imagine that so undistinguished a story could be of interest to anyone except myself, but I finally decided (with some misgiving) to promote my poor effort to the "dignity" of print. I have made few alterations to the original, but r have bestowed fictitious names upon some of my friends and others with whom I came in contact during my Service life; I trust, however, that no-one mentioned in these pages, whether under an "alias" or by his real name, will take exception to anything I may have written about him. Indeed, on re-reading my account, I seem to have paid but scanty and quite inadequate tribute to the many good comrades whose friendship, at different times and places, made my war-service much pleasanter than it might otherwise have been. Though. I have lost track of most of them during the intervening years, . I have never forgotten how much I owed to them-I hope I never shall.

In writing about such long-distant events, I had to rely almost entirely on my own memory, for I have had no opportunity to "compare notes" with any of my contemporaries, and I kept no diary at the time; the only documentary help I had in compiling my chronicle was contained in the old letters mentioned in Chapter 2, which my Mother preserved. So it is not surprising if I have made mistakes in describing things which happened more than thirty years ago, though I do not think such errors are very numerous or serious. The events of my war-service made an indelible impression on my mind and many of them seem almost as clear and detailed in my memory as though they had occurred yesterday; but the standpoint from which I experienced them was that of an ordinary private-soldier (and a not very bright or intelligent one, at that!), who often saw little beyond his immediate surroundings, and then did not always understand what he saw.

My constant aim, however, in this narrative, has been to tell of my "adventures" exactly as I remember them, without exaggeration or seeking for "dramatic" effect-and especially to avoid any perversion of the truth which might seem to display myself in an unjustifiably good light. I was far from being a "hero," even in my own eyes, and it would be futile to pretend that I was even a "good soldier." But the passing of time can play strange tricks with the memory: "the brave music of a distant drum" is apt to sound romantic, even nostalgic, as it recedes "down the arches of the years." I have done my best to confine myself strictly to the truth, and to resist any temptation to "shoot a line." Perhaps if. I had allowed my imagination more rein, and had been a more skilful writer, I might have produced a more "entertaining" story-but it would then have been other than I intended.

TRAINING

WHEN I left home, on the morning of June 6th, 1917, it was raining steadily, a straight windless downpour out of a uniformly overcast sky which looked as if it might go on for hours. The low clouds and dripping trees, the streaming gutters and general air of damp depression were in tune with my own feelings, for I was off to answer my call-up to the Army, and was oppressed by all the nervous apprehensions natural to such an occasion. I had been told many alarming things—and imagined more—about the hardships and humiliations which awaited me as a recruit, and although I was going largely by my own act and initiative, and was quite convinced that it was the right thing to do, yet I knew that at best it would be an utterly different life from anything I had hitherto experienced, and I dreaded the prospect before me. My despondency was apparently shared by the rest of the family, for my parents, sister and two young brothers were gathered at the door to see me off with melancholy faces, and my poor Mother could not suppress her tears. I must confess that I, too, had an uncomfortable lump in my throat and a sinking feeling in the pit of my stomach as I bade them farewell and set off down the garden path, clad in my oldest suit and raincoat and carrying my "luggage" in a small brown-paper parcel.

Yet gloomy forebodings were only a part, albeit at that moment the most dominant part, of my emotions as I waved good-bye with as much cheerfulness as I could muster. The brilliant green of the young Spring foliage seemed to lend a luminous quality to the grey prospect, promising sunlight to come, and in spite of my nervous apprehensions there was an underlying feeling of excitement, of adventure, of novelty; in sudden involuntary flashes of exultation I realised that, at last, I had overcome my life-long physical disabilities sufficiently to be accepted into the ranks of what, in my naive idealism, I thought of as a great crusading army, fighting for universal Truth and Justice. Even I was to have the privilege of playing a part in the "War to end War" and of helping to "make the world safe for democracy."

Although the War had already been going on for nearly three years and I had recently passed my twenty-first birthday, it was not by my own fault that I had not joined-up earlier. I had, in fact, offered myself several times since the outbreak of hostilities, but had each time been refused by the recruiting authorities on medical grounds. Most people who knew me, I think, believed—at any rate, in the early stages—that I was permanently unfit for anything so strenuous as military life, for from early childhood I had been a chronic sufferer from asthma, the frequent attacks of which had condemned me to bed or semi-invalidism during a large proportion of my life hitherto ; I had always been considered to be " very delicate," and had never been allowed to take part in games or the normal activities of other boys. As a result, I had grown up as a thin, weakly (not to say, " weedy ") youth, with little physical strength and no athletic prowess ; my education had been seriously interrupted and I made few friends, for by temperament I was shy and retiring to a degree I find it difficult to credit now ; fond of my own company and entirely lacking in self-confidence or conceit. All my inclinations were for a quiet and inoffensive life—not, one would think, the type which would ever make a soldier.

But when the War came my imagination, nourished on a love of reading which had always been my chief interest and pastime, was strongly stirred and, like so many of my generation, I was fired by a romantic, though ill-informed and uncritical, enthusiasm for the national cause. I accepted without question all the propaganda stories about the origins of the War and the crimes of the Germans, and to me it seemed to be a plain case of " white *versus* black," a struggle of light against darkness, without any qualifying doubts. And that being so, the duty of every man of military age seemed no less plain—to volunteer for the Army. " Your King and Country need YOU! "

But how could I go?—what sort of soldier could such a one as I hope to make? My whole sensitive, cowardly nature shrank in dismay from so terrifying a possibility. Yet I must at least make the attempt. I think the secret mental torment of those first weeks was among the worst I have ever suffered, before I finally screwed up my courage and forced myself to go to the recruiting depôt on September 14th, 1914. I was, indeed, at that time some six months below enlistment age, and might legitimately have held back on that account, but no-one questioned the false age I declared at the depôt. I was weighed, measured and sounded—and found wanting. Colour-sergeant Callaghan, who known me at school, tried to get me through, but without avail ; I was rejected, and dismissed with a paper to the effect that I had " tried to enlist."

That paper was my " passport " to personal self-respect during the next few months, but not for long. In 1915 I had another try, but after a much more thorough examination I was turned down even more decisively. In January, 1916, however, under the " Derby Scheme," a last attempt to make the " Voluntary System " of recruitment work, I was successful. There was no medical test, and I was formally enlisted ; I took the Oath of Attestation and the " King's Shilling," and returned home proudly wearing a khaki armlet. I was "in the Army"—or, at least, I had one foot in! But when my "Group" was called to the Colours two months later, the District Medical Board again rejected me, marking my card "Unfit for any military employment." Later I received an official discharge from my enlistment, after having served, as the document stated, "one day with the Colours and fifty-seven days in the Army Reserve!"

That ought to have set my mind at rest, so far as any imputation of not having done my best was concerned—but it did not. I knew that I should have no mental peace while the War lasted, unless I got into khaki. It was not—emphatically— that I *wanted* to go, or that soldiering held any attraction for me. I was too quiet and retiring by nature for Army life (as I imagined it) to be anything but profoundly disagreeable to contemplate. But I was continually driven, both by my ingenuous ideals of "patriotism" and by a self-conscious sensitiveness about what other people might think of me, to do what my whole soul recoiled from. I had to prove—to myself, no less than to others— that I was not the ineffective weakling that I seemed. I was more afraid, in fact, of being thought a "slacker" than I was of the unknown hardships of the Army.

Six months after my last rejection, hearing that medical standards had been relaxed and that many men, previously unfit, were now being called up, I put in an application for re-examination, and a date was appointed for me to go before a higher authority—I think it was the Southern Command M.B., at Southampton. But at the last moment I was officially notified that, in view of my previous medical record, the interview was cancelled. The Army appeared not to want me at any price! So, as a sort of "second line of offence," I enrolled for "war-work" in response to the call from Mr. Neville Chamberlain's ill-fated "Ministry of National Service," but beyond a card of acknowledgement no notice was taken of my application.

Meanwhile, I was doing everything in my power to improve my state of health. I did not believe in my own physical incapacity, and was sure that the Army would sooner or later find a job for me. It is not necessary to detail the amateurish measures I took—the long country walks and cycle rides, the exercises with a "chest-expander," the improvised "physical jerks," the efforts to harden myself against all kinds of weather and temperatures, etc. Much of this I did as unobtrusively as possible, for fearing of worrying my parents, who thought I should "let well alone" in the matter of military service. It is hard to credit, seriously, that my inexpert efforts can have done what the doctors had hitherto failed to do, but it is nevertheless a fact that my health did improve about that time. The attacks of asthma became progressively slighter and less frequent, and by the Spring of 1917 I was probably in better physical condition

3

than I had ever been. When, in May, I was summoned under the Military Service Act to appear against before the D.M.B., I had little doubt that this time I should pass for some form of combatant service. And pass I did, in the highest grade—Medical Category "A.1," or "fit for Active Service." A fortnight later I received my calling-up papers.

(It was rather ironical, though, that after all my unsuccessful "volunteering" I should finally have gone into the Army as a conscript.)

So that explains why, as I set forth into the Unknown, my timorous despondency was lightened by fugitive gleams of elation. For I had succeeded in my aim at last; I was off to "do my bit" and need no longer feel ashamed or inferior among other men. Nevertheless, although the barrier of ill-health had been triumphantly surmounted, there was still the obstacle of my weak and cowardly nature. At that moment I felt profoundly distrustful of my ability to meet the challenge of the new life without either incurring disgrace or making a fool of myself—perhaps both. But whatever might be in store for me, I do not think I would have withdrawn even if I could. A week or two earlier, I had written to a friend: "I would rather go and then wish I hadn't, than not go and all my life wish that I had." It would be useless to pretend that there were not times during the next two years when I did wish that I had taken the "easier" path, when I would have given all I had to be "well out of it"; or that there was scarcely a day when I did not earnestly long for an eventual return to civilian freedom. But, although in the event I neither distinguished nor seriously disgraced myself in the Army (the latter was probably more by luck than by merit!) and there was much about it that I detested, there were yet many things in military life and the friends I met there which now make me glad and proud that I went. I am very sure that I should to-day feel cheap and despicable in my own eyes if, professing the convictions I then did about the War, I had by any fault of my own "dodged the column" and taken no part in it.

. . . . . .

At the station I met, by previous arrangement, a young fellow of about my own age, the son of a local builder—I will call him "Harry Barnes." I did not know him well, for I had only made his acquaintance a few days previously, on hearing that he was due to report for service on the same day as myself, but I think that we were both glad that we did not have to set out on the "Great Adventure" alone. We had only about four miles to travel, and I suppose we went by train instead of by the more convenient bus because we had free railway warrants. We were both nervously anxious to do the right thing—and, besides, the bus would have cost us fourpence each!

Reporting at the Depôt in Tonbridge as directed, we were told that we should not be required for about three hours, so strolled round the town in the rain and had dinner at a café. There were about twenty other recruits waiting at the Depôt when we returned at one o'clock, and after a slight delay we entrained for Maidstone, in charge of a Sergeant of the Royal West Kent. On arrival, we formed up in some semblance of military style and marched from the station to the Barracks ; our appearance must have fallen far short of parade-ground smartness, however, for (as I remember it) the Sergeant led the way, with Barnes and I following and vainly striving to keep in step, while the rest tailed behind in a more or less straggling mob, in every variety of civilian garb.

As soon as we entered the Barrack gates we were taken to the Orderly Room, where our papers were checked and — to our surprise—each man was handed the sum of five-and-sixpence. We all thought that this was the right way to begin! But it soon transpired that the money was not given us merely in order to create a good impression, but because we were not on the ration-strength of the Depôt and should have to buy our own food in the Canteen during the day or so we remained there. At the same time, every man was required to sign a form relating to any allowance from his Army pay he might wish to make in favour of dependent relatives at home. As it happened, I had been talking to one of the other fellows, who professed to "know the ropes," during the train journey, about this subject, and on his advice I decided to allot sixpence a day in my Mother's name. My Mother was not in need of financial assistance from me, but I was advised (and rightly) that Army pay was often in arrears, especially during Active Service at the Front, where pay-days were often very irregular and determined by a variety of circumstances. The unpaid balance, it is true, went to one's credit and could be drawn on some future occasion (such as "Leave"), but that would not be of much help where day-to-day expenses were concerned. By making the allotment, therefore, I should be accumulating a fund at home on which I could draw from time to time without feeling that I was sponging on my parents.

But this laudable scheme nearly came to naught two or three weeks later, when my Mother received the official papers from the Army Pay Office. My Father wrote me indignantly—and not unnaturally, in the circumstances—to the effect that he would not permit me to contribute to my Mother's support, and declared his intention of writing to the War Office repudiating the allotment. I had quite forgotten to tell them what I had done, and to explain that my motives in this case were purely those of self-interest!

After this, my first "Pay-parade," we were conducted to our quarters for the night, and were instructed by an N.C.O. in the art of laying down our beds. We each had a set of bed-boards— three narrow planks resting on a pair of trestles about six inches

5

from the floor—a straw-filled palliasse and bolster, three grey blankets and a pair of unbleached sheets. The room was large and airy, and was not over-crowded, for the only other furniture was a deal table in the middle and shelves around the walls on which to dispose our scanty personal belongings.

Then we were dismissed for the day and adjourned to the Canteen for tea—or something stronger, according to individual taste. I was impressed by the amount of food which could be purchased for a few pence (in those days of civilian food-shortage) and the fact that the tea was generously sweetened. "We shall live like fighting cocks, at this rate!" I thought; but it was not always so!

Afterwards, Barnes and I proposed to go to the "pictures" in the town, but, being still in civilian clothes, we were turned back at the Barrack gate. So, after we had tired of watching the changing of sentries and other military evolutions about the Barracks, most of which were interesting though meaningless to us at the time, we lay on the grass beside some tennis-courts and talked. The weather had improved since we left Tonbridge, and was now brilliantly fine and warm. Our chief topic of conversation was, of course, speculation about what would happen next, and what regiment we would find ourselves in tomorrow. I knew nothing to any purpose about the respective merits of the various branches of the Service, though at the time I had some vague idea of "putting in" for the Royal Garrison Artillery—for no particular reason except that several of the other men who had come from Tonbridge that day had the same idea and I had a cousin in that corps. Barnes was quite decided: he wanted to join a motorised unit; but the internal-combustion engine was a closed book as far as I was concerned, and I had no ambition in that direction. (Of course, I knew nothing about guns, either!) But it seemed of little use to make guesses about the future—we should probably have little choice in the matter—so we had supper and, by mutual consent, turned-in fairly early. My first day in the Army had made me very sleepy, and I slept well that night, despite the novelty of my surroundings and the unaccustomed sounds of a barrack room.

Next morning there was a perfunctory medical examination—a mere matter of form, for we had all been classified by the Medical Board before being called up—and then were lined up in the Orderly Room to be posted to a regiment. It appeared that a certain latitude of choice was allowed to each recruit, subject to the intake needs of the unit chosen—though, perhaps, it would be truer to say that a show was made of giving each a free choice, for in nearly every case I saw where a man expressed a preference that unit was found to be full! Just so, when it came to my turn, the R.G.A. was in no apparent need of recruits at the moment, and the Colour-Sergeant in charge, regarding me speculatively, said, "You're about the right height—how would you like to go into the Guards?"

The Guards! I had seen them outside Buckingham Palace and read of them in histories and historical romances; I think my mental picture of this famous corps was at the moment somewhat mixed up with D'Artagnan and the "Three Musketeers," and in my romantic ignorance I believed that to be a Guardsman was a great honour — one of the greatest the Army could offer. (I still think so, but now for more substantial reasons.) I swelled with secret pride as I answered quietly, "All right, Sergeant." He then said that he would post me to the "Household Battalion," about which he would seem to have known little more than I did myself, for he conveyed the impression that this was a part of the Grenadier Guards, in close personal attendance on His Majesty the King! I walked out of the room as if I had already received the accolade!

The Household Battalion was stationed at Windsor, and I was almost immediately issued with a railway warrant for that town. After a meal in the Canteen, Barnes and I repaired to the station; my friend had achieved his ambition and was going to join the Motor Transport, A.S.C., at Grove Park. His train left a few minutes before mine, and we did not meet again until after the War.

I was the only man travelling from the Maidstone Depôt to Windsor that day—a fact which might well have made me suspect that I had been "sold a pup" by the Colour-Sergeant, but which instead I preferred to regard as a personal compliment. Naturally, not everyone would be eligible for "the cream of the Army," as the Sergeant had described my unit! I travelled by way of Waterloo and reached the Royal Borough soon after five o'clock. Feeling in no hurry to relinquish my civilian freedom sooner than I need, I strolled about the town, which was new to me, for a while, to get my bearings. There was much of interest to see, in the quaint streets, the massive pile of the Castle and the old College buildings in Eton; the river was a sheet of silver in the sunlight, dotted with scores of small boats. I had tea in a café and wrote a postcard home, full of optimism and the imagined glories of my regiment.

Presently I thought it was time that I reported somewhere or to someone, so I set out to look for my unit. I had been given no directions or credentials of any kind before leaving Maidstone, apart from a scrap of paper on which were scrawled the words, "Household Batt., Windsor," and my name, so I made my first enquiry of the sentry on duty at the gate of the Castle. He told me that the Household Battalion was stationed in the Combermere Barracks, on the southern outskirts of the town, so I walked down Peascod Street and beyond, for about half-a-mile, until I came to a wrought-iron gate, obviously the entrance to the Barracks.

But I could not bring myself to go in straight-away. Faced with the decisive moment, my courage failed me and all my old shy nervousness came back; the glamour of "the Guards" faded, and I was filled with apprehensive imaginings about what might lie before me. I suddenly felt very small and lonely, my knees were weak and the bottom seemed to have dropped out of my stomach; it was as if I was a boy again, going to a new school, only many times worse! I walked on for about a hundred yards, under a high wall with a stone coping over which some trees showed, until I reached another gate. This was, however, of solid wood and uninvitingly closed, so I turned about and slowly retraced my steps, battling with my fears and trying to screw up my courage for the final surrender of my personal liberty. It had to be done, I knew; there was no going back now, and the longer I delayed the harder it became. So at last, giving myself a mental shake and murmuring a half-hearted "Here goes!" I walked through the barrack gates and into the new life.

Just inside the gate I was stopped by the sentry on guard, and at that moment a tall, impressive figure approached from the Guard-room, dressed in impeccable khaki and a "Sam Browne" belt. He wore an embroidered coat-of-arms on his sleeve, which denoted, as I afterwards discovered, that he was the Regimental Corporal-Major of the 2nd Life Guards. It seemed that, after all, I had entered by the wrong gate; the Household Battalion shared the Barracks with the Life Guards, but the H.B. entrance was the further gate from which I had turned back. The R.C.M. demanded my name and business, and when I said I was a recruit and showed the piece of paper bearing the name of the Household Battalion he gave me a searching stare and then asked if I wouldn't rather join the Life Guards. He enumerated some of the advantages of being a member of so famous a regiment—the only time I have ever known a "Regimental" to condescend to employ the arts of persuasion in dealing with the lower ranks!— but I had no wish to have anything to do with horses, so I diffidently but firmly resisted his blandishments. At last he let me go, and directed me to the H.B. Headquarters on the far side of the Parade-ground.

Reporting at the Battalion Orderly Room, where I interrupted a couple of N.C.O.'s in a game of cards, I found that no one knew anything about me, but particulars of my name and the Depôt from which I had come were noted and I was told that nothing could be done about enrolment until my papers arrived from Maidstone. There were several other new recruits waiting about outside, and presently we were collected by a rather bored-looking Corporal and taken to our sleeping-quarters; we drew blankets for the night, were directed where to find the Canteen and the latrines, and then were left to our own devices.

I cannot say that I was particularly impressed by the warmth of my welcome into the Army. I had expected all sorts of things to happen, most of them of an unpleasant nature, but I had certainly never imagined that I should be ignored! For that was to be the fate of us newcomers during the next two days. We were not "on the roll," we were "civvies," therefore officially we did not exist; no one in authority took the slightest notice of us, though individual Troopers were usually friendly and helpful when approached; we belonged to nobody and had no duties—we were completely "spare." We slept on the bare floor of our barrack-room with our three blankets apiece—for my own part, I found it much easier to sleep under these conditions than I had expected— and got up when the bugle sounded at cock-crow or thereabouts; we got our meals in a group at the end of one of the long tables in the mess-hut, conspicuous in our shabby civilian clothes. With nothing to do all day, we spent most of the time until five in the afternoon lounging under the trees or watching the evolutions of the troops on the Square. From five until nine we were allowed to go out and wander round the town. We began to wonder why we had come!

But we did not allow our cool reception to depress us unduly. Some twenty or thirty more recruits joined us on the second day; most of them were ex-policemen from Dundee and Leith—a lively and high-spirited crowd, whose dialect was almost incomprehensible to many of us Southerners—and there were also men from widely-separated parts of England and from varied walks of life. "Schools" of "Housie" and groups of card-players soon established themselves under the trees between the blocks of Barrack-rooms, and, of course, the "wet" canteen was extensively patronised whenever it was open—as long as the cash lasted.

On the first evening I struck up acquaintance with two of the newcomers: John Redman, a precise, well-educated man who had been a bank-clerk in civil life (he was killed by a shell within a few yards of me five months later, in front of Monchy), and Lyon Mackie, who came from one of the D'Oyley Carte Opera Companies; whether or not the latter was indeed a "star," as he gave us to understand, I do not know, but he possessed a very fine baritone voice and was later a popular performer in the Batt. Concert Party. There were also "Jarman," large, genial and slow of speech, a typical Norfolk farm worker; George Egerton, swarthy and black-moustached, who had been a grocer in (I think) Lincoln; Angus MacDobbie, a powerfully-built, goodlooking youngster, one of the Scots ex-policemen; and several others whose faces I well remember but whose names I cannot now recall, among my first acquaintances in the Battalion. Most of the recruits were in their twenties, or younger, but one or two must have been over thirty—they seemed quite middle-aged to me then!

. . . . . .

I soon learned the truth about the unit I had joined. The Household Battalion was not, as I had been led to suppose, a part of the Grenadier Guards, nor was it included in the "Brigade of Guards"; in fact, it was an independent and somewhat anomalous body of dismounted cavalry, formed originally from personnel of the Life Guards and the "Blues"—the "Household Cavalry": hence the name. It had been constituted some nine months previously, at a time when the failure of all efforts to break through the trench-lines in France had rendered cavalry as such comparatively useless at the Front. The Battalion itself was in France, and we at Windsor formed the training depôt from which it drew reinforcements.

We ranked as Guardsmen, though we did not bear the title—"Household Troops," the personal bodyguard of the Crown—and because of our cavalry origin the non-commissioned ranks bore cavalry titles, such as "Trooper," "Corporal-of-Horse," etc.; but we were an infantry corps, and had nothing to do with horses. We were also paid at cavalry rates, and a Trooper in the H.B. drew one-and-nine a day instead of the usual infantry Private's "bob," which was all that even Foot Guards were paid at that time. It was this discrimination, as well as our (probably unfounded) claim to precedence by virtue of our derivation from the two "premier" regiments of the British Army—the Life Guards and the Horse Guard (or, "Blues")—which was the cause of the rivalry and bitter controversy which existed between us and the reserve battalion of Coldstream Guards who occupied the other barracks in Windsor.

Our uniform, equipment and training were, in all essential respects, identical with those of the Brigade of Guards, and most of our instructors and senior officers were seconded from one or other of the Guards regiments. In the H.B., however, a recruit's training, arduous though it was even by ordinary military standards, lacked much of the merciless gruelling which gave the Caterham Depôt the name of being "the most terrible training-ground in Europe." I have no evidence that our more "humane" regime turned out worse soldiers, either in the field or on the parade-ground, because of this omission.

The Reserve Battalion at Windsor, like the Service Battalion in France, was organised in four Companies, though, unlike the latter, these in training varied considerably from each other in size and military efficiency. No. 3 Coy. was by far the largest of the four, and was the one into which all new recruits were placed on first joining, for foot- and arms-drill and physical training—a sort of preliminary "licking into shape." No 2 was an intermediate stage, in which musketry, "company drill," hand-grenade and anti-gas instruction were the principal features; while No. 1 Company was chiefly concerned with such "advanced" matters as field-training, trench-digging, guard-mounting and ceremonial drill. Recruits "graduated" from one Company to the next when they "passed out" (attained proficiency) in each stage of training. By the time one had reached No. 1 Company one was considered to be a more or less fully-trained soldier, and it was from this Company that drafts were drawn from time to time, to reinforce the Service Battalion at the Front. No. 4 Coy. was composed exclusively of ex-casualties rejoining from hospital, men with "categories" and men holding "struck-off" (administrative) jobs; they did not come much into contact with the recruits and, as "old sweats," were regarded with something like awe by many of us tyros.

My papers, and those of most of the other waiting men, arrived on Saturday, whereupon those in authority began to take some official notice of our existence. That afternoon we were lined up and inspected by the Battalion Medical Officer—a mere formality— but nothing could yet be done about enrolling us, until we had been O.K.'d by the Colonel. It was reported that our Commanding Officer was the only Battalion Commander in the British Army who had the right to refuse a physically fit man sent down by the depôts, on grounds of personal appearance and general intelligence alone ; and it was said that a week previously he had turned down all but three out of more than thirty candidates. This was, of course, just "eye-wash," but I was taking no chances and poshed-up for the occasion with great care, even to the extent of buying a clean collar!

The interviews took place next morning, in alphabetical order. When my turn came, I was marched into the C.O.'s Office by the Orderly Sergeant and stood rigidly at attention in front of the table, while the C.O. looked at me keenly and asked a few questions about my civilian occupation, sports, hobbies, etc. I answered with more confidence than I felt and with some deliberate exaggeration about the last two items, and was accepted.

Then, after all had been inspected, we were lined up outside the Orderly Room—I soon learned how much of a soldier's time is spent in queuing-up for one thing or another!—and given our regimental numbers. Mine was "3157." There was another line-up at the Q.M. stores, where we were issued with bedding, blankets, etc., and then taken (I cannot call it "marched") in a body to our billets.

Although No. 4 Coy., the Headquarters Staff, and the officers were quartered in the Barracks, the greater part of which was occupied by the 2nd Life Guards, our three Companies in training were all billeted in commandeered houses in the near neighbour-hood, mostly in Osborne Road. The recruit-squad to which I belonged while in No. 3 Coy. was lodged in one of a row of semi-detached dwellings, No. 13 Osborne Villas—this struck me as a good omen, for my home at Tunbridge Wells was named

"Osborne Villa"!—where, with four others, Egerton, Jarman, Parks and Morley, I slept in a small room on the top floor. It was quite bare of furnishings, of course, except for our beds, which consisted of bed-boards, straw palliasse and bolster, and three blankets apiece, and we took all our meals in the mess-hut in the Barracks. Our lofty situation meant a tiring climb after parade, but it had its advantages in being less liable to sudden visits from N.C.O.'s in search of men for fatigues.

Next day we got our much-looked-for uniforms, and it was a proud moment for me, not unmixed with self-conscious embarrassment and a feeling of "make-believe," when I first walked down the road dressed like a real soldier! We all felt equally awkward at first, I think, but not nearly so conspicuous as before, and the very fact of wearing the uniform gave us a sense of being part of the corporate life of the Battalion, instead of interlopers. I posted my civilian clothes home, for non-commissioned ranks were not allowed to wear "civvies" under any circumstances—though I very often did when I was at home on leave.

Among the articles of kit included in this first issue were the following:—

> Two uniforms of khaki tunic and slacks (one for "best").
> One pair of puttees.
> One Service cap.
> Three shirts, two pairs pants, three pairs socks and a woollen cardigan.
> Two pairs ammunition boots.
> A "hold-all" containing knife, fork and spoon, and a "cut-throat" razor.
> Boot-brush, clothes-brush, brush for polishing brasses, button-stick and tin of dubbin.
> A cap-badge and set of brass numerals.
> A "housewife" with needles, thread, darning-wool, etc., for mending.
> A canvas kitbag in which to keep the above and any personal possessions.

Other things were added during the next day or two, such as, for example, webbing equipment, greatcoat, and ground sheet. All articles of official kit had to be produced in perfect condition or accounted for at Kit Inspections, and we found it expedient to have duplicates (bought or "scrounged") of many of the items, so as to be prepared in case of need with a spotless display. It was all too easy to "lose one's name" if an inspection was unexpectedly sprung on us! While in England I mostly wore my own civilian underwear and socks. It will be noted that pyjamas were not included in the "issue"—throughout my Army life we slept in pants and vest: anything else would have been considered "effeminate"!

We were now definitely "in the Army," as Sergeants and others lost no opportunity of reminding us, and had to adapt ourselves to an utterly novel way of living. Of course, it was all very different from anything I had previously experienced, and at first, in many respects, I felt "like a fish out of water"; but I had come prepared for shocks, and, compared with my worst imaginings, I found that both Army life and the men among whom I was thrown were, generally speaking, much better than I had anticipated. In fact, I think I enjoyed—for a time, at any rate— the austere conditions, the absence of "frills," the brusqueness of manner and of action, and the impersonal atmosphere of an exclusively masculine community. There was a certain satisfaction, in my early days of patriotic fervour, in doing without many of the amenities of ordinary life, in surrendering my own will to that of the Army, in working hard by day and at night going to bed tired, to dreamless slumber. Even the dictatorial powers, by no means always politely exercised, of everyone with a stripe on his sleeve, and the knowledge that I was nobody and counted for nothing, was not yet so intolerably irksome as it afterwards became. Despite my quiet and reserved nature, I got on well with my immediate comrades; indeed, I was luckier than I realised at the time in my room-mates, who were all very decent fellows and made things much easier than they might otherwise have been. On the Barrack Square, although I came in for my share of collective abuse, I do not remember that I was ever singled out for individual censure and I never "lost my name"; once or twice, indeed, the Sergeant surprisingly commended my efforts to acquit myself well.

From the beginning and for some time afterwards I was very keen on everything to do with military life, and—contrary to what seems to be the experience of most recruits—my period of training was, in fact, one of the pleasantest, though certainly not the "cushiest," episodes in my "military career." Often in later days, when the glamour and novelty had worn thin and I longed for the freedom of civil life, I would recall with incredulity the zeal with which I had then worked to become an efficient soldier. In those early days I tried really hard to learn the various drill movements and words of command, and to carry them out with all the precision and smartness of which I was capable; I bought and studied a "Manual of Field Training"; I polished buttons and brasses with zest, and felt positively ill-used when the inevitable turns of "swabbing" (billet-cleaning) or other fatigues kept me off the parade-ground!

I suppose this keenness was in large measure due to the novelty of the new life and the unaccustomed good health which it brought me, but also my sincere enthusiasm for the cause for which we were fighting and a new feeling of self-respect now that I no longer had to despise myself for being "unfit" to serve that cause, played a very large part. Despite the strangeness and discomforts (by home standards) of our living conditions, the strenuous and often exhausting nature of the training, and the frequent petty humiliations we had to endure from those in authority over us, I truly believe that those first months in the Army were the first time since 1914 when I really experienced the blessing of a clear conscience and a mind at rest within itself. For although, as I have already shown, I had remained a civilian for so long by no fault of my own, while many of my best friends were in khaki, my anomalous position had been a source of continual worry and self-reproach. Now, at least, that stigma was removed and, at whatever cost to myself, I could hold up my head with the best of them. Soon after joining the H.B. I wrote to my Mother: "We are training for Active Service, but you mustn't mind that, for everyone has to do his bit. It is such a glorious privilege, and I am proud to take my place . . . . You don't know how great it is to be doing something for the Country at last. It is worth everything to know that I am of some use at last to England." No doubt all this reads like cheap boasting, and it is almost embarassing even now to quote it, but, to the best of my recollection, it is a sincere reflection of my sentiments at that time.

.   .   .   .   .   .

Training now commenced in earnest, and our first days of idleness gave place to a strenuous activity. Each morning, reveille sounded at 5.45 a.m., and after a wash and shave we fell in on the road outside the billet for roll-call at 6.15 ; breakfast followed at 6.30 in the mess-hut in the Barracks. Then back to the billet, where room and passages had to be swept out, bedding, blankets and spare kit folded and arranged according to a strict regulation pattern ready for the daily billet-inspection, and we gave our brasses a last hurried rub-over. "First Parade," by the whole Battalion (then, I believe, about fourteen hundred strong) took place at eight o'clock. The roll was called again, and after each platoon or squad had been meticulously inspected by its own officer and reported "all present and correct" (or otherwise) to the C.O., the Colonel put us through a few formal movements and then handed us over to our separate commanders for the day's programme of training.

The Recruit-squad of which I was a member comprised about thirty men, all of whom had been passed by the Colonel the previous week-end. It was under the charge of Sergeant-Instructor Lynch, and we paraded at the extreme rear of the Battalion. Sergeant Lynch commenced our "initiation" by delivering a short informal lecture on discipline, smartness and the "duties of a soldier." Then he made us fall in, in two ranks, and explained how to come to attention, to "number off from the right," to "stand properly at ease," to "right-turn," and the rest, all of which we endeavoured to imitate with the tense awkwardness of nervous beginners and with very indifferent success. But the Sergeant was lenient towards our bungling efforts at first. "I don't expect you to do everything right first time," he said, "but I do expect you all to do your best. If you 'play the game' with me, I'll play the game with you; but if I find anyone idling or trying to 'swing it on me'—God help him! He'll wish he'd never been born!"

But this mild beginning did not last. Soon the Sergeant's unerring eye had picked out the men who were "trying," and those who were "trying it on" or were merely "dumb." The latter did indeed come to "wish they had died before they were born!" The full flood of his invective fell upon them, he "chased" them without respite, and we all suffered vicariously for their shortcomings. But I will say this for Sergeant Lynch: he always recognised willingness, and never reported anyone without good reason.

For the first day or two we drilled without equipment and learned the various words of command and the elementary movements of "foot-drill," diversified by spells of physical exercises. Then we were given an obsolete pattern of "drill-practise" rifle, with which we sloped-, ordered-, presented-, trailed-, reversed-, and piled arms—did everything possible with them, apparently, except fire them. And we marched and counter-marched, and wheeled, and right- or left-inclined, and "formed squad" and "about-turned," with gradually increasing efficiency, until we were streaming with sweat and weak at the knees with exhaustion. Our instructor was unsparing and not to be satisfied; time after time we would perform the same evolution with what to us seemed to be perfect precision and smartness, only to be told in lurid language that we were "a lousy lot of bastards" and the "worst bloody crew of knock-kneed imbeciles" he had ever set eyes on. It was not sufficient merely to perform a movement correctly and in unison; every order must be carried out with the exaggerated energy and abrupt jerks of automatons. When we marched or turned about, formed-fours or halted, we must stamp the ground (the Sergeant: "Come along, you won't crack the asphalt!"); when sloping arms or presenting, we must hit the rifle, until our hands were covered with bruises and blisters; and between movements we must remain perfectly immobile, without moving an eyelash. ("Right or wrong—keep *still*!")

Needless to say, we did not achieve even approximate efficiency on the Barrack-square in a few days or weeks, and it was a hard and difficult road of "toil and sweat" that we trod before we began to look something like a squad of real soldiers. There were some among us who seemed incapable of doing anything right—and some, at first, who did not even want to. The Sergeant had a summary method of dealing with them: they would be called out of the ranks and made to repeat the movements time after time in front of us all, to the accompaniment of unrestrained objurgations. "I can work —— miracles, I can!" he would cry. "I can make even a lousy, horrible crew of —— ——rs like you into soldiers; and I will, too, by ——!"

And perform that particular miracle he did, though certainly not "by kindness." He was relentless in the way he put us through our paces, and quite uninhibited in his criticisms of our performance. "A wet shirt" he promised us, and a wet shirt he frequently gave us. If our marching was not to his liking, he would often quicken the pace to almost impossible speeds—"left— right—left—right—left, right, left, right, left right left right left!— about turn!—as you were!"—until we were pounding along with hammering hearts and bursting lungs, convinced that we must soon crack under the strain. "If you won't do it willingly, I'll —— —— well make you!" he would shout; "you'll be glad to do it right before I've done with you. Lion-tamers have got nothing on me!" "You may break your mother's heart, but you won't break mine — Squad! 'Shun!!" One of his favourite devices for "waking us up" was to give an order, countermand it, and give it again, a score of times, with lightning rapidity: "form fours!"—as you were!—form fours!—as you were!——" until we were dizzy with dashing to and fro, breathless and thoroughly tangled up; whereupon, he would hurl imprecations upon our heads and slanders on our ancestry which, taken at their face value, were as blasphemously insulting as they were indecent. To men fresh from respectable homes his language was at first profoundly shocking, and it sounded as though he bore an implacable hatred towards us, both individually and collectively; but we soon realised that there was no malice behind his profanities, and learned to allow his abuse to slide off us without resentment.

In fact, as we came to know him better, most of us soon discovered that Sergeant Lynch was not only an efficient instructor but also a fine character. He was an Irish Guardsman, one of the "Old Contemptibles," who had been "out" at Mons, wounded during the first months of the war and sent home with a smashed collar-bone and a glass eye. His harsh "brutality" and corrosive language were largely assumed, an echo of Caterham and the "peace-time" Army. They may have been unnecessary, but they certainly achieved results. But behind his "regimental" manner he possessed a fund of humour and good-nature, and—off parade— would talk to us in friendly fashion and give us useful tips about military matters and barrack routine. Occasionally, when it was very hot and no officers were in sight, he would tell us to "fall out" under the trees in a far corner of the training-field and, while we lay around and smoked, would regale us with yarns of his experiences in the Great Retreat and "First Ypres." He was tall and lean, almost emaciated in appearance, and the rigidity of his carriage was accentuated by his war-injuries, which had permanently stiffened his left shoulder ; he permitted no undue familiarities, but in a short while he had won the unstinted admiration and respect of all but a small, incurably disgruntled minority, and it was mainly by his untiring efforts that we were transformed, in the course of a few weeks, from a crowd of the most varied and incongruous individuals into—although I say it !— one of the smartest recruit-squads in No. 3 Coy., drilling as one man and with a certain collective pride of our own. When the time came for us to leave him, when we were "passed out" and transferred as a squad to No. 2 Coy., we had a "whip-round" for his benefit and raised a very respectable sum as a testimonial.

.   .   .   .   .   .

We were known as "Sergt. Lynch's Squad," and he was in the main responsible for our training as recruits, but from time to time we would be handed over to other N.C.O.'s, who varied considerably both in ability and in character. Some of these were comparatively easy-going, whose parades were "cushy" ; others, like Corporal Prior, were "gentlemen," whose authority derived from quiet force of character and confident efficiency. Corporal Prior was our "P.T." instructor, young, fair and athletic, who led us in physical drill, gymnastics, running, and the like ; he worked us hard, but seldom raised his voice against us unduly, and never used bad language. He was well liked by all of us.

But there were also one or two who seemed to us to be examples of the worst types turned out by the pre-war traditions of "Little Sparta." One of these was a Sergeant of the Grenadiers, burly, red-faced and vulgar, who was particularly merciless in "putting us through it." No matter how long we had been on parade or how hot the weather, he would, on the slightest excuse (or on none), make us do everything "at the double"—I think he had a real sadistic delight in seeing us suffer, and often drove us to the limits of endurance. Several men collapsed under his treatment, and one—John Burdett ("Birdie"), a likeable and painstaking youngster—was taken to hospital, where it was rumoured that he died of an over-strained heart. Another Sergeant (also, I am afraid, a Grenadier) was, without exception, the most foul-mouthed man I have ever heard. His scarifyingly virulent vocabulary was inexhaustible, and he could pour out obscenities for five minutes on end without ever once repeating himself. If an officer was near he would be mild as milk, but once we were out of earshot he would take it out of us with a stream of frantically filthy language impossible to describe. He gave many of us the impression that he was half insane. The Bombing Sergeant, who later taught us how to "bowl" hand-grenades, was another of the "swine," who, when he could do so with safety to himself, would often express his dilike of individuals by physical ill-treatment.

More than almost anything, I think (because there was no escape from it, on or off parade) I hated the almost universal use of so-called "Army language"—though, of course, it was no more peculiar to the Army than to many other walks of life. I got used to it, as I got used to many unpleasant things in the Service, but nevertheless I felt (though naturally I did not say so except to like-minded friends) that it was nauseating and quite unnecessary. I never allowed myself to use the common filthy forms of speech, not from any feeling of superiority or priggishness, but perhaps because they were alien to my upbringing and my shy self-consciousness would have robbed them in my case of the spontaneity and essential meaninglessness which was their only excuse. I never thought the worse of a man for his "strong language" alone—indeed, some of the finest fellows I met in the Army were, on occasion, extremely "foul-mouthed"—and I realised that in most cases it was only a case of "habit" or the desire to "do as Rome does"; but there were times when I longed, with an intense longing, to hear the "King's English" spoken without blasphemous or sexual embroidery!

Nevertheless, little else could have been expected in a "People's Army" at that time. Recruited from the whole mass of the population, the vast majority of the troops came from the "working class," whose normal means of self-expression in those days of imperfect popular education was largely limited to that kind of "Rabelaisian" talk, and N.C.O.'s whose task it was to "discipline" them had perforce (even if it was not "natural" to them) to adopt the language of the people. It was quite unavoidable in a community which lacked the restraints of feminine society and the civilising influence of home life. As I have said, most of it was, from a literal point of view, meaningless, a means of emphasis and a habit which was almost a "manly" convention —but it was often carried to quite inexcusable extremes!

As recruits in No. 3 Company, we came very little into direct contact with the officers. The Colonel-in-Chief of the Battalion was H.M. the King—who, needless to say, never appeared on Battalion Parade!—and Lord Kitchener had been, until his death, Honorary Colonel. Our Commanding Officer was Lieut.-Colonel Hardy, M.C.; the Adjutant, whose name I have forgotten, was a Welsh Guards officer, badly wounded at the Front. Such exalted beings were almost beyond our ken, briefly visible in splendour at the head of Battalion Parade; even the Subalterns rarely appeared, except to walk down our rigid ranks on inspections, uttering criticisms of individuals which were promptly recorded in the Report Book by the accompanying N.C.O. In those days there was a considerable gulf between commissioned and non-commissioned ranks, who were assumed in theory to come from widely different social levels, and any personal contact between them was attended by official formalities. For instance, a Trooper must never presume to address an officer unless first spoken to ; he could put in an application to see the Company Officer, or, through him, the C.O., by means of a neatly-written note in stereotyped phraseology handed in to the Orderly Room, and if the application was granted (as it nearly always was) he would parade at the appropriate Company or C.O.'s Orders and be marched in by the Sergeant-in-Waiting, with all the nerve-racking "wind-up" of such functions. If he wished to speak to an officer of lower rank, he must be marched up to him by an N.C.O., and stand rigidly at attention during the interview. In comparison with and in relation to an officer, a private soldier was, in theory, "less than the dust" ; he was assumed to be ignorant, boorish and entirely lacking in the finer sensibilities of a holder of the King's Commission. But in theory only. I was soon to find out that there were as fine "gentlemen" in the ranks as in the Officers' Mess—and conversely! In justice to our own officers and those of the Guards, I think most of them recognised this, too.

There are, in truth, only two officers of No. 3 Coy. of whom I have any clear recollection as individuals ; one was the Company Officer, Captain Hibbard, a middle-aged man with a genial manner rather like that of a family doctor, who, when he questioned me one day about my antecedents, revealed a familiarity with my home town and my Father's business and acquaintance with some people I also knew there (a fact which may have redounded to my advantage, for, on the only occasion when I was brought before him on a charge of minor misdemeanour, he let me off with a mild admonishment !) ; the other was one of the lieutenants, whose name I cannot recall, who offered to recommend me for "stripes" when I had been with the Company about a month. I declined the invitation, however, because I did not feel myself to be at all competent to give orders to other men ; and also because at the time I had some romantic notion of serving in the ranks anonymously, without personal distinction or promotion!

I was told on good authority (and I can well believe it) that the tempo of our training in the H.B. was considerably higher than in most ordinary infantry units. The standards of smartness and efficiency to which we aspired were those of the Brigade of Guards, and before the war it had been reckoned that eighteen months was the minimum time needed to turn out a fully-trained Guardsman. Now, to meet the urgent calls for reinforcements from the Front, the process had to be crammed into four or five months. (Of course, pre-war "old sweats" questioned whether the products of this speeding-up were authentic "Guardsmen," but I think that on the whole we became a sufficiently close imitation for practical purposes!) It was hard work, though, for men fresh from civilian life, and in my case the exceptionally hot weather of my first weeks did not tend to make it easier ; but, somewhat to my own surprise, I throve on the unaccustomed exertions. I had never been used to hard muscular exercise in the past, and the day's parades often left me limp with exhaustion, but I always recovered my energy quite quickly, slept soundly at night and awoke in the morning free from stiffness. I had never in my life enjoyed such perfect physical health as during those first months of training.

On only one occasion did the heat get the better of me, towards the end of a spell of rifle drill ; we were standing at the slope in the blazing sun, when suddenly I felt everything start to spin round me, and I "fell out" (quite literally) in a dead faint. The next thing I knew, I was lying under the trees at the side of the Square, and the Sergeant told me to go back to the billet for the remainder of the morning. But I protested that I was quite all right, and after a few minutes' rest went back to my place in the ranks.

Strange though it may seem, at that time I really enjoyed the strenuous life and was happier than for a long time past. My Mother, at home, seemed to think that she knew better and that my enthusiastic letters were only an elaborate camouflage to hide my real feelings. I had hard work to reassure her. "Now, don't go imagining that you can 'read between the lines,' as usual, because you can't! I am *not* miserable, by a long way," I wrote ; "I wouldn't be back in civilian life, in war-time, if I could." (Would I have endorsed the last sentence, at all times, during the next two years?—I wonder!

On very few days was the programme exactly the same. Foot-drill, arms-drill and physical exercises (with or without equipment) occupied most of the time, in spells of three-quarters of an hour or an hour each, separated usually by ten or fifteen minutes' breaks, when we would scramble for mineral waters, "wads" or cups of tea in the canteen. There were also from time to time lectures on various subjects and demonstration of such things as assembling full marching order and laying out kit for inspection, practice in saluting (known to the troops as "swank parades") and sometimes a country route-march. I used to enjoy the last ; there is nothing so exhilarating as marching along a fairly level road in "drill-order," heads up, arms swinging in unison, feet beating rhythmically in step, imagining that we were making a deep impression on the people we passed. "Left—left—left-right left! Put some swank into it! Swing those arms! Put a jerk into it! You, there—Smith—d'you think you're the only one in step? Left—left!" (Thus, the Sergeant.) Sometimes we sang, but more often whistled, as we marched "at ease" ; there were some expert whistlers among us, and the squad made something of a name for itself by its rendering of popular tunes—"The Long, Long Trail," "Pack Up Your Troubles," "Keep the Home Fires Burning," etc.—as we swung along. Our officers encouraged us in this, and (so I heard) backed our musical skill against any other platoon in the Battalion.

Normally, we were dismissed for the day at four o'clock, though frequently, especially on route-march days, it might be later, and then we were—in theory—free to do as we liked until 9.30. But—and it was an important "but"—there was then "cleaning-up" to be done in readiness for the next day's parades and inspection. Every bit of metal on uniform or equipment had to be polished, bayonets burnished, scabbards and chin-straps heel-balled, boots blacked or dubbined, and webbing blancoed. There were nearly seventy pieces of brass alone—buttons, buckles, cap-badge, numerals, studs, etc.—which had to shine like the sun every day on pain of punishment-drill; for not only the articles in actual use were included, but also the metal "adornments" of spare uniform and greatcoat, and the duplicate pair of boots must be kept polished, even the insteps of the soles! My button-stick and tin of "Soldier's Friend" metal polish (moistened with "spit" and applied with an old toothbrush) were in constant operation. We were also expected to keep a knife-like crease in our slacks, which we did by soaping the insides of the folds and sleeping on them.

But with practice I soon found that this work could be got through in much less time than I had at first thought possible. There were a number of "old-soldier" dodges for lightening the toil, and I usually had a fair amount of free time in the evenings, and on Saturday and Sunday afternoons—for in No. 3 Coy. we did no guards or pickets; only if we were unlucky enough to be detailed for a fatigue, or had been "awarded" punishment drill for losing our name on parade, was our scanty leisure interfered with. But most of us did not feel inclined for anything very active after the day's parades, and often found a shady spot down by the river or a table in the Canteen or Y.M.C.A. Hut where we could sit and talk, or read, or write letters. Windsor was not well provided with indoor amusements and I should imagine would be rather dull in winter, but in summer that hardly mattered; there was always the river bank to lie on and the boating to watch, and the Great Park, with its ancient oaks, avenues of "immemorial elms" and herds of deer, was close at hand and pleasant to wander in.

I often went to the Y.M.C.A. Recreation Hut in Batchelor's Acre, near the Victoria Barracks, which was always crowded and where one could listen to concerts, join in "sing-songs," play billiards or have supper. I always felt that I had a special claim on this Hut, for it had been presented to the "Y.M." by the Linen and Woollen Drapers Association, a trade organisation to which I belonged. An annexe of the main hut was used as a "Quiet Room," in which one could read or write letters undisturbed, and there was a Post Office for the troops. I used to have the parcels I frequently received from home sent "care-of" the latter, as being safer than sending them to the Barracks, where they sometimes "went astray"; and, after one or two acute "financial crises," I obtained some money from home and opened a small emergency savings-bank account, so as to be to some extent independent of "pay-day" vagaries.

It was food that "ran away with" most of my money in those days. Our official rations were not ungenerous, either in quantity or quality—though the cooking and method of serving up often left something to be desired; we certainly got more to eat than the average civilian in that time of food-shortage—probably more than many of our number had ever enjoyed regularly in their lives—but we were nevertheless always hungry, and were impelled to supplement the rations by private purchases whenever possible. There was a small canteen in our part of the Barracks and a small shop just outside the gates, where mineral waters, chocolate and cigarettes could be bought during the short intervals between parades; in the evenings my four room-mates and I would have a substantial supper of sausages-and-mash or fish-and-chips at the "Soldier's Home" or the "Y.M.," and then, still unsatisfied, would take back with us a large loaf of new bread and half-a-pound of butter to eat before we turned in. The gallons of sweat which I must have shed on the Barrack square, making it necessary many times almost literally to wring out my shirt, demanded constant replacement by copious draughts of water, lemonade, milk or tea, when available—but not beer!

When I was first called-up, warned by several well-meaning people that I should find the Army a "hot-bed of drunkenness," I had made a firm resolution to be a strict teetotaller "for the Duration." I had not at that time acquired any liking for alcohol, but I must have had a very poor opinion of my own strength of character (perhaps with reason), for I doubted my ability to resist excess if I once started drinking. I think now that this was a foolish and unnecessary decision, for it inevitably cut me off from much good-fellowship, and some of my pals must have thought me unfriendly, or perhaps priggish, in refusing to join them in the "wet" Canteen or the "Lord Raglan" and "have one." But having made my resolution, I stuck to it to the end—with two exceptions: the first was during the Company's "Christmas dinner" in Arras six months later, and the other occasion was when three or four of us had a drink together in celebration of our transfer to the Coldstream Guards the following March. I did not, however, refuse the rum-ration which was sometimes issued on cold nights in the trenches, choosing to regard this, with convenient casuistry, as "medicinal"; and I may as well say that teetotalism was not one of my "Army habits" which I carried over into civil life.

When walking out we had to wear a webbing belt and carry a cane three feet in length. At that time saluting was performed with the right or left hand, according to which was farthest away from the officer being saluted, and I remember that the manipulation of the cane caused me some embarrassment at first. The correct precedure when approaching an officer was to tuck the cane under the arm nearest to him, count two paces, turn the head and eyes smartly towards him and salute with the other hand—a somewhat complicated manœuvre to an earnest and nervous beginner. The first time I went into the town in uniform, by bad luck I encountered an officer unexpectedly, coming round a street corner, and, being unprepared, got flustered and thoroughly mixed up with my cane! I was ready to sink through the ground with shame, but the officer evidently grasped the situation, for he returned the salute with an amused grin and passed on.

A few days after joining I had come across another man from Tunbridge Wells in the Battalion—or, to be more exact, he sought me out, having seen my name on the daily list of new recruits posted outside the Orderly Room. Returning from a Sunday-morning stroll with my room-mates, we found him waiting in our room, and he introduced himself as Arthur Brookes, son of a fellow-tradesman at home; he had been at Windsor about seven weeks, and had been told by his father that "young Mr. Noakes, of Calverley Road," had joined the Batt. He was, I think, slightly younger than I, tall and slender, with a pleasant manner which made an immediate favourable impression on me. We were both pleased at meeting someone from our own town, and did not take long to become acquainted; in the course of a walk in the Park that afternoon we exchanged reminiscences about the life we had so recently left and impressions of the Army, and discovered that we both shared a love of reading and a mutual interest in literary topics. This in itself was a sufficiently rare trait in our present environment to create a bond between us, and throughout my stay in Windsor, until I went overseas, we spent a good deal of our spare time together. Brookes had been training as a school-teacher before being called up, and was now in No. 2 Coy., billetted in "St. Swithin's," a house at the other end of Osborne Road. It was a great pleasure to me to find someone who was interested in the same things as I was and could discuss the "things of the mind" intelligently, away from the noisy gregariousness of the billet. I recall many pleasant off-duty hours spent wandering in the Great Park, lying on the river-bank or sitting on the terrace of Windsor Castle, while we argued amicably about books, politics and the war, and talked of many things:

> "Of shoes—and ships—and sealing wax—
> Of cabbages—and kings—"

Of course, we didn't see eye to eye on all subjects, especially politics and the war, about which Brookes often expressed views with which I strongly disagreed, but we never fell-out, and I think enjoyed even our differences. In the field of literature, however, we were on common ground, and sometimes bought books jointly and discussed favourite authors and poetry — especially Omar Khayyam, whose fatalistic philosophy appealed to both of us. Incidentally, to Arthur Brookes I owe my first introduction to the game of chess. Our friendship made all the difference to me during those first months.

Two anti-typhoid inoculations and vaccination, at this time, caused me little discomfort beyond a temporary lassitude and drowsiness—not an unusual condition with me in any case, perhaps!—though some of the men became quite ill as a consequence. What surprised me was to see two of the fellows—both strong, healthy men—turn pale and "pass-out" completely at the mere sight of the hypodermic, before the doctor had even touched them.

At intervals there was a Bathing Parade, when we were marched to a secluded backwater of the Thames and splashed in the shallow water for half-an-hour. We undressed under the trees, and on one occasion, on returning to my clothes, I found that someone had "won" my wrist-watch. I could not swim at that time, but I always enjoyed these expeditions, which were almost the only parades not performed "by numbers" and were the occasion of much noisy hilarity and ragging. Once, I tried to see how long I could hold my breath under-water, but after about a minute beneath the surface I found myself being hurriedly dragged to the bank by two scandalised comrades, who thought I was trying to commit suicide! Some evenings Brookes and I, armed with a towel and soap, would go into the town for a "proper" bath. There were no facilities for a hot bath in the billets (there may have been in the Barracks, though if there were I never heard of them), but we knew a barber's shop in Windsor where we could have a good one for a few pence; we would secure adjoining cubicles so that we could continue our conversation over the intervening partition.

Laundry, too, I never trusted to the official arrangements. One could have one's clothes washed free of charge at the Barracks, but I was told by many men that they were badly done and that one seldom got one's own things back; so I used to post most things home, and such things as socks and handkerchiefs I often washed myself in the garden behind the billet. What with jobs like this, and the periodical turns of "swabbing" (as billet-cleaning was called), when floors and bed-boards were scrubbed, windows cleaned and palliasses re-filled with fresh straw, I sometimes wondered whether the name "Household Battalion" had not another, and more domestic, significance!

I also found it advisable to take precautions of my own in other matters, especially with regard to the "post." Ordinary letters were delivered to the billet, but registered letters and parcels had to be collected from the Battalion Orderly Room, and after two parcels and a registered letter containing money had unaccountably gone astray and could not be traced by Post Office enquiries at both ends, I always took advantage of the Y.M.C.A. facilities previously mentioned.

Every Sunday morning there was a ceremonial Church Parade by the whole Battalion (except the newest recruits), when we marched with great *éclat* and "spit-and-polish" to Trinity Church, the garrison church of Windsor, for service at ten-thirty. The building was redolent with military history, hung round with tattered regimental Colours and panelled with Rolls-of-Honour relating to many past campaigns, and the scene, when the sun streamed through stained-glass windows on the closely-packed ranks of khaki and glittering accoutrements, was unforgettable. To me, the most impressive moments of the service were when we rose to our feet and the sound of hundreds of iron-shod boots on the wooden floor preluded each hymn with a roll of low thunder. A military band provided the music, and the National Anthem was accompanied by a crash of drums. After Parade, on fine Sundays, the Regimental Band of the Life Guards played for an hour on the Barrack Square, which was thrown open to the public.

. . . . . .

At last, towards the end of July, the stage in our training was reached when the official tests in recruit drill were made, and, with a few exceptions, we "passed out" for transfer to No. 2 Company. It was said that Capt. Hibbard was so pleased with our performance that he granted all applications from members of the squad for week-end leave without question. I had been home for the first time the previous week, from "after duties Saturday to Sunday midnight"—a short but welcome break. We took our leave of Sergeant Lynch with genuine regret, and—as I have said—expressed our regard for him in a substantial testimonial. On the last day under his command a large photograph of the squad was taken, a copy of which I still have.

Our 'prentice days were now over, and although we did not yet claim to be "seasoned veterans," we considered ourselves to be practically trained soldiers! At any rate, we considered ourselves entitled to treat with lofty condescension the raw new "rookies" who now formed the bulk of No. 3 Coy., by virtue of our seven-weeks' seniority of service.

Our "promotion" involved changes of billets, and when, a few days later, I found myself in the same house as Arthur Brookes and, by favour of the Corporal in charge, occupying the next bed to him, we considered ourselves to be "quids in." We could now carry on our discussions long after "Lights out," until shut up by the protests of our neighbours. ("Put a sock in it, you two, for Christ's sake! Some of us need some sleep, if you don't!")

Training in our new Company was intensified compared with No. 3; we were up earlier, the mid-day break for dinner was cut to little more than half-an-hour most days, and we had a good deal of drilling in full kit; but by this time we had become used to hard work and it didn't worry us much. We now had our own rifles, "Short Lee-Enfields"—hitherto, "D.P.'s" had been issued for rifle-drill and returned to the Stores after each parade—and this meant more cleaning. We became familiar with the use of the "pull-through" and "four-by-two," the magazine and the ammunition, the proper oiling and mechanism of the bolt, "fixing" and "unfixing" bayonets on parade, and a score of other details. We had a great deal of practice in loading and aiming with dummy cartridges ("ten in the tin and one in the tunnel") and many lectures on the great importance of taking the utmost care of our rifles. "Your rifle is your best friend," our Sergeant was never tired of repeating. "Look after it as carefully as you would your wife—rub it over with an oily rag every day!" Parading in full marching order and guard-mounting practice took place several times a week, and I found this back-aching work at first, for F.S.M.O. (field-service marching order) weighed something like 35 lbs. in addition to the 9¼ lbs. of the rifle, and a hundred rounds of ammunition. Before the war I doubt if I could have even lifted this weight with ease, and it is a measure of my new-found strength and fitness that very soon I was marching and drilling under it almost without discomfort. Some of the loads we had to carry about with us later, at the Front, were considerably greater.

One of the principal features of the "No. 2 Coy." stage of training was a three-weeks' course of Musketry. This, for our own and contemporary squads, took place during August. But the fine, hot weather which had lasted almost continuously since I first joined up and is an inseparable part of my recollections of my recruit-training, now broke, and heavy showers of thundery rain played havoc with the schedules for firing practice. (It was this same persistent rain-area which caused the disastrous failure of the Passchendaele offensive and turned the Flanders battle-ground into a sea of mud.) The range over which we fired was at Runnymede, the historic site of the signing of the Magna Carta by King John, but very few of the men seemed to be impressed by the fact. I mentioned it to one of my friends, and all the reply he made was, "Well, I wish he'd sign my —— ticket as well!" The plain was quite bare and open, without a vestige of cover, and on several days we were soaked to the skin without being able to fire a shot. We travelled to the range by train each morning, carrying food for the mid-day meal, and returned in the late afternoon in a like manner. Despite the unfavourable conditions, I think most of us enjoyed the course, and there was considerable competition to win prizes to which we subscribed among ourselves, for the best scores in the squad. On the day of the final classification tests there was a series of heavy downpours interspersed with bursts of hot sunshine—conditions which did not aid in marksmanship; nevertheless, the Company as a whole did quite well, and in our squad I secured the fourth highest number of points and qualified as a "1st Class Shot," which entitled me to an extra 3d. a day as "Proficiency Pay."

Then followed several days of Gas Helmet Drill, which was popular and interesting. The box-respirator had not then come into general use, and our "helmets" were of the old "P.H." type, a grey flannel bag covering the head and neck completely, coming to a point on top; breathing was through a rubber valve mouthpiece and there were round mica goggles; and the fabric was impregnated with some chemical which gave it a soapy feel. When we were "all dressed up" we looked like a cross between the Ku-Klux-Klan and the "Missing Link"! Putting the helmets on was (of course!) made into a drill movement, "by numbers," and we practised carrying out ordinary parade movements while wearing them, as well as field-exercises and firing with rifles. Also, it was necessary to learn to move by signal, for it was practically impossible to hear shouted orders in the P.H." Finally, the practical efficiency of our masks was demonstrated in a gas-chamber; we were herded into a specially-constructed hut in the middle of the Great Park, the doors were shut and a cylinder of poison-gas turned on. The deadly fumes, sufficient—so they said—to kill us all in thirty seconds, turned all our brasses green (and caused us a lot of trouble afterwards to restore their shine) but did us no harm. One or two of the men, indeed, complained of feeling ill, but all proved to be suffering from nothing worse than "auto-suggestion"—or, perhaps, were just trying to "swing it"! We also went into another hut, filled with lachrymatory gas, and, at a given signal, removed our helmets; immediately our eyes began to stream with tears and to smart as is filled with pepper, and we groped our way into the open air with yells of laughter and handkerchiefs to our faces, for all the world like a hilarious funeral scene in some outrageous farce! I think we all had implicit confidence in our respirators after that.

We also did several route-marches in F.S.M.O.—a rather different matter from our previous marches in "Drill-order"—and P.T. included cross-country runs of two or three miles. Instruction in the gentle art of bayonet fighting was given in a field near the Barracks on several occasions; it was strenuous and interesting, if one could forget what the straw-stuffed dummies we attacked were supposed to represent, though the Sergeant's blood-curdling directions to "twist the bayonet in his guts" and "jump on his face" left little to the imagination. "Use every dirty trick you know," he would say. "Kick him in the privates; bash him with the butt; its him or you!" I sincerely (though perhaps a trifle illogically) hoped that I should never be involved in hand-to-hand conflict.

Other days, or parts of days, were spent in the Park, building sandbag parapets, digging trenches, practising taking cover in open ground and attacking by sections in short rushes ; also learning how to build open fires and cook our own food on them. Windsor Great Park was ideal country for field training ; it was seemingly illimitable in extent, with wide open spaces dotted with ancient trees, shady copses and grassy slopes and crossed by avenues of elm, oaks or chestnuts. The avenue which was nearest, and consequently best known to us, was the famous "Long Walk," which ran in a dead-straight line for three miles, from the "George IV Gateway" of the Castle to the "Copper Horse," an equestrian figure of George III, bordered by a double line of elm trees nearly three hundred years old.

Field exercises, however, were not allowed to supercede parade-ground drill, on the smartness and precision of which great emphasis was laid. We spent hours on the Squqare, drilling as a separate squad or as part of the Company. Our squad was several times commended for its proficiency, and on one occasion the O.C. told us that ours was the smartest Company drill he had ever seen!

At this distance in time I find it difficult to credit that we got through such a variety and intensity of training in so short a time, but the detailed exactness with which I can still remember most of it is evidence both of the competence of our instructors and of our own youthful powers of assimilation. I sometimes think that I could repeat, from memory, everything we did then— parade-ground drill and field-training alike — were my wind as sound, my muscles as supple and my energies as unflagging, as they were all those years ago. But probably I couldn't!

During the month of August the Court was in residence at the Castle, and this, as may be imagined, was the cause of much "wind-up" among the authorities. Extra-special attention was paid (if that were possible!) to spit-and-polish, and woe betide any man whose uniform was not immaculate, whose hair was an eighth-of-an-inch too long or whose chin was not "smooth as a baby's bottom"! Dozens of orders appeared daily on the Orderly-room notice-board, detailing the procedure to be followed on any conceivable occasion, should we encounter Royalty while on the march or when off-duty. It was apparently anticipated that we might encounter the King while walking down Peascod Street, sitting on the river-bank, strolling in the Park or drinking a cup of tea in the "Y.M." As a matter of fact, we never once set eyes on His Majesty, though on one occasion we saw the Queen, in rather embarrassing circumstances which apparently had not been provided for in the regulations. We were doing physical exercises with rifles in the field opposite the Barracks and, it being a very warm morning, we had been allowed to discard most of our clothing. Suddenly, without warning, Her Majesty appeared in a horse-drawn carriage, driving along the road close to where we were drilling. Our Sergeant was seized with panic and lost his head for the moment; he called us hurriedly to attention and gave the order to "present arms"—quite incorrectly, in our state of "undress." We must have presented a rather unorthodox spectacle, for the Queen turned in her seat and stared at us for as long as the carriage was in sight.

About this time air-raid warnings were fairly frequent, by day and by night. One or two of these, no doubt, were genuine, for although Windsor had never been attacked, London was only twenty miles away and had been bombed several times. One, in particular, if "phoney," was realistically staged-managed. We had just finished Battalion parade and had fallen out for a few minutes' break, when an R.F.C. despatch-rider roared through the gate on a motor-cycle and handed an envelope to the Colonel. (Why not have telephoned?) He (the C.O.) immediately summoned all officers, with the result that we were fallen-in and doubled back to our respective billets, with orders to get into full marching-order at once. The reason given (unofficially) was— "an invasion and a raid by a thousand planes"! After standing by our beds and sweltering for a couple of hours, we were told to take off our kit and go to dinner, and shortly afterwards were instructed to go on afternoon parade as usual—somewhat to our disappointment, for few of us had then so much as heard a bomb burst and were ready for some excitement. But apparently the "invasion" had been beaten off without our assistance!

During another raid-warning we were turned out in the middle of the night and marched into the Park, with what object no one seemed to know. After that, we had orders to keep F.S.M.O. in readiness by our beds every night. One evening we were warned to be ready to leave Windsor at five-minutes' notice, and it was reported that we were to guard the railways in the event of a threatened strike. Next day, it was credibly stated that we were to be rushed to the East Coast, to meet yet another "invasion," but this report, too, turned out to be a "furph." ("Furph" was a slang word apparently peculiar to the H.B., signifying "baseless rumour" or "wind-up.")

Nevertheless, all these furphs caused us serious concern—not because they might be true, but because they repeatedly interfered with (or so we imagined) the realisation of our "Draft Leave." This was the statutory five-days' Leave given to every recruit before he could legally be sent overseas, but as it was the custom in the H.B. to give it from No. 2 Coy., after one had passed-out in Musketry but before training was complete, it did not necessarily indicate an early overseas posting. I had had two short week-end leaves previously, but the prospect of five clear days at home was as exciting as breaking-up for school holidays! After several disappointments, those of us in the squad who qualified received our passes on the evening of August 28th. They were made out "as from" the following morning, but in consideration of sixpence dropped in the Corporal-Major's cap, we got them twelve hours early—one could do much in the Company Office by a little judicious bribery—and I made a bee-line for the train to London. Arriving at Charing Cross, however, I found to my disgust that I had just lost the last connection for Tunbridge Wells, so I boarded a train which only went as far as Tonbridge, intending to walk the remaining five miles. But by the time I got to Tonbridge, about midnight, a gale was blowing and it was raining in torrents, so rather than be soaked to the skin I spent an uncomfortable night trying to sleep on a seat in the station waiting-room. About dawn I got a lift in the guard's van of a milk train, and arrived home unannounced at a quarter to five.

On returning to Windsor after midnight on the following Sunday, in company with a crowd of our fellows whom I had met at Paddington, we drew our kit and bedding, rifles and bed-boards, from the Company stores, where they had been handed in before we left, and carted them to Osborne Road, only to find that the squad had been moved during our absence to another house, and that adequate accommodation had not been reserved for us. Consequently, we had to squeeze in between the other beds, on the floor, by the light of matches and to an accompaniment of curses from the disturbed sleepers. Next day we managed to sort things out satisfactorily.

That week was one of almost daily ceremonial drill in the Park, with the Colonel and the Adjutant as audience, and the word went round that we were shortly to be reviewed by the King. But that, too, like so many other rumours, proved to be without foundation.

The move to "Elgin Lodge," and then, two days later, to "Ashstead House," meant that Brookes and I were again separated, as he, not having done his Musketry Course, was shifted to another house. He was in the signallers, who were a race apart from the rest of the Company, and did not parade with us but pursued their own esoteric mysteries in the Park. We could, of course, still meet after duties, but not so often as hitherto.

.   .   .   .   .

On September 10th, a number of men from our own and other squads, myself among them, were selected for transfer to No. 1 Company, for the final stages of training. This resulted a few days later in yet another move, the sixth and last at Windsor. The new billet was called "Elmsfield," a large mansion at the corner of Osborne Road and King's Road, which overlooked the Park and housed the greater part of the Company. No. 1 was organised on more regular lines than either of the other two Companies, being composed of four platoons of equal strength instead of an indeterminate number of squads at varying levels of proficiency. Discipline was, in some respects, more strict, but as we were now (in theory, at least) practically trained soldiers, we had somewhat more freedom when off parade, and, as prospective members of the next Draft for the Front, we enjoyed a much greater prestige in the Battalion. The Company was commanded by Capt. A. T. Legge, an officer of the Coldstream Guards, a martinet but a man whom we all came to admire and respect, whose "bark" was considerably worse than his "bite"—and "bark" is the best word to describe his parade-ground voice and manner.

Almost as soon as I joined the Company I was detailed, with a score or more others, to undergo a course of instruction in the mechanism and use of various types of rifle-grenades. I found this a very interesting subject and I think I did fairly well at it. Most of the tuition was by means of lectures in a large room in "Elmsfield," where we sat in rows on wooden forms, taking notes, while the officer-instructor illustrated his points by drawing diagrams on a blackboard. It was rather like being at school again—and some of the "pupils" behaved like overgrown school-boys, too. Some were intelligent and painstaking, others were just "stupid," and a few tried to treat the class as a joke (though in the Army the "schoolmaster" could deal with any attempt at ragging or inattention far more drastically than at school!) At the end of a week a morning was spent putting to practical test the knowledge we were supposed to have acquired. A Major from Brigade Bombing School was present, and expressed himself as very pleased by our performance. The target was a pit some ten feet in diameter, into which we fired bombs from a distance of fifty or sixty yards, from behind a sandbag parapet. Most of us were successful in exploding our grenades more or less in the centre of the target—to fire, the rifle-butt was placed on the ground and aiming was largely a matter of correctly estimating the angle at which the muzzle should be elevated—though one man, probably through nervousness, sent a bomb nearly straight up, so that it fell only a few yards in front of us and we had to throw ourselves flat behind the parapet while it burst. After the demonstration I and several others were posted in "Orders" as having qualified as "Rifle Bombers."

Another day was spent in carrying out (or, in attempting to carry out) "manœuvres," which were rather unrealistic because the opposing forces were entirely imaginary. According to the announced "scheme," we were conducting a fighting withdrawal from Windsor towards London, while the "enemy" was assumed to be attacking from the direction of the Great Park. The weather was unspeakable and rain came down in torrents all day; nobody seemed to have a very clear idea of what we were supposed to be doing, and the whole affair was literally a "wash-out." My platoon saw little of the action almost from the start, for the officer in charge took us the wrong way and we completely lost touch with the rest of the Company; in default of orders from H.Q., therefore, we "occupied" the village of Datchet and, as our officer did not seem to know what else to do with us, we stayed there until afternoon. Rain fell unceasingly, and although our greatcoats and groundsheets were in our packs, they could not be used without spoiling our "smart" appearance, so we had to put up with being soaked to the skin. For two hours I stood on guard on a bridge over the Thames, with water running down inside my clothes all the time. About half-past three the battle was apparently given up as a bad job, and we marched back to billets for a belated dinner. The evening was spent in drying our clothes and trying to restore the shine to our tarnished brasses.

Next day's inspection revealed a spot of rust in the socket of my bayonet which I had overlooked in the candle-light by which we had cleaned up, and for the first and only time at Windsor I "lost my name." At "Company Orders," Capt. Legge, while admitting the extenuating circumstances, awarded me an hour's extra drill—the most serious consequence of which was, from my point of view, that it automatically cancelled the week-end pass I had put in for.

Other exercises in field-training included advancing by sections along the three miles of the Long Walk, from near the Castle gate to the "Copper Horse" at the far end. We would rush forward for twenty or thirty yards, throw ourselves flat and provide "covering fire" for the next section to advance, after which we would go forward under cover of their fire, and so on. We never failed to "capture" our objective in good time for the return for dinner!

Sometimes during these "actions" the Captain would hold up operations while he walked along the line of our recumbent figures and apportioned praise or blame to individuals for such things as the blancoing of equipment or the rolling of puttees. It often seemed to us that the authorities considered "spit-and-polish" more essential than tactics to the winning of battles! On one such occasion I received special commendation for the neat appearance of my pack—but the Captain didn't know that it was lined with special boards which I had had cut for the purpose.

I do not remember that we had any route-marches while I was in No. 1 Coy., but we went everywhere, of course, "on our own flat feet," and when not marching "to attention" we were usually singing. We had our own (not always strictly "respectable") words to fit many of the popular marching-tunes, and whether passers-by understood them we neither knew nor cared. Every ex-Serviceman knows the Army version of "Colonel Bogey"; there were also "You'd be far better off in a Home," "At the halt, on the left, form platoon," and the Coldstream-

Mozart March: " By the right, by the left, by the centre . . . . "
and many others. Well-known hymn tunes were pressed into
service, with words quite otherwise than the original—such as
" The Church's One Foundation " (" We are Fred Karno's Army
. . . . "); " What a Friend we have in Jesus " (" When this
flicking war is over . . . . "); " Holy, holy, holy " (" Grousing,
grousing, grousing—always bloody-well grousing "), etc.; and, of
course, many current music-hall songs and more-or-less repeatable
ditties. To hear us swinging along the road, one might think
that " grousing " was unknown in the H.B.—but we did some
of that, too!

Among the dozen or so of very decent fellows with whom I
shared a room in " Elmsfield," I can now unfortunately remember
clearly only one—a lively, high-spirited lad of near my own age, Ted
Barker, who was by way of being rather a chum of mine at the
time, and who was usually known by the nickname of " Brother."
When we both went to France he was put into another Company
and I lost touch with him, but I encountered him again nearly two
years later, when we were both in the London Motor Ambulance
Column at Kensington. I only saw him once after demobilisation,
but we still exchange greeting-cards every Christmas.

.   .   .   .   .

Soon after my return from Draft Leave I had begun to have a
slight recurrence of my old malady, Asthma, a respiratory trouble
of long standing which, as I have told, had spoiled my childhood
and was mainly responsible for the failure of my earlier efforts
to enlist. At first the spasms were slight and occurred only
during the night, when they caused me little inconvenience beyond
broken rest, and I was able to carry on with my normal duties
during the day ; but towards the middle of September they began
to get worse and I could no longer conceal my disability. The
other fellows in the room were very forbearing and uttered no
word of complaint when I would sit up in bed and pollute the
air with the stifling fumes of " asthma cigarettes "—my " Chinese
fags," as they chaffingly called them. Once, rather reluctantly, I
" reported sick " ; but such is the unpredictable nature of asthma
that, after the long wait outside the M.O.'s office in the early
morning, by the time my turn came to see him all signs of the
malady had vanished, and I was given " medicine and duty,"
with an implied suspicion of malingering.

But a day or two later, on the 27th, I had a really bad turn
which did not clear up, and the M.O. excused me from duty. I
returned to the billet, but during the afternoon became worse, and
the Corporal-Major, coming into the room as I sat on my bed
labouring for breath, was so alarmed by my appearance—asthma
often scares people who are not used to it—that he despatched me
" toute suite " to the Battalion sickroom. The M.O., in his turn,
got the wind-up, and sent me in charge of an orderly to the Life

Guards Hospital in the Barracks, which was fully equipped for cases of real illness. There I was soon installed in a large, airy ward and a comfortable bed, and provided with every hospital comfort.

I was rather bad that night and the next day, but the attack followed its usual course and I soon began to recover, though the spasms continued intermittently for about a fortnight, during which I had a quiet and restful time, with several congenial fellow-patients and plenty of reading-matter. The only drawback was that I was forbidden to smoke, though smoking had never done me any harm as regards asthma—rather, I think, the reverse. But this difficulty could be overcome occasionally, with circum-spection! While I was in hospital, Brookes also was admitted to another ward, suffering from a bad abscess, and as soon as I was more or less convalescent I was able to visit him and exchange notes on our respective clinical symptoms!

I do not know why that scourge of my childhood, asthma, should have returned at that time, just when I had thought it finally eradicated. It was certainly not due to my general health, for I had never been in better physical condition than I was then, and I had no "cold" or other ailment at the time. My own theory, for what it is worth, is that asthma is much less a pathological than a psychological condition, and that may suggest a possible explanation. Until my Draft Leave I had had no sign of the trouble; it was immediately after my return to Windsor that the attacks commenced. Perhaps — despite my genuine keenness to "do my bit" in the Army—five consecutive days at home had revived in my subconscious mind a longing for the easy comforts of home life with which asthma was associated and a return to which the attacks had often in the past been the cause. Many times during my boyhood, asthma (and over-indulgent parents) had been a means of escape from "uncomfortable" conditions at school or elsewhere, and it may well be that now, against my conscious will or desire, the old suppressed mental habit was reasserting itself. I am no psycho-analyst and I do not know whether this is a scientifically plausible explanation, but to me it seems at least a possible one.

The Doctor at the hospital expressed surprise that I should ever have been passed as "A.1," and spoke of sending me before a Medical Board to have my "Category" lowered; it looked as though my career as a "first-line" soldier was about to come to an inglorious end. But on October 16th I was unexpectedly discharged from hospital, and returned to full duty.

. . . . . .

The reason, however, was apparent the following day, when it was announced that a large draft, comprising nearly every trained man in No. 1 Coy., was to leave for France at the end of the week. Rumours of a draft had been current for several weeks past, but there had been no official confirmation and many of us had begun to think that there was no truth in them. Now it was learned that the Service Battalion had suffered heavy casualties in the Passchendaele battle, and that we were required to make up their numbers.

The next few days were a whirlwind of preparation. Kit inspections, medical inspections, the issuing of Active Service pay-books, the filling up of innumerable forms and the answering of endless questions, parades for this, that and the other, followed in bewildering succession. In response to a telegram telling of our imminent departure, my Mother and Father came to Windsor on the Thursday, and we spent part of the evening together. My poor Mother, who watched us parading outside the billet, was horrified at the "brutal" way in which Capt. Legge shouted at us, and refused to believe me when I told her how we all liked and respected him!

My own feelings were chiefly ones of excited anticipation. The general air of stir and bustle, the prospect of going abroad and of seeing for myself things I had so often read about, rather overlaid for the time being any regrets I may have felt at being still further separated from my home and the possibility that I might never return. And at that time, too, the romantic idealism with which I regarded the war was still undimmed by disillusion-ment; it was still to me a holy crusade for the salvation of the world. "If by going," I wrote at the time, "I can help in the smallest degree to shorten the war, and to free the world from the terrible curse that seems laid upon it, it will be well worth while."

As the Prince of Wales (himself a Guardsman) wrote, years later, about his own departure for the Front: "My generation had a rendezvous with History, and my whole being insisted that I share the common destiny, whatever it might be."

So, I think, it was with many of us—a big adventure and a high endeavour, about the sordid realities of which we had then no knowledge—and there was no lack of high spirits in the Company that week. (Although I must admit there were moments when I felt—as, no doubt, many of us did—a secret foreboding of what the unknown future might hold for me.)

We did not leave on the Saturday as expected, after all, and the week-end was thick with flying rumours, often of the most wild and contradictory nature. We were going to Italy, to Salonika, to Egypt, we were to form part of an army of invasion to land on the German coast—every possible or impossible destination was assigned to us by reports which claimed to have come straight from the Orderly Room or the Officers' Mess. But there was no real doubt in any of our minds that we were going to France, to our own Service unit—we were only "kidding" ourselves!

On Saturday evening there was a concert, given by the Battalion Concert Party, in the Windsor Constitutional Club Hall, to which all members of the Draft were admitted free. One of the items on the programme (which had been printed before the Draft was ordered on Active Service) was the well-known " Oh! Let Me Like a Soldier Fall! " and I was amused to find, when the " turn " came on, that the singer—Lyon Mackie, who had joined on the same day as myself—had substituted " Annie Laurie " for this rather too appropriate title.

All was now ready for departure, and on Sunday, after Church Parade, which was an impressive service of dedication and farewell for the Draft, there were no duties. I spent the afternoon alone (Brookes being still in hospital) in re-visiting for the last time favourite spots in the neighbourhood — the Castle terrace, the Y.M.C.A. Hut, the river banks, the Long Walk and the Park, etc. Windsor held, and still holds, for me many memories, by no means all of them unpleasant ones, and often when I was abroad I would look back on those days with something of the nostalgic sentiment with which other men remember—or so I am told—their public-school or university days. Not that I will pretend that I " enjoyed every minute " of my training in the Army! No-one enjoys being sworn at and ordered around, and having no privacy at all. But there was something—an indefinable feeling of deep satisfaction—in working with other men for a common purpose, a pride in the Uniform and the Regiment, and in having become (in spite of my previous puny health and sense of inferiority) a Soldier, which for me outweighed the drawbacks. Windsor will always be associated, in my memory, with sunlight and physical well-being, with the plaintive but heartening notes of bugles sounding the " Last Post," with the Drums beating Tattoo on the Barrack Square in the westering rays of the setting sun, with the " shr-up, shr-up, shr-up " of marching feet . . . . Sentiment?—yes; but there it is!

We finally departed on Monday, October 22nd. The last evening had been spent in riotously high spirits ; in my room at " Elmsfield " we had a roaring fire, for the weather had turned somewhat chilly, and on this occasion a liberal allowance of coal was issued to the billet ; boisterous ragging, songs and jokes (many of which I cannot possibly repeat here!) were kept going until a late hour, and no-one took any notice of " Lights-out." In the morning we were up betimes, kits were finally assembled and the rooms swept out for the last time.

The Draft paraded on the Barrack Square, two hundred strong, at 11.15 and was inspected by the Colonel, who afterwards addressed us in glowing terms, saying that we were " the best draft the H.B. had ever sent out." (I suppose every C.O. has said the same thing to departing overseas contingents everywhere, and it has never failed to rouse the same self-congratulatory cheers that it did from us!) He then distributed packets of cigarettes to all of us, and Capt. Legge gave each man several pears said to have come from his own orchard. It was clearly "Our Day," for officers and N.C.O.'s alike made a most unaccustomed fuss of us, and to the rest of the Battalion we were already almost heroes!

At last the final orders were given: "Draft . . . shun! Slope . . . arms! Form . . . fours! Move to the left in column-of-route . . . Left! By the right, quick . . . MARCH!"—and, headed by the band and all the senior officers, we swung through the gates to the vociferous cheers of the assembled troops. Brookes had been discharged from hospital that morning, and was just in time to wring my hand and wish me luck as we passed.

It seemed a long time ago—though it was, in fact, only four and a half months—since the evening when I had crept timidly up to those same gates, a nervous and miserable recruit entering upon the terrors of an unknown existence. Much had happened since then. My worst fears about life in the Army had proved to be groundless, and in many ways (as I have remarked) I had been happier than I could have believed possible in the circumstances. I felt myself to be a different man, and in some ways, perhaps, I *was* different; my bodily health and strength were vastly improved, and I had the beginnings of a new confidence in myself; I had learned (as I then imagined!) to put up with hardships and to live without civilised comforts; and I was proud—much too proud, and with far too little justification—of having become a "trained soldier." As we marched through the gates in all the panoply of war, towards our first "baptism of fire," it was well for me that I did not know all that lay ahead, or how much I had still to learn—and to un-learn—in the months to come.

Our progress through the town was almost a triumphal march. Traffic was suspended, and crowds lined the route, cheering and breaking into the ranks to press gifts upon us and wish us "God-speed." At the station we were joined by a draft of three hundred Coldstreamers, and the bands of the two battalions combined to play us out. Colonel Hardy and Capt. Legge went down the line of carriages, shaking hands with each of us and wishing us a speedy and victorious return—the latter was visibly distressed at losing what he called "his best Company"—and even the Regimental Corporal-Major "roared as gently as any sucking-dove." As the long train drew out of the station the massed bands played "Auld Lang Syne" and the roof re-echoed to the sound of cheers and singing.

.   .   .   .   .   .

We travelled to Southampton by way of Basingstoke, and drew up at a large covered platform near the dock-side. Having de-trained and piled arms, we assisted in unloading the baggage of the Draft, but after waiting about for an hour it was announced that, as our boat was not ready, we were to stay in Southampton for the night. Consequently, about five o'clock we fell in once more and marched to a rest-camp about a mile outside the town, where we were installed in large corrugated-iron huts accommodating about fifty or sixty men in each. During the night I had a slight attack of asthma, which quickly passed off and was notable for being the last sign of the malady which I was to experience "for the duration." France was to prove the final cure! Next morning we had little to do except wander about the Camp, which was a large one and at that moment contained drafts of the K.R.R.C., the Rifle Brigade, the "Buffs" and the R.A.M.C., besides the Coldstream and ourselves, all waiting to cross to France. There was also a number of American troops, vanguards of the armies which were soon to follow and, according to their own boasts, to "win the war for us." Another huge camp was under construction near-by for them.

We embarked during the afternoon in a converted Irish cargo-boat, the s.s. *Antrim,* and glided away from the wharf at about five o'clock. Passing down Southampton Water and the Solent, and leaving the Needles on our left hand, we encountered a stiff breeze as we emerged from the shelter of the land, and began to roll a good deal. We sighted dimly in the distance a number of craft which we thought were destroyers and submarines lying off the entrance to Poole Harbour, and then England faded away in the mist and darkness of the night.

The weather was wet and dismal, and the wind increased until it was difficult for us landsmen to keep a footing on deck. Before long nearly everyone appeared to be sea-sick, and men were lying about in all sorts of postures or hanging desperately over the rail. I, however, although I had never been more than a mile off-shore before, on a pleasure steamer, was quite unaffected by the motion, and was able to get a good deal of amusement from the scene, in the usual unsympathetic manner of a "good sailor." I would see someone from my platoon come staggering up the companionway, and would say, cheerfully and maliciously, "How goes it, chum?" "Christ Almighty!" (or words to that effect) would come the answer, and there would be a frantic rush to the side. We were, of course, sailing without lights, for fear of lurking submarines, and smoking was strictly forbidden on deck, so I soon determined to go below and try to get some sleep. But when I reached the quarters allotted to the troops (in the hold of the vessel, apparently) the sight and the sound and the smell of hundreds of men being ill in concert drove me hurriedly on deck again. I should not long have retained my immunity from sickness in that veritable "Black Hole of Calcutta!" It was not inviting in the wind and the drizzle, and I thought longingly of my bed-boards and straw palliasse at Windsor, but I took my greatcoat out of my pack and, wrapping myself in it, settled down in the most sheltered corner I could find, prepared to make the best of it in the open, wet with rain and spray, and soon half-numbed with cold.

We made the French coast about 1.30 a.m. and entered the port of Le Havre. Soon after the ship came to anchor tea was made, and those of us who were still capable of appreciating such things were very thankful for the hot drink, supplemented by a few biscuits and a much-needed cigarette. There was a long wait in the harbour, and disembarkation did not commence until after daybreak. At half-past seven we filed off the boat, crossing two other ships on the way to the quay, and at last set foot on the soil of France—most of us, indeed, in a rather limp and un-Guardsman-like condition.

IN THE TRENCHES

IT was a cheerless morning, with lowering clouds and an intermittent drizzle, when we filed ashore, and at first sight "this fair land of France" presented a far from inviting prospect. A slimy quay, dirty cobbled roadways strewn with all kinds of litter, ramshackle buildings which looked as though they had never known a coat of paint, and a general air of grime and neglect—that was my first impression of Le Havre, the second-largest seaport of France ; and those other parts of it through which we passed that morning did little to increase my admiration. The town was like a slatternly woman rousing from a drunken slumber, unkempt and bleary-eyed, and at first I attributed its sordid appearance to the effects of the war, though I afterwards realised that it was not unlike most other dock areas. I think what first brought home to me the fact that we were now in a foreign country was the absurd momentary surprise with which I noticed that all the advertisement posters were printed in French !

Disembarkation was a somewhat lengthy process, with all sorts of inexplicable delays, but at last we were all on shore and lined up ready to move off. The men who had suffered from sea-sickness during the voyage had all recovered sufficiently during the long wait in harbour to fall in with the rest, though indeed, to judge from the greenish complexions around me, there seemed to be few who had passed a pleasant night. For my own part, I was only too glad of the prospect of exercise at last to restore the circulation in my cramped and chilly limbs.

As we marched through the streets the inhabitants, for the most part, regarded us with sullen indifference ; no doubt such sights were a daily occurrence to them. But we were pursued by a horde of ragged urchins, who followed us like a swarm of gnats, refusing to be shaken off and clamouring insistently for " biskeet ! " " bully-beef ! " and " Penny, p'eese ! " and making offers which my knowledge of pidgin-French was then, perhaps fortunately, hardly wide enough for me to translate.

Our destination was the Base Camp at Harfleur, about four miles beyond Havre ; we were heavily laden, and marching was not made easier by the deplorable state of the roads, which were full of ruts and pot-holes, with thick mud everywhere. Even where an attempt had been made to camouflage the worst patches, it seemed to have been done by a method which I have sometimes seen adopted in country lanes in England, where stones are thrown down and left to be rolled in (or out) by the passing traffic. In addition, the weather was very bad, and a heavy shower of rain at starting was followed by three successive hailstorms en route. "So this is 'la belle France'!" I thought. "Germany could hardly be worse!"

The Camp, when at last we reached it, was a veritable city of canvas; an immense collection of tents, marquees and huts, covering a valley, the adjacent hillside and the plateau above. It was one of the main Base Depôts of the British area, and accommodated many thousands of troops coming from or going to the battle-zone, as well as an almost equally large body of people engaged on administrative jobs, supply services, etc. At that time (and, I think, throughout the war) it enjoyed the reputation of being the safest of all the big Base camps, being well beyond the range of the biggest guns and never having been visited by hostile aircraft.

The H.B. Base Depôt was situated on a hillside overlooking the river Seine; just below us was a small railway station, used apparently for goods traffic only — at any rate, troops never entrained there but had to march into Havre—and adjoining, on the inland side, the Depôt of the Guards Division. The ground sloped steeply towards the east, and a very little rain sufficed to make it slippery with mud. On one side there were a number of Army huts which served as Depôt Headquarters, Mess-room, Medical Office, Stores, etc., and several other huts near the top of the slope were the officers' quarters. The centre of the field (for such it was) contained about a score of bell-tents with wooden floor-boards, in which we "other ranks" were housed, fourteen men to each tent. On arrival, we divested ourselves of our kit and crowded into the dining-hut for a much-needed meal, and afterwards there was a medical inspection. Then we were free to explore the amenities of the neighbourhood.

The military population of the Base Camp was very varied and was composed of men from many different British regiments; and it was continually changing. I suppose there was scarcely a man in any of the many Divisions which were based on Harfleur who did not pass through it at least once, though in nearly every case their stay was extremely brief—except for the permanent staff, whom we "fighting soldiers" called "Base wallahs." Drafts like ours were arriving almost daily and departing to reinforce their respective units at the Front, casualties discharged from hospitals and convalescent-camps in France spent a few days here for re-equipment on their way back to the line, men on "courses," men going on leave and men coming back from Blighty. I myself visited the Base on four separate occasions while I was in France, but I was never there for more than a few days.

This first time we were there for four days, during which we had another gas test, some bayonet fighting exercises and several kit- and rifle-inspections. Any remaining deficiencies in our equipment were issued, as well as some additional items, including, for the first time, a "tin hat." (I notice that my initial entry in the debit page of my Active Service Pay Book is a fine of 2d., for a new cap-badge, but I have no recollection of how or where I lost the original one.) Although most of us were eager, novice-like, to get to the Front and "see what the trenches were like," we were somewhat reluctant to leave Harfleur, for the camp was pleasantly situated in fine weather (the rain ceased after the first day) and there were many amusements provided by the numerous recreation-huts for our off-duty hours ; the food was generous in amount and the cooking good ("better than at Windsor.") Certainly, we were somewhat cramped for room in the tents, especially at night, when fourteen men slept with our feet to the central pole and our heads touching the sides, and it was impossible for anyone to get out or hardly to turn over without disturbing his neighbours. When it rained, water would drip from numerous unexpected places! Nevertheless, we thought ourselves to be quite comfortably situated —as indeed we were compared with much that came afterwards.

We left on the twenty-eighth, after a long wait on parade for the Camp Commandant to inspect us, and after he had addressed us at some length—an oratorical display which we, standing in the sun in full marching order for nearly an hour, did not altogether appreciate. We were thoroughly tired by the time we reached the rail terminus at Havre about five o'clock, under a greater accumulation of impedimenta than I had ever carried before, and we lost no time in staking out our claims in the waiting train. We did not move until nine o'clock at night, however, and then jogged along very slowly. I had thought myself lucky in having secured a seat in a "4th-class" compartment, and a window seat at that, so that I could watch the scenery in comparative comfort ; but as the night wore on I began to wish that I was in one of the cattle-trucks in which most of the men were travelling, for, although they were crowded and dirty, in them one could at least lie down. The seats of those "4th-class" compartments were unpadded and there seemed to be no springs underneath the coach, so that every bump and jolt was unfailingly registered on my anatomy and by morning I felt very stiff and sore. The journey lasted for about twenty hours—not on account of the distance covered, but because the speed of the train seldom exceeded about six miles an hour, and it constantly stopped or backed into sidings for no apparent reason. Indeed, many of us occasionally jumped out and ran alongside the train for the sake of the exercise, and were hauled in again when we were tired. During some of the halts we would take our mess-tins with tea and sugar in them to the engine, and prevail upon the driver to squirt hot water from the boiler into them ; the resulting pale amber liquid with a thick scum of floating tea-leaves was a parody of "tea," but in the chilly hours of early morning it tasted like nectar!

Our journey's end was reached at about nightfall; the place where we alighted from the train was apparently in the midst of open country, and I could see no signs of a station in the deepening twilight. This, so it was said, was as far east as trains were allowed to go, and was not far from the village of Aubigny, some fifteen kilometers from Arras. The Divisional Reinforcement Camp was quite close at hand, and we were soon settled into our tents.

If we had been crowded at Harfleur, we were like sardines here! And mud was the only flooring of the tents; we had to rely on our ground-sheets alone to keep us dry when we "got down to it." We were getting nearer to the battle-front and could now hear the guns distinctly, while all night the eastern sky was alive with their distant lightning. Some time before dawn I was awakened by my neighbour to listen to the sustained thunder of barrage-fire, which at that distance sounded like a continuous rolling of drums or the pounding of thousands of feet on a hollow wooden floor. Evidently a raid was taking place on some part of the Line in front of us; the sky scintillated with a thousand flashes and even here the ground seemed to quiver beneath us. It was my first introduction, a distant recognition as yet, to War.

The next day the Draft had a short route-march, and I had a chance to see something of the surrounding rural district. I cannot say I was very favourably impressed by my first view of the Picardy countryside, so often praised in song and story; it seemed to me to be poverty-stricken, neglected and uninteresting, and I could not imagine a time when it could be true to say, "Roses are blooming in Picardy"—mud, rank grass and bare branches were all that met the eye. The farms we passed looked untended and the cottages in bad repair, many of their thatched roofs being covered with a thick green moss and their broken windows stuffed with pieces of sacking. No doubt the ravages of three years of war (though this district had never been a battle-ground) and the universal decay of late autumn was to blame for much of this uninviting aspect; and the depredations of thousands of occupying troops, although they were friendly, must have contributed. The country could be beautiful enough in spring and summer, as I was to learn later.

There was a little hamlet close to the camp, consisting of a few dilapidated cottages, a sugar refinery and a church which seemed much too large for the needs of the population; it was neither venerable nor picturesque. But there was a much larger village about two kilos away—this was probably Aubigny, though no-one seemed sure of its name—which I visited in the evening by walking along the railway track, and where the Y.M.C.A. hut seemed to be the social centre for the military population of the whole district and was crowded to capacity. I was glad that we were not going to stay long in the neighbourhood.

.   .   .   .   .   .

We left the Reinforcement Camp after two days, and marched away along the poplar-lined "route-nationale" to join the Battalion in Arras, where we arrived in the late afternoon. I shall never forget my first view of the city as we entered through the West Gate. Outside, on the St. Pol road by which we had come, there had been few very obvious signs of war, apart from the infrequent boom of guns in the distance and an occasional party of Royal Engineers working near the road. But as we emerged from the dark archway of the mediæval gate into one of the main thoroughfares of the city, we seemed to step directly into the battle-area itself.

The closely-packed rows of shops and houses extended right up to the gate, and there was — in this part, at any rate — no gradation into suburbs and villadom: one passed straight from country to city. And what a city! On both sides of the street were smashed and mutilated buildings, some gutted by fire, some with their roofs a mass of splintered rafters outlined against the sky, others with their fronts blown out, exposing with a sort of dreadful indecency all the intimate details of the interior—the pictures hanging on the walls, the homely furniture, beds on sagging upper floors still strewn with the tumbled sheets of their last occupants. Shutters hung askew on their broken hinges, and here and there a wisp of tattered curtain fluttered from a glass-less window. The side alleys and shop-fronts were blocked by piles of debris cleared from the road, which was crowded with a busy throng of troops passing to-and-fro, ration-carts and limbers clattering over the stone-paved road, cavalrymen on horseback and Staff-officers in motor cars. There were even some civilians, clinging obstinately to what remained of their homes ; some had even contrived to re-open their shops, and carried on a precarious though no doubt profitable travesty of business amid the ruins. They lived, I presume, in cellars and vaults, wherever they could find shelter, for such houses as still remained habitable had mostly been taken over by the military. Perhaps the most unexpected and incongruous sight in that place of paradox—a city smashed and dead, yet active with the noise and bustle of an unnatural parody of life—was the children, dirty, unkempt, uncared-for little urchins, hollow-eyed and skeleton-like yet shrill and clamorous with their external demands for "souvenirs." Truly, this was no place for children ; yet there seemed to be quite a number of them still— how or where they lived, no one seemed to know.

The Household Battalion, when we arrived, was quartered in the "Ecole Communale," a large school building in the Rue de l'Arsenal which was still mainly intact, though one wing had suffered badly. We marched past the entrance to the front court-yard and, turning up a side street, entered the quandam "playground" in the rear of the main block which served the Battalion as a parade-ground. Under the critical eyes of our new comrades, we wheeled smartly into position and came to a halt. The C.O. welcomed us with a brief address, and the formalities attending the reception of new members into the Battalion were soon completed. When the Draft was distributed among the four companies of the Batt., I found myself in No. 1 Company, 2 Platoon ; several of my friends from Windsor were also posted to this platoon, and our Corporal-of-Horse proved to be a very fine N.C.O.

By some oversight, there were no rations for us on arrival—it seemed that we should not be on the ration-strength of the Batt. until the next day, and should have been issued with food for twenty-four hours before leaving the Reinforcement Camp. As we had had nothing to eat since a rather early breakfast, we naturally felt the situation rather keenly! However, the cooks were mobilised and a scanty meal was scraped together, which we were afterwards able to supplement to a slight degree with purchases of chocolate at a neighbouring estaminet.

Next morning it was announced that the Batt. was to go into the Line the same evening, and the day was spent in preparations. My introduction to the trenches was not to be long deferred.

Daylight was fading when we left the Ecole Communale on the seven-mile march to the sector of the Line held by our Brigade. We proceeded up the Boulevard Carnot to the broad ruin-encircled Place de la Gare, where the chief railway station of Arras was a vast skeleton of glass-less steel girders through which no trains had run for three years. Crossing the grass-grown track by means of a road-bridge, our way took us through the suburb of St. Sauveur into the Arras-Cambrai " grand'route," which ran, poplar-lined and straight as an arrow, across the bare rolling country. It was a highway which, I believe, had been the scene of many " International Trophy " automobile races before the War. On the outskirts of St. Sauveur was a board calling attention to the fact that we were now entering the Danger Zone, where civilians were strictly forbidden and gas masks were to be carried at the alert. A few hundred yards further on we passed the last shell-torn villa of what had apparently once been a pleasant bourgeois neighbourhood, and darkness fell as we emerged into open country. I was only just able to make out, in the gathering twilight, where the old British front line had run before the Battle of Arras last Easter.

It was an eerie and unforgettable experience, this my first journey " up the line." There was no moon and the darkness was profound before we had covered half the distance, save for a faint gleam of ineffectual starlight, the occasional lightning flash as guns fired on either hand, and the ghostly glow of Verey lights on the eastern horizon which, as we got nearer to them, could be seen soaring above the sky-line in graceful parabolas like brilliant will-of-the-wisps or earthbound stars. On each side of us was unrelieved blackness, save when a sudden gun-flash showed up a riven tree-trunk or a heap of broken brickwork, or a tangle of barbed wire reared itself against the light of a distant star-shell like writhing tentacles. Every now and then would come three sharp, staccato cracks as a battery of field-guns fired, or the deep boom of a giant howitzer from far behind would be followed by the "accelerando" and "diminuendo" of a big shell high overhead on its way to the German lines. From No Man's Land came at rare intervals the distant rattle of a machine-gun or an isolated rifle-shot. It was all much more peaceful than I had imagined.

The road ran in a series of gentle undulations from ridge to ridge, and was paved (or had been, for it was much broken in places) with the square stone blocks which formed the surface of most French highways. Such roads were firm and durable, but they were not ideal for marching on, for the blocks (about six inches square) quickly became slippery with slime in wet weather, especially to iron-shod boots! At "Fosse Farm," a point about seven kilos from Arras, we halted for a time and indulged in a surreptitious smoke, carefully shielding the glowing ends of our cigarettes in our cupped hands, for there was only one rise which separated us from direct observation by the enemy. When at last we moved forward again, long intervals divided the platoons, and we were warned to make as little noise as possible. We skirted several shell-holes in the roadway, some old and full of water, and one or two new ones; about a kilometre further on the night was suddenly rent by the screech of two shells in quick succession, one of which struck the side of the road about twenty yards behind 2 Platoon. These took us by surprise and, raw hands that many of us were, sent us racing forward down the road as fast as we could go in the darkness. Fortunately, the entrance to the trenches was near at hand, and we tumbled in, thankful to get below ground-level. But those were the only shells which troubled us that night, and we finished our journey calmly and a bit ashamed of our temporary "wind-up."

We had entered the Support line close to where Battalion Headquarters were situated in a deep dugout under the Cambrai road. Although we did not know it at the time, the road down which we had come was in daylight in full view of the Germans, and consequently usually under machine-gun fire, but it was a short cut which saved us a long tramp through the winding communication-trench; our officers had taken a considerable risk by bringing us that way, and it was lucky that we had not been spotted. We were still some distance from our destination, however, and the trench we followed led roughly in a northerly direction, though I should have been completely fogged by the erratic twisting of the narrow way, but for the fact that the approximate position of the Front line, to the east of us, was indicated by the Verey lights. Every few minutes one would soar out of the gloom and shed a bright and sudden light into the trench, throwing the tumbled earth of the parapet into hard relief against the white glow, and rendering the subsequent darkness blacker than ever by contrast. In one or two places the trench had been blocked by a direct hit and filled nearly to surface level with debris ; these we had to pass on hands and knees, and freeze into immobility if a star-shell went up. A moving object might be spotted in the glare from " over the way," but one was usually safe from observation if one kept perfectly still, even if standing in the open. At another place a shell on the parapet had caused the zinc revetting to bulge inwards, and it was only just possible for men of moderate proportions to squeeze through side-ways. But in the main it was dry and easy going, and at last we reached our allotted post and took over from the troops we were relieving.

. . . . .

The Household Battalion was a unit of the 4th Division, but I forget the number of our Brigade and the names of the other Battalions composing it. I do remember, however, that one of them was a Scottish unit, for when we were in barracks in Arras a week or two later, this Battalion used to shatter our dreams with Reveille on the bagpipes every morning ! At that time the 4th Division was holding that part of the Front immediately east of Arras, and the H.B., in rotation with the other units of the Brigade, was responsible for the sectors in front of the village of Monchy-le-Preux. It was a quiet and fairly " cushy " area just then—though of course, being new to the trenches I did not realise it at the time ; conditions seemed sufficiently rigorous at first, though in later months I was often to look back on them as a comparatively " bon " time. Hardship and comfort, in war-time, are largely matters of com-parison, and I certainly did not know then that I was well off. I was lucky, too, in being able to accustom myself to trench warfare before having to take part in more active operations. Had my overseas posting been delayed a few months, I might have found myself (as did my friend, Brookes, and others who had been with me at Windsor) rushed straight into a major battle. Yet—I don't know ! Winter in the trenches was bad enough.

" The Line," in sectors such as this, consisted of three main systems of trenches : the Front line, separated from the enemy by a No-man's-land of varying width ; the Support line, about a hundred to two hundred yards to the rear ; and the Reserve line, farther back still. These were battle-positions, constructed with fire-steps, defence posts and " strong points " at frequent intervals ; though they did not run straight in any case, but followed a course dictated by the nature of the ground, strategic requirements and many other factors, and were rendered still more sinuous by the construction, every fifty yards or so, of " traverses "—double right-angled turns, with the object of preventing enfilade fire. The trenches themselves were—in theory and the best examples—about eight feet deep, six feet wide at the top narrowing to four feet at the bottom, floored with wooden duck-boards and revetted with sheets of zinc or hurdles. But few of them were, or remained long, in that state of perfection : most were just deep, narrow ditches in the bare earth, frequently disrupted by shell-fire and hastily repaired. The three main lines were connected with each other and with the rear by "communication trenches," deep narrow ditches usually only just wide enough for two men to pass, and winding very erratically.

It fell to the lot of No. 1 Coy. to hold the Support line for the first four days of this "tour," and 2 Platoon occupied a post in "Hoe Support"—all the trenches in this sector were named after tools ; e.g., "Spade Avenue," "Pick Alley," "Trowel Trench," etc.—to which was attached a fairly large dugout, in which we lost little time in installing ourselves. Dugouts in the Line varied considerably in size, depth and comfort, according to circumstances, and this one was a subterranean chamber about thirty feet below ground-level, rectangular in shape and measuring about forty feet by ten. Entrance was by way of steep shafts cut into steps, one shaft from each end of the dugout, and in it the troops not on duty could sleep secure from any but the heaviest shell-fire, which at that depth could be heard only as muffled thuds overhead. The only danger was the possibility of a direct hit on the entrance (hence the two shafts), but such accidents were rare. The floor was strewn with loose stones, but it was dry, and we soon made ourselves comfortable in the two blankets which we each carried. Some of the more "luxurious" dugouts were fitted with wire bunks, which were considered to be the last word in trench comfort, but as many of us were newcomers it was no doubt considered best not to begin by pampering us (!) and in this one the only "furniture" was a blackened brazier made from an old biscuit-tin, left behind by the previous tenants. A sentry was posted in the trench outside each entrance, to be relieved every two hours, and the rest of us turned in. I was so tired after the long march from Arras that, despite the excitement and romance of my first visit to the trenches, I was quickly asleep.

In the morning we all turned out half-an-hour before dawn for the customary "Stand-to," this being in theory the time when an attack by the enemy was most likely to begin. But on this occasion everything was very quiet, and "Jerry" evidently had no ambitions except, like us, those directed towards breakfast. Indeed, as the light increased, one of our fellows, who claimed keener eyesight (to say nothing of a more fertile imagination) than most, declared that he could see the German field-gunners on the opposite rise about three miles away drinking coffee—though he didn't explain how he knew it was coffee! The Orderly Officer appeared and received the Corporal-of-Horse's report, and as the sun began to show above the horizon the order to "Stand-down" was passed along the line ; upon which we all, except the sentries, descended to our underground abode and attacked our breakfast.

Rations for the ensuing twenty-four hours were brought up by fatigue parties every night—Jerry permitting—and were shared out by the N.C.O. in charge ; they usually consisted of bully-beef, army biscuits, bread and tea-and-sugar (already mixed) ; sometimes rashers of bacon and at intervals a small lump of butter or cheese and a pot of jam between a Section of seven or eight men. The bread normally amounted to a quarter of a loaf per man, though if supplies were short or interrupted it might be a case of "six-in-a-loaf" or an even smaller ration. The biscuits were hard and square, very like the larger type of dog-biscuit, but they were not unpalatable to hungry men with good teeth. In addition to these daily rations, we each carried what was known as an "iron ration" of bully and biscuit, in a special calico bag, but it was strictly forbidden to break into this except in great emergency or by order of an officer. Whenever possible, we made tea or fried our "sandbag" ham over small fires built in the trench outside, but at night the brazier in the dugout had to be made use of, both for culinary purposes and for warmth—and a very smoky, choking business it usually was. The brazier was placed near the foot of one of the shafts, which acted in part like a chimney, but quite enough smoke remained below to be far from comfortable, until the fire had reached a steady glow.

To this day, the smell of coke-and-wood smoke in a confined space will vividly recall to me the scene in a dugout—the dim light of candle-ends stuck on mess-tin lids or in niches cut in the wall; the figures of men squatting on the ground among a clutter of equipment, some cleaning rifles, others trying to read letters or old newspapers, or searching the seams of their underwear for lice; the confused clamour of voices, talking, arguing or singing; the stifling atmosphere, made up of coke fumes, tobacco smoke, musty earth, stale sweat and damp khaki—how cosy and home-like it could seem when returning from a tiring night-fatigue or a cold and lonely spell on sentry !

After we had fed, that first morning, most of us attempted to have a wash, or what passed for a "wash" in the Line. Because water was scarce—it all had to be brought, like our rations, from the rear—no more than a mess-tin-full could be spared for the joint ablutions of five or six men, and by the time all had finished it had the appearance, and almost the consistency, of thin grey mud. But it was better than nothing, and had a freshening effect —we soon learned not to be particular in matters of toilet while in the trenches ! A little later, I was detailed to form one of a party to carry water to the Front line, about a hundred and fifty yards distant, I suppose, in a direct line, but a great deal further through the narrow, twisting communication trench. We walked in single-file, necessarily, each with a couple of two-gallon cans (which had previously held petrol) slung over one shoulder and a rifle on the other; it was fairly easy going for the most part, though we encountered patches of glutinous mud, and in some places the trench was so narrow that we could only pass anyone coming in the opposite direction by spreadeagling ourselves against the wall. However, at length we reached the forward positions held by one of our other Companies—the Front Line itself !

I was surprised at the peacefulness of the scene. Everything was very quiet in the sunlight, and it was difficult to believe that this was the actual frontier between two great nations locked in the greatest war in history ! It seemed almost incredible that the enemy was only a few score yards away. I don't know what I had vaguely imagined it would be like—attacks, bayonet-charges, constant rifle-fire, hand-to-hand fighting, shouting, excitement ? Probably I had had no very definite picture in my mind. But this silence ! And no one seemed to be bothering about the war. Two sentries lounged against the trench-wall at each post, nursing their rifles, while the rest of the men sat around on the fire-step, smoking and talking, or else snatched a short sleep in the " bivvies"—shallow holes dug into the side of the trench under the parapet, the only shelter available in the Front line. The general atmosphere seemed to be one of bored indifference.

One could just see, in places where the parapet was broken, the barbed-wire entanglements and rank grass of No-man's-land, but it was not advisable to look over the top too often or too long, for snipers on the other side were usually on the look-out to correct indiscretions of that kind. There was very little gun-fire to be heard, most of it from our own artillery, and the only active sign of the enemy was an occasional reconnoitring aeroplane high over-head, followed by the faint white puff-balls of anti-aircraft shells, whose distant explosions sounded like the pop of drawing corks.

After dumping our load at the appropriate places, we retraced our steps through the muddy trench, and in due course arrived back in the Support line, with considerably more of the soil of France on our boots than we started with.

At dusk we stood-to again for an hour, and the Verey lights resumed their nightly dance. Artillery fire increased somewhat during the first hours of darkness, but was almost entirely directed on the rear, presumably with the object of hampering the bringing up of supplies. After midnight it died down, and except for an occasional shell now and again the rest of the night was quiet. Quiet, that is, in a comparative sense, for there was spasmodic bursts of machine-gun fire from one side or the other and occasional rifle-shots; and it was seldom, even in the quietest periods, that more than a few minutes would elapse without the sound of a shell passing over, far or near. The long-drawn-out scream, starting on a low note, rising swiftly to a high shriek and then descending in a deep moan, soon became the most familiar and inescapable background of our life in the trenches—though in this case, at any

D

rate, familiarity did not breed contempt. If the top note did not pass a certain degree of intensity, the shell was "well over " and of no concern to us; but if, on the contrary, instead of descending the scale it increased to a tearing scream, like the ripping of a thousand yards of calico, we knew it would burst near and took hasty cover. There were many variations in the orchestra of the artillery, ranging from the short, sharp whizz and almost simultaneous explosion of " whizz-bangs "—the hardest of all shells to dodge—to the extraordinarily accurate imitation of an express train given by the biggest longe-range shells, and one soon learned to distinguish the type of shell by the sound of its passing. "Crumps," "five-nines," "Jack Johnsons," "Coal-boxes," "Pip-squeaks," "Minnies " — those were some of the names we gave to the various disturbers of our peace.

But it is not my intention to write a detailed diary of the three months I spent on the Arras front. I could not do so if I wished, for, clear and vivid though my memory is of many events and conditions during this period, much has faded with the lapse of years, and I am sometimes unable to determine the exact chronological order of certain incidents. This is perhaps because the purely physical discomforts of that winter—the cold, rain, frost, snow, etc.—were so much greater than any I had hitherto known, and so impressed themselves more firmly in my subconscious mind than did actual events and personalities. Also, I was then quite new to the conditions of warfare, and they have— in retrospect, though probably not at the time—a sort of nightmare unreality which is difficult to disentangle from the actual happenings. Not that there was, in truth, anything unreal about life in the trenches; its sordid actuality was an extremely concrete fact, and any feelings of fantasy with which I remember it lies in its complete unlikeness to what we call " ordinary " life. Sometimes, today, I find it hard to realise that it was indeed I myself who experienced the things recorded in these pages. Yet I had an easy time during the War, compared with most men.

It would be easy, perhaps—in the extreme unlikelihood that this book will ever be read by anyone who knew me at that time —to represent myself as a sort of "war-book hero," indifferent to hardships and danger, and to whom life in the trenches, once the first novelty had worn off, became merely boring and monotonous. Some men may have reacted in that way—to judge from many published books of reminiscence, the writers usually did !—but it was not so with me. There may be, no doubt, a few lucky men who are literally without fear—though I doubt if this rare quality is ever due to anything higher than a complete lack of imagination. Fear is a natural concomitant of intelligence, and he who is most mentally alive has thereby the greatest capacity for being afraid. The truly brave men, the real heroes, are those whose self-control is so strong that they can overcome their fear and act as though it did not exist. Most men are capable of this kind of bravery on occasions—there are times in war when the least of us may be " keyed-up " to a point of self-forgetfulness when personal danger is ignored—but not many can maintain a cool demeanour by sheer strength of character under all circumstances. To pretend that I was one of these, or that I soon " got used to " shell-fire and the other hazards of life in the Line, would be entirely false. Each day in the trenches, indeed, so far from deadening my sense of peril, increased it, and I must confess that I felt " windy " during most of the time I spent in the line. True, I endeavoured—and, I think, fairly successfully on the whole—to conceal my true feelings from my companions, yet I often felt secretly ashamed that I could not " face danger with a smile," as I thought a soldier should. But I do not think I was alone in this. We were all, in varying degrees, afraid ; and all, with greater or less success, tried to hide our fear from each other —and from ourselves. I have heard veterans who had been " out" since Mons or Gallipoli (some of them wearing decorations for bravery) admit in unguarded moments that every time they went up the line they felt windier. " Going over the top," although actually more dangerous to life and limb, was probably less of a strain on the nerves, because less protracted, than life in the trenches.

During my first days at the Front, it is true, I thought that the dangers had been over-rated; I had expected something much more adventurous. In writing home, I asserted cheerfully (though perhaps it was more to reassure my Mother than because I believed it): " it is really as safe as, for instance, London at the present time," and spoke with a fine air of romantic nonchalance, of " reading Browning under shell-fire "—though the shell in question had been at least a hundred yards away! But this, of course, was the bravado of ignorance, and it was not long before I had reason to change my opinion.

Those three months in front of Arras were an alternation of holding the line—in Front, in Support or in Reserve—and of fatigues, ration-parties, digging-squads, marching up and down the Cambrai Road and the adjacent country ; of moving from one sector or post to another, from one camp to another, and, occasionally, back to Arras for a few days so-called " rest." There were no big events, nothing to compare with what came later, but plenty of incidents and danger, and each time " up the line " I liked it less. There were also one or two good interludes, or what seemed good by comparison, though by any ordinary standards of physical comfort the best of them would seem but squalid today.

.   .   .   .   .   .

However, my first spell in the " forward area "—that is, of actually living by night and day in the trenches—was short. The Company held the Support line on this occasion for only seven days, during which, although everything was extremely novel to me, nothing of outstanding note occurred. I took my turn from time to time in mounting sentry on the fire-step, and in the fatigue-parties which went back after dark to fetch rations from the limbers at Fosse Farm. For two days I was detailed with five other men and a Cpl.-of-Horse to act as a gas-guard at the Battalion Aid Post, a dugout in a " blind-alley " trench a short distance behind the Support Line, where our only duty was to watch, by turns, for the possible smell of gas. One night, while I was on sentry, there was an enemy raid on a sector to the left of our position; a fierce bombardment started up, and our troops fired a number of red and green rockets into the air—the " S.O.S." signal, calling for artillery support—and a strong counter-barrage was laid down. For a time pandemonium reigned, but the raiders soon withdrew or were beaten back, and, after our guns had plastered the trenches opposite for about half-an-hour, the night settled down into quiet once more.

The Battalion's next move was back to Fosse Farm, a reserve position near the Cambrai road about two kilometres behind the Front line. I never discovered the system by which the rota of reliefs in the Line was determined ; there was a common belief among the troops that the programme was (or was meant to be) as follows: four days in the Front line, four days in Support, eight days in Reserve, and then a fortnight " out of the line "; but in my experience no regular sequence was ever adhered to. There was, one supposes, some logical plan which governed our movements, but to us they seemed to be as haphazard as the moves on a chess-board would appear to an individual pawn. We never remained for longer than a few days in one spot, but would be shifted from post to post, and from camp to camp, apparently according to the whim of some remote Headquarters, and for no discernible reason.

At Fosse Farm, however, for the three or four days we spent there, conditions were much more comfortable than in the Support trench, and our quarters were, to me at least, quite unexpectedly fantastic. We were billeted in a series of caves deep below the earth, under the farm buildings which lay in ruins and apparently deserted beside the Cambrai road, and which showed no indication of the busy population they covered. The caverns, of which there were several, opening one out of another, were sufficiently spacious to accommodate the entire Battalion with ease (including an officers' Mess), as well as a Company of Royal Engineers. It was reported —with rather doubtful credibility—that they had been formed by the quarrying of stone used in the building of Arras Cathedral, and had been sealed up and forgotten for centuries ; after the bombardment of the city, so the story went, their existence had been revealed by the discovery of some old documents among the ruins, and after Fosse Farm had been recaptured in April, 1917, the caves had been re-opened. This romantic story may have been the truth, but to me they looked much more like natural formations, especially as a spring of pure water bubbled in a rock basin in the uppermost chamber and formed an underground stream which I had no opportunity of exploring, but which probably drained into the River Cojeul, some distance to the south. This spring was a very convenient "water-point" from which to supply the troops in the line, the more so because there was no fear that it could become contaminated by gas, like streams in the open.

The caves were lofty and well-ventilated, and it was a pleasant change, after dugouts and tents, to have plenty of room in which to move about. They were fitted with wire bunks in tiers, on which we slept, and were lit by electric light, the power for which was supplied by a dynamo on the surface, whose humming could be plainly heard in the Front line. Some years later, I read a book by a German soldier who had been on this part of the front at about the same time as I was; in it, the author mentions this humming sound, which was apparently no less audible in the enemy lines, but he evidently did not know what caused it or whence it came. Indeed, the Germans did not seem to be aware of the existence of the caves, for the entrances had never at that time been shelled; had they used them during the two and a half years they had occupied this area, they could hardly have failed to realise the value of the caves to us.

This subterranean world exercised a romantic fascination upon me; I never visited the caves—the twisted, narrow stairway from the upper air, the splashing of running water, the mysterious shadowy rock corridors—without being reminded of the lunar world that H. G. Wells imagined, or of Wookey Hole in Somerset. The underground stream recalled to my mind that other river which ran

> ". . . . through caverns measureless to man
> Down to a sunless sea."

Even the darkness, when the light was switched off at night, had a velvety profundity which seemed almost substantial; the luminous dial of my watch was like a pale planet floating alone in an infinite black void.

But life at Fosse Farm was by no means a troglodyte holiday, and I had little time for literary musings. Every day there were working parties in the line or the surrounding areas, under the direction of the R.E's, and ration-carrying fatigues at night, of which I of course came in for my share. It was while on one of the former expeditions that I had my first introduction to shell-fire at close quarters, when the enemy spotted us digging in a Support trench and sent over a few salvos; no-one was hit, but work had to be abandoned for that day.

The Subaltern in command of my Platoon, Mr. Whitehouse, a very pleasant and popular youngster, celebrated his twenty-first birthday while we were in the caves on this occasion, and loud sounds of revelry could be heard coming from the officers' quarters until long after our own lights had been switched off. Another of No. 1 Company's junior officers bore a name universally known in the "Wine and Spirits" trade ; whether or not he was indeed one of the firm, as was widely believed, he certainly had a taste for the products for which his name was famous, and was more often than not half intoxicated. He was not a bad sort, though. Officers were allowed to take what stimulants they liked into the line, but anything beyond the official "rum ration" was strictly forbidden to the rank-and-file—which, we considered, was distinctly unfair!

At Fosse Farm I was able to write home for the first time since I joined the Battalion in Arras. Letters could not be dispatched from the trenches, though the in-coming mail was sent up regularly with the nightly rations. All letters from the Front to England were, of course, subjected to a strict censorship, normally by our own officers, but before leaving England I had arranged a code by means of which I could circumvent the regulations and indicate the name of the place from which I was writing. The scheme worked well (when I remembered to put it into operation) and was never spotted, though if it had been "rumbled" I should doubtless have been in for serious trouble. From time to time I managed to secure one of the prized "Green envelopes," which were exempt from Battalion scrutiny, though they might be opened at the Base ; the writer had to sign an undertaking that the contents referred to none but "private and family matters." In these letters, of course, I did not attempt to use any kind of code, being "on my honour" not to mention military matters, but we all considered ordinary letters to be "fair game," if we could get away with it! A "Field Service Postcard" was also available in cases where it was not convenient to write a letter ; it bore a series of stereotyped phrases like "I am quite well"—"I have been admitted to hospital, wounded/sick"—"I am being sent to the Base"—"I have received your letter/parcel dated . . . ."—etc., the inapplicable sentences to be crossed out but nothing added. I made frequent use of these cards, but I also seem to have been an indefatigable letter-writer throughout my overseas service. My Mother kept all those addressed to her, and they have been of considerable help to me in compiling this account—not, indeed, so much in the actual narration of events or description of scenes (for I was always extremely circumspect in what I wrote and often deliberately misrepresented the truth in order not to worry her) as in the memories which they revive of the things I did *not* say. Very often, the re-reading of these hasty, scrappy, crude epistles will recall to my mind the circumstances and emotions amid which they were written more vividly than anything else, although the words themselves may be commonplace enough and betray no hint of what I might have written. For instance, there is a letter written the night before I went "over the top"—one might almost gather from it that I was in a rest-camp, miles behind the Front!

.   .   .   .   .

When the Battalion was due to return to Arras I was sent with a small advance-party under a Corporal-of-Horse, two days ahead of the rest, to prepare billets. We were all men from the last draft, chosen probably with the idea of letting us down lightly to begin with, and we set out during the afternoon in good spirits at our luck. Before we had gone far along the Cambrai road, however, the Germans, who had an observation balloon up in the distance, detected us and, although small parties were not usually considered worth spending long-range shells upon, they probably thought that to march openly in the middle of the road in broad daylight was an inexcusable affront to their dignity. The first shell struck the road ahead of us and after a few seconds another burst behind ; these were evidently ranging shots, and the next one would probably score a bulls-eye, so we decided to move the target. We left the road in double-quick time and took refuge in some shell-holes a few dozen yards away, feeling that in the circumstances discretion was the "better 'ole" of valour! There we waited until the enemy tired of peppering the empty road with high-explosives, and then continued our journey ; but in order not to expose ourselves again we took advantage of whatever cover was available, and crossed the bare summit of the ridge on hands and knees, crawling along a dry ditch in single file behind the N.C.O.

At Arras, this time, we were quartered in part of the Schramm Barracks, a rather gloomy collection of massive rectangular buildings not far from the St. Pol Gate ; it was a fortress in itself, and within its confines the part devoted to Officers' Quarters was more heavily fortified still—which led me to wonder whether, in the French Army, the officers distrusted their own men more than they feared a possible enemy! By the ironical chance of war, the Barracks had been hardly damaged at all by the bombardment which devastated the city, though there was not a whole pane of glass in the window-frames. The rooms we occupied were large and bare, three or four storeys above ground level ; we slept and sat on the floor with only our two blankets apiece to soften the boards, and each room housed a platoon of about twenty-five men. But even so we were not overcrowded, and considered ourselves very comfortable for "active service" conditions. The windows were covered with oiled calico, for the most part—which, though fairly effective in keeping out the wind, did not admit much daylight—heating was by means of the ubiquitous biscuit-tin brazier, and lighting by candles (as and when procurable). Normal sanitary arrangements in the Barracks appeared to have broken down, for field-latrines had been dug in the spaces between the blocks of barrack-rooms, but on the ground floor some water-taps functioned intermittently, under which we performed our ablutions as best we might. In cold weather they were frequently frozen up altogether.

Beyond the rear gate of the Barracks, on a large open space which had been, I think, a cavalry exercising-ground, there was a Y.M.C.A. recreation hut, an improvised cinema and a large wooden structure which, on Sundays a church, on other days did duty as a theatre, in which the Divisional Concert Party, the " 4th Division Follies," presented two or three shows a week. Some of these entertainments, necessarily with an all-male cast, were very good (or, at least, they seemed so at the time), and played to crowded houses. Every concert began with the " Follies' " " signature-tune " (as it would be called now), which the audience knew by heart and in which everyone joined with great enthusiasm and feeling:

"When the great red dawn is shining,
    And the waiting hours are past,
When the tears of night are ended
    And we see the day at least,
I shall come down the road of sunshine
    To a heart that is fond and true—
When the great red dawn is sh-i-i-ning,
    Back to Home—back to Love—and You! "

.   .   .   .   .   .

The normal length of these "rest" periods was, as I have said, supposed to be a fortnight, but there was no certainty about this. We might be out of the line for about three or four weeks, or orders might come through for a move at any time without warning. It was all according to the caprice of Headquarters—or so it seemed to us. And the term "rest" was a euphemism which by no means indicated a lazy time; intensive field-training took up most of our time, and there were many parades and kit inspections; we were expected to "posh-up" almost to Windsor standards. Nevertheless, it was an easy life compared with the trenches, and I don't think many of us hankered to get back to the line. Although Arras was within range of heavy artillery and was surrounded by batteries of our own guns, it was never shelled at that time, and we could sleep at night undisturbed. It was said— with the confident but doubtful veracity of such rumours—that there was a tacit understanding between the two armies that if they did not shell Arras we would not shell Douai, which was about the same distance on the further side of No-man's-land. At any rate, no shells fell on the city while I was there.

Two or three days after we had taken up our quarters in Schramm Barracks a party of eight men, myself included, was detailed from the Battalion for a week's Brigade Course of hand-grenade bombing. There was a similar party from each of the three other units in the Brigade, and we were billeted in a couple of empty villas on the other side of the city. The district had apparently been a pleasant "bourgeoise" residential quarter, now of course deserted by civilians, and many of the houses were comparatively little damaged, so we found ourselves in very cushy circumstances. We slept in real beds, only three to a room, and had plenty of fuel for fires, and generous rations; the officer in charge of us was "a real good sort" (*vide* "Letters") whom everyone liked, and we all enjoyed the course, which was very different from the grenade-throwing instruction at Windsor. We marched out into open country soon after daybreak every morning, and after several hours' practice in hurling Mills-bombs, returned to the billet for dinner; afterwards we were usually free for the rest of the day, and could take advantage of such sight-seeing as poor shell-torn Arras offered. The ruins of the Cathedral and other public buildings were interesting at first, and the famous iron spiral-staircase which stood straight up out of the flattened ruins of a block of offices, like a Jacob's ladder leading—whither? But one soon sickened of the universal scene of destruction, and in any case the early fall of darkness limited the time available for exploration. Arras after dark was pitch-black. The city, however, was not badly provided with indoor amusements for the troops. Several good military concert parties gave performances from time to time, and there was the cinema at Schramm Barracks, the "Y.M." and other recreation huts, and a large "Expeditionary Force Canteen" where many things could be purchased. One evening I discovered, to my delight, a small French shop among the ruins which had many of the chief English newspapers, not more than two or three days old, and the sight of the familiar titles so thrilled me that I dived inside and bought a copy of every one I could lay my hands on!

This short "hand-grenade" Course is an example of the way in which certain scenes and incidents in this initial period of my Active Service, when everything was strange and novel to me, could be overlaid in my memory and apparently completely forgotten. After the Course ended, I do not think I ever consciously recalled anything about this rather pleasant interlude: subsequent events just crowded it out of my mind. It was not until long afterwards, after the end of the war — while, I think, I was jotting down a summary of the events of my war-service which was the germ of the present account—that something touched a hidden chord in my memory, and I suddenly remembered the whole episode in all its details. It was an unimportant incident in itself, but it is one instance among many of the way in which submerged memories can be brought to light by the appropriate stimulus, and leads me to believe that we never really "forget" anything that has ever happened to us. The mental exercise of writing these pages has already recalled many things to my mind that I have not consciously recalled since the day they happened—many more, indeed, than I have space or time to set down—and yet others are dimly glimpsed but which I know actually occurred. Could I but hit on the right kind of mnemonics, I could doubtless remember everything about my war-service, in every smallest particular.

A few days after we had reluctantly rejoined our respective units at the end of the Course, the Battalion moved from Schramm Barracks back to the Ecole Communale ; but this, like most of our moves, was only a temporary migration, for less than a week later the Brigade "rest" came to an end and the H.B. went into reserve positions at "Bois-de-Bœuf" Camp, about half-way between Arras and Monchy, and not far from the cross-roads at Feuchy Chapel. Inevitably, it was popularly known by the troops as "Bully-Beef Camp," and was composed of Nissen huts ; these were semi-cylindrical tunnels of corrugated zinc, with a window at one end and a door at the other ; they were somewhat dark and close, but not uncomfortable to live in, being waterproof and wood-floored, and much to be preferred to tents at this season of the year. Here our principal duty was to provide working parties for the Royal Engineers, in or near the trenches, though we also had a certain amount of drill and rifle-practise at times. The "R.E. fatigues" were, generally speaking, not over-strenuous, though the four or five mile march back to camp after a long stretch without food could sometimes be rather exhausting. Once we were taken back to Arras for a few hours, to receive instruction in the art of constructing "concertina" wire—coils of barbed wire which, when pulled out, formed an easily-erected barricade across a trench.

One of those days at "Bully-beef Camp" sticks in my memory as providing the hardest endurance test I had yet had at the Front, though, of course, it was in reality nothing to what I was to have later on.

We left the camp at eight o'clock in the morning, and after following the main road to Fosse Farm turned off to the left across open country and descended into the slight hollow behind Monchy which was known (heaven knows why !) as "Happy Valley." Here we entered some trenches which wound along the northern slope of Monchy hill, and came to the entrance to a tunnel which was being bored beneath the village. This may have been designed to provide protect access to an Observation Post on the forward slope of the hill, which dominated the German positions over a wide area and was consequently under constant fire. Our task was to assist in the excavation, some in the actual digging and others in hauling truckloads of loose soil to the dump outside. We worked hard and without a break until after mid-day and then started off back to camp.

The first part of the way led across a stretch of ground which sloped towards the enemy lines, through a trench known as "Orange Reserve," which was inadequately screened by a low parapet, and as we went some look-out post must have seen the flashing tips of our bayonets above the sandbags. Suddenly a battery opened fire on us; they evidently had the range of the trench to a yard, for the shells fell very close and we had a remarkably narrow escape. One burst just across the parapet, and the concussion flung me into a corner of the trench and showered me with earth, while another about twenty yards further on fell squarely into the trench and practically filled it in. No one, fortunately, was hurt, but the sudden bombardment put the wind up us and we all bolted back to a dugout which we remembered having passed a few minutes earlier. We tumbled into it, pell-mell, and remained their until the shelling ceased and it seemed safe to proceed. We were very careful to keep our rifles well down! The rest of the journey was without incident, and reached the camp about two o'clock, tired and very hungry.

During the afternoon an emergency call was received for a large carrying-party to unload an expected cargo of munitions and transport it to the Front line; so we were called out again and marched back to the "railhead" some distance behind Monchy. The railway line by which the load was coming was a narrow-gauge single track from Arras, which ran as far as the head of Happy Valley, from which point a duckboard track led to the entrance to the trenches. When we reached the "terminus," however, we found that the train had not yet arrived, and we were told that we must wait until it did so, for the trench-mortar bombs it carried must be taken to the line that night "at all costs."

We had a long and dreary vigil, for it appeared that the railway line had been damaged by shell-fire in several places and the train was held up until it could be repaired. The duckboard track on which we passed the next five or six hours, alternately walking about and sitting on our heels, was on a high and open spot, the summit of the rise behind Monchy—a place very often shelled by the enemy, but by good luck Jerry was "taking a night off" and not a single round came over. The sky was cloudy, though the moon showed through at intervals, and the rain, frequently threatening, held off; it was not cold for late November, but we were exposed to a wind which held the promise of winter, and soon no amount of stamping and arm-flapping could keep us warm.

At long last, shortly after half-past twelve, the little train came snorting up the incline, and we lost no time in loading ourselves up with its freight. The tramp along the duckboard track and then through the maze of trenches to the Front line, burdened as we were in addition to our usual equipment and rifles (without which no one was allowed to go anywhere in the "forward zone") was very exhausting, and by the time the Front line was reached we were all streaming with perspiration. However, our load was safely deposited in the " bomb store " at last, and the return journey by a different route, was effected without mishap. We got back to Bois de Bœuf shortly after three a.m., after having been " on fatigue " for seventeen hours out of the twenty-four, and needless to say were very ready for the meal of hot tea and bully which awaited us. We finally rolled up in our blankets about four o'clock.

Next day, or the day after, Brigade Orders contained a special paragraph about " the creditable way in which the work had been carried out under trying circumstances." The " circumstances," however, might well have been much more " trying " if the enemy's artillery had chanced to be active that night. Twenty-four hours later the place where we had waited for so long was heavily bombarded and the duckboard track blown to splinters.

I had now had a month at the Front, and imagined that I had been initiated into all the hardships and horrors of war ! I had been cold, wet, weary, muddy, lousy, hungry, and at times afraid ; but these things, though very disagreeable, had so far made little difference to the idealistic enthusiasm which had inspired my first months in the Army. Surviving letters of that period contain several passages which, even though they may read like crude heroics, to the best of my recollection are a sincere expression of my feelings at that time, and were not just written for effect. As, for example, the following effusion, dated from Bois-de-Boeuf Camp :—

" Believe me, I want peace as much as anyone, but it must be a *real* peace. In a great and just cause, such as is given to us to defend, we cannot—we dare not—turn back. For my own part, I count it an honour to take part in the most righteous war England has ever fought . . . I know people are getting 'fed-up' and 'war-weary'; the romance and glitter of war has gone, the time for drum-beating and flag-waving is over. Now is the time when we must summon our resolution and set our teeth to carry it through at whatever cost, for the sake of the future welfare of the world, the freedom and happiness of future generations, and for the sake of those who have given everything for the cause. Germany is not yet beaten, but we have her with her back against the wall. Victory is in our grasp, and we should be utterly unworthy of the trust reposed in us if we turn back now."

Truly, the romance and glitter had gone ! It seemed a far cry to the facile enthusiasms of August, 1914. The winter of 1917-18 was perhaps the darkest period of the whole war, when every ambitious effort on the Western Front had failed, at enormous cost, to break through the enemy's lines, and there seemed to be no possibility of ending the fearful wastage of life, money and material. After the bloody failure of Passchendaele the war seemed to sink down into a hopeless stalemate, a grim holding-on to established positions in the cold, rain and mud, waiting for the thrust which was bound to follow the release of the German Eastern armies by the collapse of Russia. As a foretaste of what might be expected, the Austro-German offensive against Italy had broken the Goritzia front and swept back the defenders almost to Venice. A few days after the letter just quoted, came news of the brilliant British surprise attack towards Cambrai, but that, too, proved to be a " flash in the pan " and was speedily reversed by the German counter-attack. The only visible gleam of hope on the horizon was the approach of the armies of our newest and as yet untried ally, America. Could they get here in time ?

Active Service was too new to me then to have yet dimmed my credulous idealism, though it was later (and perhaps inevitably) succeeded by a more or less temporary wave of disillusionment. But among the troops generally there was a good deal of cynical, almost defeatist, talk during that winter, though most of it I think was no more than the normal habit of grousing for which the British soldier is notorious in times when nothing spectacular is happening. I do not think it indicated anything more serious than a general feeling of frustration, and I also (despite what I said earlier) did my share of "moaning," for the endless routine of fatigues, sentry-go and squalid living-conditions became at times excruciatingly boring. At such times—and indeed at all times—my thoughts would return with longing to memories of home comforts, and I wondered how I could ever have been dissatisfied in the past ! Letters from home were the brightest spots in my life (as they were to all of us) and I must acknowledge that I was far luckier than I deserved in this respect, for a mail seldom arrived without at least one for me. To quote again :—

" I wish I could give more detailed descriptions of the places I visit, but that I suppose can't be helped. What yarns we shall all spin, in the glorious days ' when the boys come home! ' I can imagine us all sitting round the fire, living over again the days when we were not only winning the war, but winning ourselves. For that is what it means. Life in France is ' bringing us out ' in ways that would never have been possible but for the war. For all that, though, we are going to finish the war as soon as possible—or, rather, as soon as we can gain a complete victory. And that is not so far off."

And again :—

" You say the news from home must seem trivial compared with my experiences out here. Please don't get that impression. Out here, news of home is like food and drink to us, however ' trivial ' ; indeed, this life is like a dream, and the old life the only reality. We ' live on memories.' Our constant thought is ' what are they doing at home? ' "

63

In addition to letters, I frequently received parcels from home, newspapers and magazines, much of which, of course, I shared with my immediate comrades. I had only to mention anything I needed for it to be sent, if obtainable, and a large part of my own letters was taken up by lists of such things, at my Mother's urgent request. No man at the Front can have had more generous parents, and I only wish that I could feel that I merited a half of their unselfish solicitude.

Among others, I often heard from my former " half-section," Arthur Brookes, who was still at Windsor, and about the time of which I am writing he told me that he had had his " draft leave " and expected to come out before long. I was in hopes that if he did so he would be in No. 1 Coy., and even with a bit of luck in my own platoon. But as things turned out, he did not come to France until the following September. I was not, however, the only representative of Tunbridge Wells in the Service Battalion at that time, though strangely enough, I was not aware of the fact until the very last moment, just as I was leaving the Batt. for hospital. One of my fellow-townsmen was Cpl. John Hawker, whose home was in the High Street, and the other Corporal-Major Davies, of No. 3 Coy. I also made the acquaintance of a man from Tonbridge, and one from Forest Row, with whom we eagerly discovered mutual friends in the old country.

When we left " Bully-beef Camp," it was to return to Arras— somewhat to our surprise, for we had expected to do another spell of trench duty. The reason may have been that the 4th Division was being held in readiness in case it was needed on the Cambrai front, where the Guards Division was already in action. Whether or not this was so—and we of the rank-and-file were not, of course, told—we remained in the city until December 10th, at the Ecole Communale, and had a good deal of battle-practice. One day the Battalion went out into the open country to the south-west of the city, and carried out a realistic attack on imaginary enemy positions, in battle order and using live ammunition. It was strenuous and rather exhausting work, but quite exciting, and in the absence of retaliation we had a great time blazing away an immense quantity of S.A.A. at nothing and making as much noise as possible ! The rifle-grenade section of No. 1 Coy., of which I was a member, gained considerable kudos by our accurate bombing of an old chimney-stack, supposed to represent an enemy machine-gun post. There was one real casualty, however; a man of No. 2 Coy., in the excitement of the moment, dashed across a stream in advance of his platoon and was struck down by a Lewis-gun bullet. It was said that the M.O., when hastily sent for, thought the summons was only part of the general " make-believe," and delayed coming until it was too late to save the man's life.

Since the Battalion returned to Arras many of the officers had been busy rehearsing a concert which they intended to present for the entertainment of the " other ranks." The show they eventually produced, after less than a week's preparation, was excellent and revealed considerable talent in unexpected quarters. Colonel Portal himself gave a realistic impersonation of George Robey, and after " brought the house down " with a spirited rendering of " The Flowers that Bloom in the Spring, tra-la! " with dance accompaniment. (One man remarked to me, with surprise, "Who'd have thought the old man was such a decent old b——r ! ") The star of the show, however, was my Company Officer, Capt. Cazlitt, who was made up as a really " fetching " young lady: during the interval, the Colonel appealed to the audience to refrain from sending notes to the Prima Donna, who, he assured us, was already engaged ! There were several well-acted satirical sketches, poking fun at military regulations, brass-hats, politicians, etc., including one (which especially appealed to me) depicting a draper's shop run on military lines after the war. The hall which did duty as a theatre, an ex-lecture room, was only large enough to accommodate about half the Battalion when crowded to its utmost capacity, and the show was so popular that it was repeated on four successive nights. The performers themselves seemed to enjoy it at least as much as the audience, many of whom (myself included) saw it at least twice.

We of the Household Battalion were, I think, exceptionally fortunate in our officers. They were nearly all young, and most of them were as popular as they were efficient. It is difficult to estimate the C.O.'s age; at the time he seemed to me to be almost elderly, though I doubt if he was actually more than forty. The Major was about the same age. Capt. Cazlitt, O.C. No. 1 Coy., and Lieut. Whitehouse, my Platoon Officer, both celebrated their " coming-of-age " during the last two months of 1917, and each, in his own sphere, was as good an officer as one could wish to serve under. Almost everyone in No. 1 Coy. swore that they were the best officers in the best Company of the Batt., though this may have been prejudice on our part.

In the Army, one of the cardinal rules is that authority derives from " the King's Commission," and not from any personal quality of leadership in the man who holds that commission. It is the rank that counts, not the individual. That, at any rate, is the theory, and may be—no doubt, is—in general a wise principle. But armies, after all, are made up of men who are human beings and not just parts of a machine; there will always tend to be more all-round efficiency in a unit or company whose leaders command the personal trust and admiration of their men, as well as their obedience. That, anyhow, was my impression in the Household Battalion, where discipline, " morale " and mutual respect between all ranks combined in an " esprit-de-corps " at least as high as in any other unit. We knew and liked our officers and N.C.O.'s (in the majority of cases) as individuals, while they treated us as reasonable human beings and knew that they could rely on our willing co-operation in any task that had to be done. I am sure that there was a real feeling of personal loss in all of us when—as I shall tell— the Battalion was disbanded.

The short period of field-training came to an end on December 10th, and we went back into the line, in front of Monchy but a little further north than before. We entered the line by a communication trench which ran through the outskirts of the village and was somewhat exposed as it wound down the hill-side towards the Front line, and a few shells greeted us as we proceeded, but they were only part of the "evening hate " and I do not think the enemy could have seen us in the darkness. Our new post was on ground which sloped towards the north-east, and over the parapet at dawn next morning we had a wide view of the ground towards the German lines, with the village of Hancourt plainly visible on our right front. There was little in the early morning panorama to indicate war, and it was only as the light increased that one realised that the buildings which seemingly nestled among trees were only roof-less shells and that the poplars lining the road in the distance were bare and splintered stumps. As the daylight grew we caught sight of a number of Germans scuttling across the open ground below us towards their own lines, from a mine crater which they had occupied during the night; it was the first time in this underground warfare on which I had actually seen the enemy " in his wild state," and we were all much too interested to remember to fire at them until it was too late.

The next fortnight was an alternation of spells in the Front line and in Support line ; it was one of those periods to which I referred earlier in this chapter, during which I have many vivid memories of incidents and conditions, but in general am now unable to arrange them in the order of their happening. I cannot, therefore, claim that this part of my story is chronologically accurate, though all the incidents described occurred during this " tour of duty."

For two or three days after we " took over " things were a good deal more lively than they had been during our previous spell. There was a good deal of hostile shelling on our rear, especially towards Happy Valley and Monchy village, and trench-mortar bombs exploded at intervals among the barbed wire entanglements in No-man's-land, necessitating wiring-parties at night to repair the damage. Once or twice volleys of rifle-grenades were sent over, but failed to reach our trench. One evening, soon after dark—I think it was our second day in—there was a raid on part of the Brigade's sector, and although the post at which I was stationed was outside the area attacked, we came in for a heavy dose of " minnies " (minenwerfers)—in some ways the most unpleasant form of bombardment. The trench was blown in on both sides of us, and we lost two men killed and one wounded.

But this sort of thing, though extremely disagreeable, was part of the normal happenings of trench-warfare and was to be expected on any part of the front. The worst of our physical discomforts, during this spell, could hardly be laid to the enemy's account. The weather had turned cold at about the same time as we came into the line, but it was not until three or four days later, when No. 1 Coy. took over a new part of the Front line, that the frost set in in earnest. It lasted, with scarcely an intermission, for nearly a month.

Exposed as we were to its full rigours in the open trench, it seemed to me that I had never been so cold, and indeed by the standards of an English winter I think that the frost was exceptionally severe, though probably in normal circumstances, with plenty of food and exercise, it would have been no great hardship. In our situation, however, it was a tax on the strongest constitution. The temperature dropped lower and lower, the ground hardened and the trench walls were as if moulded in cast iron, while the duckboards underfoot were slippery with ice. Across the parapet hoar-frost an inch thick outlined every strand of the barbed-wire entanglements and in the moonlight gave them the look of a delicate band of white lace. A slight sprinkling of snow fell at the outset, but for the most part the weather was fine— pale ineffectual sunshine by day, and interminable nights of steely stars glittering endlessly in a frozen universe.

The cold pervaded everywhere and penetrated everything. It crept under our clothes, our fingers and joints ached with it continually, it seemed to congeal our blood and to chill the very marrow of our bones. We had not been allowed to bring great-coats into the line, for fear of hampering our movements, and almost the only addition to our ordinary clothing was a sleeveless leather jerkin, woollen gloves and mufflers. Fires of any kind were, of course, impossible in the Front line, with the Germans only just across No-man's-land, and, unable to leave the post, we would have welcomed any kind of physical activity as a means of keeping warm. But, with nothing to do when not on sentry, we were obliged to rely on stamping and arm-flapping to stimulate the circulation; naturally, not even this could be kept up indefinitely, and our feet were soon so numbed by the cold as to lose all sense of feeling. It was, in fact, several weeks later before I fully regained conscious possession of my own toes!

Here in the Front line there were no deep dugouts to retire to when not on duty; the only shelter available—if shelter it could be called—was a shallow excavation in the wall of the trench, hardly big enough for two men to squeeze into at the same time. Even so, it was not a comfortable resting-place, for in order to lie down the sleepers had to stick their feet out into the trench, where they were a trap for every unwary passer-by and the occasion of much profane language on both sides.

One of the consequences of the Arctic spell was that, although our water supply was brought up regularly every night with the rations, it often froze solid in the cans, and only during daylight, when trench-cookers could be lit, that it could be thawed and we could have a drink. Rifle oil, too, became too viscous to be used, and the metal parts of our rifles stung the hands if handled without gloves.

Under conditions like these, it is hardly surprising that hostile activity died down on both sides. Long-range shelling went on intermittently, especially the nightly strafe on the supply lines, and machine-guns were watchful over No-man's-land, but there was very little firing on either side in the Front line. Evidently, the Germans had troubles enough of their own, without trying to add to ours; and, for our part, we were quite willing to let sleeping dogs lie. Once or twice at night we would loose off a few shots into the dark, in order to let Jerry know that we were still there and to keep our rifles in trim, but otherwise we seldom had occasion to use them.

On completion of our first spell in the Front line—five days, I think, for we did not remain there continuously during the fortnight, but alternated with one of the other Companies—we moved back to the Support line. There, although the weather was no less severe, conditions were a good deal easier, for we were able to enjoy a brazier fire and some small measure of sleep in the dugout attached to the new post when not on duty. True, it was scarcely a dugout in the best sense of the term, being little more than a large "bivvie" on trench-floor level, by no means impervious to shell-fire and only able to accommodate five or six of us at one time, but it sufficed to furnish us with an occasional degree of shelter from the weather which had been altogether lacking in the Front line. It must not be supposed, however, that we spent most of our time "keeping the fire warm," for, in contrast to our previous lack of exercise, we were now kept constantly busy. In addition to the regular two-hour spell on sentry, the Platoon was frequently called upon to provide a quota for ration-carrying, digging and water-fatigues, and the greater part of our personnel was almost always absent on some working-party or other. These expeditions usually involved a tramp of several miles through twisting trenches, heavily ladened with sacks of food, water-cans or munitions, in addition to our rifles and equipment, and were not rendered easier by the slippery condition of the ice-bound duck-boards. The journey from the Support line to Fosse Farm, where the limbers unloaded, back with a load of supplies through the maze of trenches to the Front line, and then "home," invariably took several hours to accomplish, and quite often we would return only to find orders awaiting us for another trip. Usually, we would consider ourselves lucky if we got three consecutive hours of sleep during the night, and we made up what we could at odd times, whenever we happened to be free for half-an-hour or so.

In these circumstances, it is not to be wondered at that when we did have a chance to " get down to it " we needed no rocking, despite the cold. But a frequent cause of disturbance, however tired we might be, was inflicted on us by the activities of lice. These disgusting vermin were among the most irritating (literally) and universal of the minor " horrors of war," both in the line and out of it, and they became more lively as soon as we had rolled into our blankets and got reasonably warm. When I first reached the Front I was inclined to disbelieve what the old hands told us about the inevitability of lousiness ; like most of the newcomers, I thought that it must be due to personal neglect and that if I took reasonable care of myself I should never get into so repulsive a state. I soon found that I was wrong. The loathsome parasites were quite unavoidable at the Front, for the conditions under which we were obliged to live made personal cleanliness impossible, and the soil and everything with which we came in contact were infested with the vermin. No matter what precautions were taken, everyone was lousy ; insecticides were of little avail, and the utmost one could do, in our circumstances, was to wage an unending war against the pests by cracking them between thumb-nails or burning their eggs out of the seams of our clothes with a lighted cigarette-end or candle flame. They were slow-moving and easily caught, but they bred so fast that the most unremitting efforts could do no more than keep their numbers down. We made a joke of our lousiness, as we did of most things that were unavoidable. In common parlance, a louse was known as a " chat," and the word was also used as a verb: " to have a " chat" meant, not light conversation, but to hunt in the folds of one's shirt! Newcomers from England were solemnly assured that on the other side of No-man's-land all the lice bore iron-cross markings on their backs and did the goose-step in formation.

Very occasionally, we would be taken back to an improvised bath-house at Tilloy-les-Mofflaines, and had a wash under the warm reluctant shower and a change of underwear, but as often as not the " clean " clothes we received in exchange for our dirty ones were already lousy before we put them on. One night, coming back to Arras from the line, I drew fresh blankets from the Battalion store, only to find that they were in a worse state than the ones I had handed in. I spent much of the night picking lice off them in the dark, by touch alone!

The only times during my overseas service when I was, or could be, completely free from the pests was during the brief and blessed interludes in hospital, and in time, like everyone, I came to regard them almost as a matter of course, an inescapable evil of active service—yet, like so many things in war-time, such squalid conditions seem almost incredible to me now.

.　　.　　.　　.　　.　　.

Despite the continuance of the cold and the constant succession of exhausting fatigues, life for us was considerably more endurable in Support than in the Front line. Yet it was then, on one particular day, that I reached what I thought was the climax of "fed-up-ness." Immediately after the morning Stand-to I was detailed for "gas-guard" at the entrance to a dugout some little distance from the platoon's post, for the usual two-hour "relief"; but shortly after I went on duty an order from Battalion H.Q. took every man of the platoon, with the exception of the Cpl.-of-Horse, away on fatigue for the greater part of the day, and I was left with no one to relieve me. I was on sentry the whole day, with the exception of half-an-hour at mid-day, when the Corporal took my place while I snatched a hurried meal; there was nothing to do but stand in the trench and keep a look-out for possible (but rather unlikely) gas-shells, in which case I was to sound the klaxon alarm near-by; there was nothing on which to sit—just bare clay walls and the duckboards—it was bitterly cold; I could not, of course, read, and I hardly saw a soul the whole day. I do not even know if the dugout I was "guarding" was tenanted. I tried repeating to myself all the poetry I could remember, but the hours seemed endless; by the time evening came, I was "fed to the teeth." The Batt. was moving to a new sector that night, and when the fatigue-party returned I had just time to hurry back to the post and get my kit together before joining in the trek to our new post in Happy Valley, which we reached about midnight. But I was not to rest yet, for I was immediately put on sentry for another two hours. Not unnaturally, I felt very hard done by, and expressed myself in terms which very nearly led to my being "put on a charge" for refusing duty. Yet, after all, I suppose it was only fair, though I did not realise it at the time, for the other fellows had been on fatigue all day and were probably more tired than I was. I am not proud of this episode.

While we occupied this post—probably for a couple of days only—we were allowed to send letters to England, the only time in my experience when this was permitted direct from the trenches. The concession was made, probably, because otherwise our Christmas greetings would not have reached home in time. At that time we were expecting to spend Christmas Day in the line, but a day or two later came the welcome news that we were to be relieved on Christmas Eve.

When, in due course, we "took over" in the Front line for another spell, the rigours we had previously experienced were repeated. The frost still held, and far from showing any sign of abatement, seemed to have settled down immovably for the rest of the winter. There was no wind, the sky by day was a clear pale blue, and the rays of the sun, striking the earth at a flat angle, were reflected away again in a million frost-sparkles without noticeably affecting the temperature. The time I liked best was the dawn, when we lined the trench for the morning Stand-to and watched, beyond the jagged edge of the parapet, the smoky red mist rise like sacrificial fires on the altar of the approaching sun, whose first rays touched the frosted wire into a network of pale rubies and flung a fanfare of rose and lilac over the eastern sky.

Dawn, too, brought relaxation; for the long night hours, in this queer inverted existence of ours, was not a time for rest, but was filled with a tense alertness, an unacknowledged and suppressed "wind-up," which the coming of daylight did much to relieve.

This time we were a little further to the north of our previous post, on the extreme left of the Brigade front ; probably we were quite close to the village of Pelves—or what was left of it—but I cannot be sure. In the trenches one could see little of one's surroundings, and here we were somewhat overlooked from a ridge in front and consequently were forbidden to risk giving away our position by looking over the parapet by day. The troops opposite seemed to be a rather more aggressive lot than previously, for "minnies" occasionally fell in the wire ahead, and several volleys of rifle-grenades were fired at the post, though without causing any damage. One of our own trench-mortar sections made itself extremely unpopular by sending a few bombs into the German lines from a near-by position—unpopular, because, having loosed off their bombs, they were away with their mortar to another part of the line, while we had to stop and receive the enemy's acknowledgments!

One night, soon after midnight, a sudden burst of rockets and a crashing bombardment heralded another German raid. We were again lucky in not being the point selected for attack, but we were in the midst of the box-barrage with which the enemy's artillery surrounded the threatened area, and for half-an-hour we lived under a deluge of explosions, as hundreds of shells crashed on every side, shrapnel whistled and thumped into the ground and richochetting bullets whined overhead. Standing on an unusually high firestep and firing at random into the dark, I felt most uncomfortably exposed ; I could see the red spurts of flame in the German front line as batteries of mortars were set off, and once a piece of shrapnel hit my tin-hat a resounding whack. But no one at our post was injured—a quite remarkable piece of luck, considering the violence of the bombardment. Further up the line, about 100-150 yards to our left, however, a few of the raiders succeeded in reaching the trench, and there were several casualties on both sides before they were driven out. Our artillery then strafed them heavily for a full hour.

But that was the only lively night of the present spell ; the others were " quiet "—interminable hours of tension, when nothing happened but anything might at any moment. I shall not easily forget those winter nights in the Front line. Darkness fell about four in the afternoon and dawn was not until nearly eight in the morning—sixteen hours of Stygian blackness, broken at intervals by gun-flashes or the gleam of star-shells ; punctuated by the scream of a shell, the crack of a rifle or the sudden heart-stopping rattle of a machine-gun. The long hours crept by with leaden feet ; sometimes it seemed as if time itself were dead. In the darkness, we were a prey to all sorts of unreasoning fancies, and often imagined we saw things out in front which were not there. Such ordinary object as a tree stump, a hummock of earth or a coil of barbed wire took on new and menacing forms and in the wavering light of a star-shell could seem to be moving towards us. We talked in low voices, as though afraid of being overheard ; and, indeed, there was always the possibility that a hostile patrol might approach within ear-shot. No one, of course, admitted being windy, and would have indignantly denied the charge, but I am fairly sure that few were entirely easy during these long vigils.

The Arctic cold was ever present, probing with icy fingers beneath the thickest clothing, freezing feet and fingers, and making it impossible, even when not on sentry, to sit still for long at a time. Most nights we got a tot of rum, brought round by an N.C.O. and measured out to each man under the supervision of the Orderly Officer ; it helped, but it was not strong enough nor was the tot large enough to have much effect. One night (the night of the raid just described) Mr. Whitehouse was Orderly Officer and, with a Corporal, dispensed the rum-ration to the Front line posts. But he had apparently been sampling it himself on the way, for by the time the post next to ours had been reached the jar was empty and he himself was distinctly "merry." Finding that the jar, when inverted over our waiting mess-tin lids, refused to imitate the Widow's Cruse, he ordered the Corporal to take it back to Coy. H.Q. and swear that it had been only half-full to begin with, and in the meantime he crawled into a bivvie and tried to entertain us with incoherent and often unrepeatable songs. Our amusement was tempered somewhat by the fear that his attempts at singing would be audible in the German lines and provoke retaliation. As the raid commenced shortly afterwards, it almost seemed as if our apprehensions were justified. But as soon as the bombardment started, Mr. Whitehouse was completely sobered ; he went from post to post with the utmost coolness, and when he spoke to me in passing, I can vouch for it that there was no trace of intoxication in his voice. But we got no rum that night !

We were relieved soon after dark on Christmas Eve. Getting out of the trenches was a long and somewhat exacting task, owing to the slippery state of the duckboards and the frequent confusion caused by men falling down and losing touch with the files in front. When at last we emerged on the road leading to Arras the going was easier, though the frosted stone "pavé" surface was not much better to march on, and we were not in very good trim for the five or six miles journey before us. The prospect of a spell out of the line, however, was sufficient to overcome our weariness, though by the time the camp was reached our only thought was to turn in with as little delay as possible. Fortunately, all was ready for us; "details" and H.Q. men had prepared the huts in "Wilderness Camp," extra blankets were issued, and after a welcome meal of hot tea, bully and biscuits, we lost no time in "getting down to it." Although it was Christmas Eve, no one suggested that we should hang up our socks—which was just as well, seeing that we had worn them continuously for the past fortnight !—and the Corporal's satirical offer to dress up as Father Christmas and sing carols to us fell on deaf ears.

Christmas Day was heavily overcast and as cold as ever. We were allowed to lie late on this occasion, and there were no duties for any of the men who had come from the line, all guards and pickets for the day being found by "details"—the Battalion nucleus which had remained in Arras while we were in the trenches. Needless to say, we fully appreciated the holiday. I had difficulty, though, in realising that it was indeed Christmas, so very different was it from any Yuletide that I had ever spent: Most of the others, too, had the same feeling of unreality, for there was hardly any exchange of the customary wishes for "a Merry Christmas"— anyone who spoke the words did so in a humorous or ironical tone. A touch of festivity, however, was lent by the arrival of the Post Corporal after breakfast, with the accumulated mail of the past week, and we crowded eagerly round as name after name was called, and letters and parcels were claimed by the fortunate owners. I was particularly lucky on this occasion, for several large parcels of Christmas fare and a whole sheaf of letters fell to my share, as well as newspapers and magazines. In my section, at least, we were not lacking in good food or smokes that day.

Later, there was a Church Parade of the whole Battalion on an open stretch of ground just outside the hut lines. A military "drum-head" service is impressive at any time, but on this occasion, on this particular day, I was oppressed by a sense of the essential hypocrisy of it all. Here were we, five or six hundred men, trained in the art of killing their fellows, formed up in seried ranks around a Chaplain whose white surplice barely concealed his military uniform, and singing of "Peace on earth, goodwill towards men," while all around the guns thundered their unanswerable and derisive commentary. It seemed to me to be little short of blasphemy. The very ground we stood on had not long since witnessed a welter of bloodshed, less than five miles away the slaughter continued, and soon we should be going back to kill or be killed. How then did we dare to speak of the Christmas message, or offer praise to the Prince of Peace ?

When the Parade dispersed a few white flakes were drifting down from the grey pall overhead, and before long it was snowing in earnest. There was no special menu for dinner, just the ordinary fare : stew and boiled rice, if I remember rightly. Afterwards, the occupants of my hut, almost without exception retired beneath the blankets, to overtake some of our extensive arrears of sleep, and the afternoon was a blissful blank until—only a few minutes later as it seemed—we were roused by the shout of '' Tea up ! ''

Outside, the scene was now completely changed. The snow was coming down in a steady blizzard, driving in clouds before the wind, and the ground was already covered to a depth of several inches. Everywhere the hut roofs and tent-tops gleamed white in the darkness, and the gaunt arms of shell-shattered trees stood out like skeletons. To this extent Christmas had lived up to its traditional reputation, though we were not in a position to enjoy to the full its old-fashioned charm. Not for us were the blazing fires, the holly, the crackers, the mince-pies and plum pudding, the cheerful family gatherings and all the other time-honoured joys of Yuletide. But at least we had a stove in the hut, we were warm and dry, and above all we had the blessed realisation that we were no longer in the trenches. It was the most un-Christmas-like Christmas I had ever spent, yet no one could say that we were low-spirited. After tea, we went along to the Canteen tent, near the camp '' gate '' ; the big marquee was thronged, and filled with a babel of voices, with every now and then a rousing chorus as someone at the piano thumped out the air of a popular song. It didn't matter whether we knew the words or not—everybody joined in—even the booming of the guns outside was drowned by the din we made. I stayed until about eight o'clock and then, still feeling tired, went back to the hut, intending to turn in early. But before doing so, I settled down to write a letter home, for naturally on this day above all others our secret thoughts were far across the Channel, in the homes we longed to return to and where we well knew we were not forgotten. This done, I rolled into my blankets and in a few minutes was sound asleep.

. . . . . .

Next day the Battalion returned to Arras, but my luck was out. A large working-party was detailed for carrying-fatigues in the line, and we set out early from Wilderness Camp for Happy Valley. Our packs were taken to Arras with the rest of the Battalion stores, but otherwise we had to go in full equipment. All day we were kept hard at work, carrying tools, sand-bags and coils of barbed wire from the railhead to the various dumps, with short rests and on '' haversack '' rations. Backwards and forwards we went with our heavy loads, over snow-covered ground or through frozen, slippery trenches. It was not easy to walk crab-fashion through narrow twisting ways, holding on to the end of a box of S.A.A. with one hand and fending off the wall of the trench with the other, at the same time trying to maintain one's footing on icy duckboards and prevent one's rifle-sling from slipping off one's shoulder! And carrying a length of duckboarding on one's shoulder across the open was equally difficult, for gusts of wind would catch it and tend to swing one round, with awkward results to the balance and to one's neighbours! Our lines of dark burdened figures, trudging doggedly across the white landscape, must have looked like gangs of Siberian convicts, and before the end of the day the victims of the Czardom could hardly have felt more exhausted.

At nightfall we started back on the seven-mile tramp to Arras. The snow-storm of yesterday had made the roads hard and slippery, and even had we been fresh, marching would have been somewhat difficult; but we were all already dog-tired, and could have slept by the roadside where we were. That march is like a long-drawn-out nightmare in my memory. Every limb ached; my equipment seemed to weigh tons and to become heavier with every mile; my rifle-sling cut into my shoulder. my spine felt like breaking and my feet were as leaden weights. Although the temperature was several degrees below freezing, we sweated freely and were tormented with thirst; after our water-bottles were emptied (most of us had emptied them already during the day) we scraped handfuls of snow from the roadside, and during the brief halts we did not dare to sit down for fear of dropping to sleep, but propped ourselves up on our rifles or against tree-trunks or telephone poles. The road seemed to lengthen into eternity. During the later stages I am convinced that there were times when I was actually asleep while marching, and moving automatically with the monotonous rhythm of the tramping feet around me. I might have doubted the possibility of this kind of "sleep-walking" had not other men afterwards admitted that they had had the same experience. After what seemed an endless purgatory, at long last we reached Arras and stumbled through the gate to Schramm Barracks; but when we halted and drew up in a ragged line on the Barrack-square, we could only maintain a standing position by propping ourselves up with our rifles, and on reaching our quarters just threw ourselves down on the floor in all our kit, and slept like the dead, despite the icy draughts which blew through the empty window-frames. That was a Boxing Day "bank-holiday-outing" to remember!

Reveille was allowed to pass unheeded, for the next day was No. 1 Company's own "Christmas Day" and the twenty-first birthday of our Company Officer. By about ten o'clock, after a wash and shave, I felt quite refreshed again, although still very stiff and "leg-weary." In the afternoon we assembled for our Christmas dinner, provided at the expense of Captain Cazlitt. Tables sufficient to accommodate all of the rank-and-file of the Company had been laid in adjoining rooms, which were gaily decorated with paper garlands and holly. (There was no mistletoe —alas! we had no use for it). A most liberal fare was provided, including many of the traditional items of a Christmas menu— turkey, fresh vegetables, fruit, chocolates and crackers, besides home-made plum-puddings and mince-pies which were reported to have come from the Captain's Sevenoaks home. There was enough and to spare for everyone, and plenty of beer. The officers and N.C.O's acted at waiters, and joined unreservedly in the general festivities, while the Colonel wandered from room to room, greeted with vociferous cheers, especially when he promised that our next Christmas dinner should be in Blighty!

Three days later, we were back in Wilderness Camp, where we had been on Christmas Day. The camp, which was about two kilometres east of Arras, only just off the Cambrai road and nearly opposite the turning which led to Tilloy, was well named, for all around was the most utter and complete wilderness. The ground was pock-marked with old shell-holes and trenches, and bare of every sign of civilisation; a few splintered stumps in what had been, until the previous spring, No-man's-land, were all that was left of trees and copses, with here and there a heap of stones marking the site of a cottage or barn. The only intact buildings were the huts and tents of the Camp, and an occasional nissen hut. But at that moment, all the desolation was blanketted beneath a universal covering of snow, so that it looked like a scene in the Antarctic wastes.

The next five days were much like those at Bois de Boeuf, with working-parties every day, from which we returned at night tired and very hungry. None of these expeditions were as exhausting as the one on Boxing Day, but they were quite sufficiently so to make us disinclined for anything but bed when we got back; though usually, as soon as we were dismissed, I would throw off my kit and make a bee-line for the Canteen, where I would wolf any sort of food that was available, before turning in. Some of it was food which I wouldn't dare to eat at bed-time now-a-days (once it was a whole tin of pineapple chunks!) but the only time I was kept awake by indigestion was after enjoying a hard-boiled egg just received from home!

The Battalion took over a sector of the line again on January 3rd, but to my surprise I was ordered, with about thirty others drawn from each of the four Companies, to return to Arras with "Details." Our pleasure at the unexpected respite was, however, somewhat tempered when we learned that we were a special squad to carry out a projected raid on the German lines, and were going back to rehearse the "scheme." It was not a prospect to look forward to, but it meant another week out of the trenches at least, and we were promised special (unspecified) privileges if the raid was successful. On Active Service during the Great War, one did

not think—one did not dare to think—too much about the future ;
the present was what mattered.

      " Tomorrow?—why, tomorrow I may be
      Myself with yesterday's sev'n thousand years."
and, with old Khayyam, we were disposed, fatalistically, to " take
the cash in hand and waive the rest."

Our return to Arras was, indeed, a rather hilarious journey,
for even in the main streets no attempt had been made to clear
the snow, which was trodden hard by passing traffic, until the
surface was a sheet of solid ice. It was almost impossible to keep
a footing—skates would have been more appropriate—and marching
down the incline of the Boulevard Carnot we slid about in all
directions, clutched at each other and fell over each other (not, I
am afraid, always involuntarily!) and all the shouts of the Corporal
to " Pick up the step, there!" as he, too, went down, failed to keep
us in the ranks. We were bruised, but in good spirits, by the time
we reached Schramm Barracks.

Practice for the bombing raid was carried forward vigorously
during the following seven days. On some open ground a short
distance from the Citadel a facsimile of the ground over which the
operation was to take place had been constructed, both our own
and the German trenches being reproduced in rough detail, as well
as the principal irregularities of the surface and the barbed-wire
entanglements between the lines. Over this terrain—the exact
resemblance of which to the original we had, of course, to take on
trust—we made repeated assaults to a prescribed time-table, until
each man knew exactly what his part was to be and could have
found his way in the dark—as, indeed, he would have to do when
the time came. As far as we were concerned, the rehearsals went
" like clockwork "—but there were one or two slight omissions
which might make a difference on the " opening night ": the enemy,
and his barrage, for instance! A partial thaw set in one evening,
and we had hopes that the snow might be cleared off before the raid
took place, for it would render us rather conspicuous even at night,
but next day it snowed harder than ever.

One evening the Major, who was in command of the raiding
party and of Battalion " details " in Arras, treated two hundred
and fifty of us to seats at a concert organised by another regiment
in the city. The concert hall was some distance from our quarters,
and the pitch dark streets were so slippery that, in order to get along
without falling at every step, we were obliged to link arms in rows
of six or more. But the concert was well worth while, and the
Major was voted a " jolly good fellow."

But after a week of intensive " assault-practise," interrupted
once or twice by blinding blizzards, word was received that the raid
was " off," and we were ordered to rejoin our respective Companies
in the line forthwith. No reason for the abandonment of the project
was given us, and we did not feel inclined to question the decision.

I will not pretend that we were not profoundly relieved, for we knew only too well the hazardous nature of these attempts to "twist the tiger's tail" and that there were long odds against many of us getting back from such a raid unscathed. The ostensible object of these "shows" was to secure "samples" (dead or alive) of the troops opposed to us, so as to determine their regiment, strength, etc.—and this was sometimes done—but I think their main purpose was "to keep the war going." Certain "high-ups" among the Brass Hats of both sides feared, perhaps, that if the armies were allowed to sit facing each other indefinitely, the soldiers might begin to think (a thing soldiers should never do!) and end by agreeing with their "opposite numbers" to end this misery by shaking hands and going home! So the High Commands evolved this plan of frequent "pin-prick" attacks, as a means of "fostering the offensive spirit" and "keeping the men on their toes," regardless of the useless waste of life involved.

Going into the line in the ordinary way was almost pleasant in comparison with going up in order to "go over the top," and we set off the same evening in good spirits. The journey was uneventful, and we entered the line by way of a communication-trench on the south side of the Cambrai road. We did not proceed at once to join our respective Companies in the Front and Support lines, but passed the night in a post just off the c.-t., where there was a small dugout; this, however, was already occupied by a sergeant and about ten men, who considered that there was no room to spare for visitors, so we settled ourselves in a near-by bivouac roofed with corrugated iron and sandbags. Just as we had left Arras, I had been handed a parcel from home, and we now proceeded to investigate its contents. There was a large cake, some chocolate, a tin of condensed milk and other dainties, but before we had had time to dispose of many of them some big shells began to fall in the vicinity, too close to be pleasant, and we had to make a hurried retreat to the dugout, where we thrust our company, willy-nilly, on the protesting inhabitants. Unfortunately, in our hurry we left most of the parcel behind, and in the morning I found that a direct hit had completely demolished the bivouac, parcel and all.

I rejoined No. 1 Coy. in the Support line, and after a couple of days the longed-for thaw set in. We then wished it hadn't! The temperature rose abruptly, and everywhere the walls of the trenches began to cave in and covered the duckboards with mud and water, which the persistent rain did not improve. It was not until the night on which the Batt. was due to be relieved, however, that we realised the full meaning of the word "Mud."

At first, when starting off for the rear, it was fairly easy going, although we had to wade through at least a foot of water in several places and our boots were soon full of it. But soon, in the deep narrow communication trench, we encountered mud that was like glue, and the farther we went the worse it became. Every vestige of the duckboards disappeared beneath the mud, into which our feet sank deeply at every step ; progress became slower and slower, for soon it was necessary to tug each leg out with both hands, and then to haul each other out bodily. Presently, we were in above the knees, and despite the most violent struggles it was impossible to go on. To add to our discomfort, a number of shells burst not far away. Although in the normal way the narrow trench, whose top was about a foot above our heads, would have been good protection against any but a rather unlikely direct hit, there was now a considerable danger that the concussion of an explosion anywhere in the vicinity might bring down the sodden walls upon us and bury us alive. However, as we could not go forward, and were already too exhausted by our struggles to go back without a short rest, there was nothing we could do about it. Two men further along the line, I heard afterwards, did manage to extricate themselves and climbed out of the trench ; but, in trying to find their way back across the open ground, they were both killed—by shells or machine-gun bullets, or perhaps by drowning, for two or three days later the bodies were found in a flooded shell-hole.

At last a message was passed along from the rear that a new route had been found where the mud was not so deep, and by dint of the most violent exertions we succeeded in turning round, and moved slowly back. For some distance, however, it was only possible to make any progress at all by literally dragging each other bodily out of the mire at every step. When at last we reached a trench known as Spade Reserve, the mud was found to be less deep and softer, and farther along still it was liquid, so that we were able to move more quickly. But still death dogged our footsteps. At intervals along this trench deep holes, some five or six feet square, had been dug for drainage purposes, leading out through the parados by an opening much the same width as the trench itself. One of our fellows, who must have lagged behind the rest, was probably hurrying to overtake the others when he mistook one of these unprotected openings for a continuation of the trench, blundered through it in the darkness and was drowned in the liquid mud which filled the sump. He was not missed until the roll was called two or three hours later.

The going was much easier for the remainder of the journey, but in order to avoid sticking fast again we were obliged to leave the trench at the point where it passed under the Cambrai road, and go up the road itself along a stretch where it was directly exposed to enemy fire. We were not observed, however, though several times random bursts of machine-gun bullets whined high over our heads. We trudged limply past Fosse Farm and, some distance beyond, came to our destination, a reserve position known as " the Brown Line," consisting of a half-ruinous trench with broken-down bivouacs and some empty gun-emplacements. Here the roll was called, and we turned in and slept the sleep of exhaustion, lying in quondam " shelters " hardly raised above the floor of the trench, soaked to the skin, half-frozen, plastered with mud from head to foot, and with our feet resting in mud and water. Next day, many of the men reported sick with rheumatism, trench fever and other ailments, but—rather to my own surprise—I was none the worse for the exposure, which would, I am quite sure, have laid me up for months before the war.

I was lucky, that afternoon, in being detailed for the Advance Party which was sent ahead to prepare quarters for the Battalion, which was due to come out of the line for a short rest in a couple of days. We set off for Arras in high spirits, despite the fact that we were all rather limp after last night's " adventure," and many were hobbling with rheumatism, swollen feet or ruined boots. We marched to the tune of " We all go the same way home " and " This is the end of a perfect day," but before we had covered the six miles of road which separated us from our destination the song had quavered into silence and some had fallen out, to be picked up by passing lorries.

.   .   .   .   .

As soon as we had made ourselves comfortable in a room in Schramm Barracks and I was able to take my clothes off for the first time in a week, I found that several sore places on my legs, of which I had been conscious for the last couple of days without being able to do anything about them, were inflamed and suppurating ; and a finger of my left hand, which I had scratched on a strand of rusty barbed wire yesterday, commenced to fester and swell to double its normal size. As they showed no sign of improvement, as soon as the Battalion returned to occupy the rest-billets we had meanwhile prepared for them, I decided to " go sick." The M.O. ordered hot fomentations and put me on the " excused duty " list ; he rated me for not having reported earlier, saying that in another day or so I might have lost the finger. But although I had daily dressings, and the finger improved—it was very painful at first, and I still have a scar—the sores on my limbs registered " no change." The Batt. moved again to Wilderness Camp on the 23rd, and I went with them, still excused duty, but when the short " rest " came to an end on the 27th and they went back into the line, the M.O. sent me back to Arras with " Details."

During the next four days I was given a different kind of treatment each day, by doctors of other units in the Division, who apparently took sick-parade duty in turn. I am not surprised that the remedies prescribed did no good, for they were very casually applied by the R.A.M.C. orderlies who carried out the " dressings " —the " hot " fomentations, for example, were nearly always only luke-warm ! The last of the M.O.'s to see me, an American, gave me a very thorough examination, and decided that I must go to hospital. He did not tell me his diagnosis, beyond saying that my blood was thoroughly out of order, owing to the conditions in which we had been living.

Consequently, on the afternoon of February 1st I reported at the 10th Field Ambulance Station. It was only a few minutes' walk from the Barracks, for which I was thankful, for I had to go in full marching order, carrying all my kit and belongings (except, I think, my rifle). It was one of the extraordinary rules on Active Service that, if one was wounded, no matter how slightly, a casualty was entitled to " dump " his kit at once ; but if one was merely sick one was expected to carry everything to the F.A., so long as one was able to stand at all ! At the Ambulance Station I was seen by the doctor in charge, and was then taken by motor ambulance to the 19th Casualty Clearing Station at Duisans, about ten kilometres west of Arras. Although I did not know it at the time, I had taken my final leave of the Household Battalion ; before I returned to the Front, the Batt. had ceased to exist as a unit. I was kept at the C.C.S. for two days, and then entrained with hundreds of other sick or wounded casualties in a Red Cross train, bound for a Base hospital.

This was the first time I had been obliged to " go sick " since I came to France, and so far I had completely refuted the prophesies of my relatives, most of whom had predicted that " of course " I should never be able to " stand " the conditions of Active Service. I heard afterwards that, when I first crossed the Channel, it was confidently expected that I should be invalided back within a week ! And, to tell the truth, I, too, was surprised and somewhat proud of myself, that I had been able to " stick it," with my medical history and despite hardships which would have been unthinkable before I joined up. Not only was there now no sign of asthma, but I several times boasted, in letters, that I could not even catch an ordinary cold ! But it was now, when I was living for a time in comparative comfort and safety, that I realised how much the last three months—and particularly the last six weeks—had " taken out of me." I had not had a worse time than other men—in truth, as many front-line soldiers could testify, I had endured much less and for a shorter period, than many of them—but I doubt if I could have stood much more without the spell of rest, mental and physical, which hospital gave me. The transformation of the weakling I had been, into a strong and hardy soldier, was not, it seemed, as complete as I had imagined !

The train journey from Duisans to the coast took eight hours, not so much because of the distance covered as because of the slow rate of travel and the frequent stops. However, I was very comfortable, and would not have minded had the journey been much longer. The coaches were of the latest " corridor " type, smoothe-running an luxuriously appointed ; each compartment accommodated three passengers a side, and there were a couple of bunks overhead, in place of the luggage racks, for stretcher cases. The nurses and orderlies who looked after us were attentive to our every need, and even our meals, daintily cooked and served, were brought to us on trays. It was an unwonted change, to be waited on as if I was a wealthy tourist! I asked one of the orderlies where we were going, but his reply, "Lee Tree Port," conveyed nothing to me, until I realised that he meant Le Tréport, a small seaside resort not many miles from Dieppe.

On arrival at our destination, soon after dark, we were conveyed by motor ambulances and buses to the 16th American General Hospital, high up on the cliff overlooking the sea. Here we were met, literally on the threshold, by a bevy of nurses bearing bowls of cocoa and biscuits, and as soon as we had refreshed ourselves the inevitable forms were filled up and questions asked, after which we were conducted to our respective wards. Then came a hot bath, which to me was more welcome than almost any other of the comforts of hospital, and I settled down into a real bed and quickly fell asleep, blissfully conscious that I was "down the line" and out of hearing of the guns, whose continual thunder had not left my ears during the past three months.

.   .   .   .   .   .

The hospital was part of the American Red Cross organisation, and the wards were spacious wooden huts about fifty feet long, arranged in a radiating circle around the dispensaries, etc., while the Heaquarters Offices, and the Sisters' quarters, were situated on the outskirts. Doctors, nurses and orderlies were all American volunteers, and I was immediately impressed by their cheerful friendliness, efficiency and lack of "red tape." The doctors, despite their "Commissions," showed no consciousness of their superior rank but talked to us "as man to man," and nearly all the hospital personnel had the same typically American manner—bright, breezy and independent.

There were no events worthy of special record during the three weeks I spent at Le Tréport. The war might have been a thousand miles away, and we led a lazy life of complete rest—just what I needed! —spending most of our time talking, reading or sleeping, a welcome contrast from the previous months. None of the patients in my ward was confined to bed—most of them were suffering from boils, abscesses or other superficial troubles—and, apart from the daily "dressings" and a visit to the doctor every three days, there was little to prevent us from passing the time as we pleased, though we were not allowed to leave the hospital. The ward contained a good supply of books, magazines and games, and there were concerts at the Y.M.C.A. and a cinema, as well as a gramophone in the ward, so we did not lack for amusement. There was no fixed time for getting-up in the mornings, and we rolled out of bed when we felt inclined, usually about 7.15; breakfast was officially between seven and seven-thirty, but one could always obtain it later, and we found by experience that late-comers often fared best for "buckshee" rations. Then, after a wash and shave, we made our beds and lay on them for a leisurely smoke. The only " work " we were expected to do was to wash the floor of the ward every morning, which " duty " we took in turns. The afternoons would be spent in slumber, and the evenings in conversation or cards round the stove, with perhaps a visit to the before-mentioned Y.M.C.A. or cinema. While in hospital I struck up acquaintance with several men of kindred interests, and we had many interesting and keenly argued discussions, which were sometimes prolonged far into the night.

.   .   .   .   .   .

During the past few weeks, I have to confess that my feelings about the War, and about many other things, had changed quite a bit. I had had three months at the Front, and the impact of the hard facts of war seems to have had a gradual but drastic effect on the illusions with which I had come to France. I knew now that the " glory " of war consisted mainly of dirt, discomfort, filth, weariness of mind and body, " wind-up," and endless effort. Of course, I had known, in theory, that Active Service would be like this, but it is one thing to contemplate, from a distance, hardships " bravely borne for a noble cause," when one is well-fed, warm and rested—but quite another thing to endure them in cold and rain and mud, when hungry and half-dazed from lack of sleep, and without prospect of permanent relief. I suppose few men survived life in the trenches, especially in winter, for long without disillusionment, and some reaction from my earlier emotional idealism was inevitable, but now—for a time—my mood swung to an extreme of equally crude scepticism. This may have been in part a reflection of the widespread feeling of vague disgruntlement among the troops during that winter, to which I have already referred, but it was also due to a belated realisation that the actions and war-aims of the Allied Governments were not always in accord with the ideals for which I had believed we were fighting.

During my stay in hospital I had time and opportunity to think things out and to discuss them with my companions, and I thought I could now see that, whatever might be the attitude of the soldiers and common people, the Foreign Offices and politicians—the " Chancellories of Europe "—were still playing at " power-politics," and using us as pawns in the game. What brought my grievances to a head more than anything, I think, was the flat refusal of the French Government to listen to a proposal that after the war the people of Alsace-Lorraine should settle their own future by referendum. This seemed to me to be a direct denial of the Allies' joint pledge for the " self-determination of small peoples," because France wanted a strategic frontier on the Rhine. And I disagreed with the official attitude towards the Russian revolution. Quotations from a contemporary letter will serve to express my feeling of discontent and disillusionment at that time, in contrast to the high-flown sentiments of two or three months earlier :—

E

" The conclusion of peace by the various Russian nations has put an end for ever to our hopes of starving Germany out (!), if it was ever possible.   There is, of course, a lot of hot air flying about in that connection, and Russia is denounced as a traitor who has ' let us down,' etc., but I cannot see that it is justified.   In my opinion, the Russian people are actuated by principles far higher than the war-mongers are capable of realising—the principles of Christianity and humanity—and they can see that the continuance of the war only means playing the game of the diplomats and the politicians.   The Russian people have awakened, and it is we who as a nation are asleep to the facts.   Yes, I too have experienced that awakening, bitter though it may be, from the splendid dream of national integrity, of a fight for right under the leadership of a Government who really desires the triumph of justice without a thought of national ambition.   Now I see how I was mistaken, how I and all of us were hoodwinked.   We were undoubtedly right in going to war; under the circumstances and according to what we were told, we could do nothing else, and the People, then as now, were fighting for justice.   The Government has deliberately fostered that spirit, all the while knowing that *their* aims were political, not cosmopolitan.   Now that there is such a demand for " war-aims," we are beginning to get at the truth.

" For instance, Mr. Lloyd George is loud in his demands that the ex-German colonies shall settle their future fate by vote, but if that principle is the only just one, why should it not be applied to some of our own colonies, the Boer states, for example, and India ?   Again, France, firm champion of international concord as she professes to be, refuses to have anything to do with a ' League of Nations '—it would stand in the way of her national ambitions and render impossible her revenge against Germany for 1870.   Also, she professes and advocates the principle that a nation or people should be allowed to settle their own government by popular vote, yet she refuses to listen to the proposal for a referendum in Alsace-Lorraine.   If she is so sure that the inhabitants want French rule, she can have no fear for the result.

" No, we have been hoodwinked into giving ourselves over, bound hand and foot to the workings of that same secret-diplomacy machine which we were assured had perished for ever.   The majority of the people do not realise this yet, but when they do—there will be trouble !

" Everybody I have met is highly indignant with the Prime Minister for making the question of Alsace-Lorraine a vital part of our war-aims.   What has Alsace-Lorraine to do with us ?   What do we care for the private ambitions of France ? It only demonstrates how the high ideals for which we went to war have been debased. . . . If we were still fighting for the great purposes which inspired us at the outbreak of the war, I would by all means say, ' Fight on ! '—but we are not. It is national ambition, national advantage, that we are fighting for now, and, in the slang phrase, ' it's not good enough! ' "

That was the kind of schoolboyish nonsense I was writing and thinking at the beginning of 1918. (How some of it got past the censor I still do not understand!) In the light of subsequent history, my ignorance of the facts on which I based my criticisms was almost pathetic—especially with regard to Russia—though in some respects I still think I was right. But this period of grousing was a temporary phase. The events of the following month and the danger of final defeat, had the effect of reviving, to some extent, my enthusiasm for the national cause, though my " patriotism " was never afterwards so unqualified and my devotion was more critical, than they had been in the past. About this time, too, I was strongly attracted by the idea of a League of Nations, which seemed to me to be the only possible way of guaranteeing the world against the recurrence of war; but it was not merely an alliance of sovereign states, for the prevention of war only, that I looked for, but a real super-national Government of Mankind, a Federation of the World. That, reasonable or not, was, I believe, the earnest hope and faith of great numbers of people in 1918 and 1919, but events proved once again that the instincts of the people were ahead of the prejudices of their official representatives.

. . . . . .

By the end of the month the sore places on my limbs were completely healed, and I was feeling great benefit from the long rest. I still do not know the official name of the ailment from which I had been suffering, except that it was some sort of blood disorder due to general fatigue and trench conditions, but on March 1st I was passed by the M.O. as fully recovered, and left Le Tréport at dawn two days later, in company with one other man. We spent the night in a rest-camp at Dieppe, and reached the Base at Harfleur at about eleven the next morning.

I found that during February a general reorganisation of the Army had taken place, the exact object of which, being no tactician, I did not understand; but the effect was that the number of battalions forming a brigade, and the number of brigades forming a division, were reduced, thus—on paper—increasing the number of divisions at the Front. In some esoteric fashion this was supposed to have increased the strength of the Army ! I presume the " big-wigs " of the High Command understood this; I confess I didn't.

One of the by-products of this rearrangement was that the Household Battalion, by the time I returned to duty, had been disbanded. It was reported that the Army Council considered that it was too expensive to maintain the Reserve battalion at

Windsor to serve a single unit at the Front, and—if rumour can be relied on—there had been a good deal of jealous intrigue in high places in the Guards directed against our Battalion. There had been a certain amount of talk about our impending dissolution for some time before I went to hospital, but nothing definite, and it was not until I arrived at the Base that I learned that the disbandment had actually taken place.

So the old H.B. was no more ! Probably no single battalion in the Army had a better record for so short a period of existence (my eight-months of service covered nearly half of its total life) and I think that all ranks profoundly regretted its passing. It had never " hit the headlines " in the newspapers and most people had never heard its name; even in the Army other units with whom we came in contact outside our own Brigade had to have our badge and initials explained. (Disrespectful " grabby mobs " called us variously " the Ham Bones," " Holy B——s," or even " Horatio Bottomley's Own ! ") I have never come across a reference to the H.B. in any book of war-reminiscence, and the Encyclopædia Britannica does not mention its name ; for all the documentary evidence I have seen, it might be a figment of my imagination ! But its old Colours still hang in the Garrison Church at Windsor. Nevertheless, the Household Battalion was not inferior to the older regiments of Foot Guards, either in smartness on parade or in bravery in the field, though some of the latter were inclined to regard it somewhat as a " poor relation." It had rendered valiant service on the Somme, and had won high recognition on the bloody field of Passchendaele, than which no troops could have had a more stringent test. However much we might grouse among ourselves, it was a Unit to be proud of, and we all felt—a prejudiced view, maybe—that the Authorities had shown great lack of imagination in disbanding us.

I found, however, that there was still the remnant of an H.B. depot at Harfleur—now under the aegis of the Guards Division— where stray casualties like myself were being collected before being transferred to other units, and I was still nominally a member of the Household Battalion until I returned to the war area. This was not long delayed, for after receiving a new outfit a party of us left for the Guards Division Reinforcement Camp four days later. After a very cold night journey and a short halt at Rouen in the early morning, we reached Agnez-les-Duisans and the Reinforcement Camp, in the Arras district, where the Division had been stationed since December. Immediately we arrived, before even we had taken our kit off, we were lined up and called upon to decide then and there which regiment of the Foot Guards we preferred to join. We were only allowed a choice within the Guards Division, so I elected to become a Coldstreamer, and was despatched with others who had chosen the same regiment to the Coldstream section of the camp. Here I remained for several days, while the formalities of transfer were completed, and on March 18th I paraded before the C.O. to have my pay-book altered, and was thus formally " invested " with the rank and title of a " Private in the Guards," with the regimental number " 22766." That evening, for the second time, I broke my self-imposed " pledge," when three of us ex-H.B.'s had a drink together in a neighbouring estaminet, to celebrate our transfer to the Coldstream Guards.

The personnel of the late Battalion was by now widely scattered. The rank-and-file and the N.C.O.'s were, as far as I know, without exception, distributed between the various battalions of the Coldstream, Grenadier, Scots, Irish and Welsh Guards, and most of the officers also ; though I believe some of the latter transferred to other regiments, and one or two secured "cushy" Administrative appointments. I never heard what became of Colonel Portal, our late Commanding Officer. Captain Cazlitt was employed in some important capacity on the Staff of the newly-formed " Allied High Command " at Versailles. My late platoon officer, Lieut. Whitehouse, joined the Welsh Guards and was reported "missing" after the German offensive. Six months later, when I was drafted into the 1st Coldstream, I found that my new platoon-Sergeant was none other than Cpl.-of-Horse Reed, who had been in charge of No. 2 Platoon, H.B.

But one of the most outstanding examples of "Time's revenges" was Corporal-Major Maker, whom I had known in the H.B. at Windsor (if, indeed, a recruit could be said to "know" a Corporal-Major!) In "civvy life" after the war, he became a Commercial Traveller, and for several years he used to call on me regularly and solicit *my* "orders" !

Many other members of the old Battalion I came across from time to time, some of them in the most unexpected places, but of my late comrades in No. 2 Platoon none accompanied me to my new Company in the 3rd Coldstream. It almost seemed as if it was a deliberate policy to break up old associations as thoroughly as possible, for even the small party of ex-H.B. casualties who came with me from the Base and who chose the Coldstream were split up among the four battalions of the Regiment, and the only other man who at that time was drafted with me to the 3rd Battalion was put into another Company.

So ended a chapter in my Army life, and in a sense I started military life afresh, in the oldest, instead of the youngest, regiment of Guards. The change was a signal for a whirl of new experiences and adventures to crowd swiftly upon me, making the previous months seem almost uneventful by comparison.

THE "MARCH DO"

THE COLDSTREAM GUARDS, as everyone knows, is one of the most renowned regiments in the world. It is believed—by itself, at any rate—to be the oldest in the British Army, though other corps have disputed the distinction; of the five great regiments which compose the "Brigade of Guards," it is certainly the earliest-formed, though not officially the "senior." "General Monk's Regiment of Foot Guards" was constituted in 1650, as part of Cromwell's "New Model" Army, and at the time of the Lord Protector's death ten years later it was lying at Coldstream, a border village in Berwickshire. General Monk's declaration in favour of the Restoration, and the Regiment's subsequent march on London, led to its recognition by Charles II as the "Second Regiment of Foot Guards," and it later took the name of "the Coldstream Guards." The Regiment has made history in every great European war from that time to the present day, as well as in many other parts of the world, and its Colours are emblazoned with the most famous battle-honours in military annals. During the Great War, it was one of the first regiments to come into action at Mons, and was in the line when the last shots were fired before the Armistice.

Until recently, all the Guards battalions serving with the B.E.F. in France had been integrated in one division—the Guards Division—but now, owing to the general reorganisation of which I have spoken, three battalions, the 3rd Coldstream, 2nd Irish and 4th Grenadier, had been detached and sent to the 31st Division, where they were known as the 4th Guards Brigade. The 31st Division was, for the moment, out of the line and resting in and around the village of Tincques, about mid-way between Arras and St. Pol, where I joined the 3rd Coldstream on the afternoon of March 19th. The Battalion was billeted in a farm just outside the village; H.Q. were established in the farmhouse, which was also still occupied by the farmer and his family, and the Company to which I was detailed was lodged in a large barn on the opposite side of the farmyard.

Joining a new regiment was rather like going to a new school, with new faces and surroundings, new customs to learn and new traditions to assimilate. All were complete strangers to me, and as far as I knew there were no other ex-H.B.'s in the Company. Naturally, I felt a little strange at first, but everyday routine in the Army was much the same in most units, and it did not take me long to shake down in my new environment. I experienced a much better reception than I had half-anticipated, in view of the rivalry which had existed between the Household Battalion and the Coldstream Guards at Windsor. I had previously had some qualms about my wisdom in choosing the latter regiment, for that reason, but, in fact, my entry into the new Battalion was such that I was immediately able to dismiss my apprehensions, and indeed I never had serious cause to regret my choice. On the contrary, later on (as I shall tell) I became very proud to call myself a Coldstreamer, however little I merited the honour, and would not willingly have transferred to any other regiment in the British Army!

The barn in which we were billeted was a large and fairly roomy one, and the floor was covered with a thick layer of straw (not more than usually verminous) which made it comfortable for sleeping; but the building was badly in need of repair, draughts whistled through innumerable crevices and the roof was far from watertight. In the centre of the farmyard, opposite the door of the barn, there was the usual immense dung-heap, over which fowls fluttered and clucked, and from which a pungent odour arose. Fortunately, it was too early in the year for flies, but there were plenty of rats. By Active Service standards, it was a snug enough billet, though I suspect that my phrase, "we are staying at a farm," evoked a rather different picture in my Mother's imagination!

When I arrived, I found that a football match was in progress between the Battalion and the Brigade Ammunition Column, so after securing my "bed" and disposing of my kit I went down to the field and added my voice in support of my new side. Some people would say that it was an ·"omen" that our team was defeated—though what the omen signified I am unable to say.

Next day, also, we had bad luck. There was to have been a musketry competition for the Batt., in which prizes were offered for the best scores in each Company. We marched out to the range in the morning, but the persistent drizzle made visibility so bad that the match had to be abandoned without a shot being fired, and we returned to the farm somewhat damped in spirits as well as in person. In the evening, a number of us went to the cinema in the village, an improvised affair in a small hall, but after a long and rather noisy wait it was announced that the apparatus had irreparably broken down, so our entrance-money was refunded as we filed out with many colourful sarcasms.

I remember very little about Tincques—which is, perhaps, not surprising, since I was only there for two days. It was, apparently, a quite uninteresting village of shabby-looking cottages, most of which showed notices announcing "Café" or "Eggs and chips" at exorbitant prices, and several estaminets. It was, of course, at that time crowded with British troops, who furnished a fine harvest for the inhabitants. My impression of the French peasantry, at that time, was that they were hard-working, stolid and quite remarkably imperturbable under the stresses of war (the worst disasters would be met with the phrase, " C'est la guerre ") ; but also that they were, most of them, entirely unscrupulous in their dealings with the troops. They were (perhaps not unnaturally) out to make money all the time, and the general level of the prices they charged for whatever they had to sell was governed by the capacity of their "customers" to pay. One always knew, for example, if Canadian or American troops were in the neighbourhood, because then everything was fifty- or a hundred-per-cent. dearer than elsewhere. No doubt they suffered considerably from the depredations of our men, but their demands for compensation were often so exorbitant that one might think the British were an invading army rather than allies.

Yet, after all, there may have been much to excuse their attitude. To them, no doubt, we were as alien as would be the Germans ; we occupied their towns and homes, we spoiled their crops, filched their fowls and often, I fear, "ruined" their daughters (not always without encouragement!) The British soldier in France was not, at all times, a "knight in shining armour." And there was constantly the danger that the tide of war might roll over their homes and set them in hopeless flight. They had not wanted this war, and were the chief sufferers from it. So perhaps it is not altogether surprising that they felt themselves entitled to take what they could, from whom they could, though to us—their "protectors"—it seemed like black ingratitude, and one often heard them cursed for "a lousy lot of thieves."

The following day was the fateful Twenty-first of March, the day on which the long-expected German offensive began. The dawn broke clear and brilliant after a slight ground-mist had cleared, and it was not long after Reveille that we became aware of a heavy and continuous barrage-fire thudding away in the distance from the direction of the line. We did not take much notice of it, however, for raids at any time of the day or night were of fairly frequent occurrence, though the firing was unusually prolonged and intense on this occasion. Officially, no mention of anything unusual was made, and the day's programme was carried out as previously arranged. This consisted of "field operations" in which the whole Brigade took part. We marched out some three or four kilometres towards Arras, and then conducted a sham "attack" in the homeward direction. The distant bombardment continued throughout the morning, and at intervals of about ten minutes or so a long-range shell screamed far above our heads on its way to St. Pol, which was about 25 kilometres behind the front. This unusual phenomenon led to some speculation, and made us think that something out of the ordinary must be taking place in the line, but no-one seemed to imagine—or at any rate nobody gave voice to the thought—that the long-talked-of German attack had actually begun. It had been so often rumoured and vainly predicted on so many dates during the last three months—for instance, it had been confidently stated that it was to take place on the Kaiser's birthday, January 27th—that at last most of the troops came to regard it as a mere newspaper "scare."

In the meantime, the immediate and urgent problems of keeping to the rules of the sham fight occupied our minds to the exclusion of other matters. For two or three hours we crawled on the damp ground and at intervals rushed forward breathlessly with rattling equipment, to flop down behind the next bit of cover; it was tiring and rather warm work. Once, several British aeroplanes passed overhead and circled low above us, as if uncertain who we were or what we were doing. The pilots must have been considerably puzzled, in view of what they probably knew was happening in the line only a few miles away, to see a large body of troops advancing westwards in full order of battle. I imagine that their first thought must have been that we were Germans who had broken through past Arras with unbelievable rapidity!

When the operations had been concluded according to plan, and we had "fought" our way back to Tincques shortly after mid-day, we were dismissed for dinner, and spent the rest of the afternoon sleeping and cleaning our kit. I remember that I was specially industrious in polishing my brasses and buttons, which had become very much tarnished from the damp grass, as I was anxious to create a good impression in my new Battalion. The weather had turned suddenly warm and golden, and the sun set that evening in a blaze of glory; it was the first day, in fact as well as according to the calendar, of the longed-for Spring. I wrote a letter home after tea, full of hopes that the miseries of winter were now over; it was not finished when the mail was collected, so I stuffed it into my haversack and, in the event, it was never posted.

We turned in as usual about ten o'clock, without the slightest premonition—at least, as far as I was concerned—of the dramatic events in which we were soon to be involved. The distant gun-fire had almost ceased and the night was quiet and star-lit. It seems almost incredible that the morning's bombardment should have excited so little attention in the ranks—"Wolf!" had been cried too often. Anyhow, that night the orders for the following day's programme of training were posted as usual, and we rolled into our blankets without any apprehensions.

.   .   .   .   .

It seemed as if I had only been a very short while asleep, when a sudden bugle-call shattered my dreams. It was—no, it couldn't be!—yes, it was Reveille! I rolled over, and sat up in complete darkness, and saw from the luminous dial of my watch that it was only half-past three. Muttered groans and curses came from the recumbent forms around me, but we soon realised that something momentous was afoot and began to dress hurriedly. We had hardly pulled on our socks, when the door of the barn was pushed open, admitting a rush of cold air, and a voice shouted " On parade, and ready to march off at 5.30 ! "

Thereupon arose a wild scrimmage, and in the light of glimmering candle-ends there was for a time an apparently hopeless confusion of men dressing, collecting their kit, assembling their equipment and rolling up blankets in " bundles of ten " for handling in to the Stores, amid a deafening babel of voices. We were all ready by the time stated, but were then told that parade was postponed until eight-thirty. Breakfast followed, and many were disposed to think that it was only a trial turn-out ; but at eight o'clock we were ordered to fall-in, and marched to the Arras-St. Pol road, which passed within a mile of the village. It was obvious, now, that we were going into action, but none of us had the slightest idea of our destination, and such officers or N.C.O.'s who possessed reliable information kept it to themselves. The Arras front was nearest, and it was only reasonable to suppose that this was where we were going, especially as we could hear the artillery working vigorously again in that direction. We were entirely without news and ignorant of any details of the battle, so of course did not know that the danger-point was far to the south of Arras.

By about eight-fifteen the whole Brigade was deployed alongside the St. Pol road and after a brief wait a procession of motor-buses and lorries appeared from the west ; there were about two hundred of them, and they made an imposing array as they swept past us with a roar of engines and a cloud of dust. To our surprise, they did not stop to pick us up, but passed out of sight eastwards. It was only a short while later, however, that the same or a similar convoy appeared, coming from the direction of Arras, and pulled up as it arrived abreast of the Brigade line extended along the side of the road. The order to embark was immediately given, and we clambered aboard the nearest cars. They were mostly covered A.S.C. lorries with the side curtains rolled up, but the one I was in was an ex-charabanc fitted with transverse wooden seats and a low canopy overhead. We were packed in so tightly that it was scarcely possible to move hand or foot, and although we carried rations in our packs it was found to be impossible to get at them throughout the day. Long before the end of the journey we were envying the occupants of the lorries, who were sitting on the floor and although no less crowded, could at least stand up from time to time and ease their cramped limbs.

It was a fine example of organisation. The loading-up of the whole strength of the Brigade was the work of a few minutes, and at once the long cavalcade was on the move. To our intense surprise and bewilderment, we found ourselves travelling away from the line—not towards Arras, as we had expected, but westwards to St. Pol. As we rolled through the town the inhabitants crowded to their doors and windows, and seemed immensely puzzled and disconcerted at the sight of so large a body of troops tearing at full tilt *away* from the battle. They must have thought that some terrible disaster had taken place, and that the British Army was in headlong flight ! It was hardly remarkable that there were few attempts at cheers or greetings—some, indeed, shook their fists as we passed, and shouted curses.

On the further side of the town we turned south. I was sitting near the side of the car, and by watching the shadows of the telegraph poles was able to judge our general direction fairly well. After a run of about fifteen miles, not very fast because of the size of the convoy, we passed through another town, which I made out to be Frevent, but we did not stop. Later, during the afternoon, we touched Doullens and, crossing a bridge over a river, turned sharply north-eastward. A long and uninterrupted run brought us to Beaumetz, and here the convoy left the main road and took to what appeared to be a series of country lanes in a general easterly direction. We passed several villages and hamlets, one of which was almost certainly Blaireville and another possibly Handecourt— though I should point out that I was not at all sure of the geography after Beaumetz, and it was some weeks later before I had a chance to trace our probable route on a map. It was after sunset when we at last came to a halt, at the cross-roads north-west of Boisleux-St. Marc (?), and were able to alight and stretch our aching limbs. No sooner was everyone in the road than the lorries rolled away empty, and we were ordered to form up on some high sloping ground a short distance away ; permission was then given us to take off our equipment and make ourselves as comfortable as possible until midnight.

Our first thought was for the "inner man," for we had had nothing to eat since breakfast ; the rations with which we had been issued before starting were in our packs but, as I said before, we had been so tightly packed in the lorries that they had been useless. We were very glad of them now, however, though our greatest need at the moment was for something to drink. Our water-bottles had long since been emptied, and our throats were parched with the heat and the dust of the journey. Never was I more thankful than when, shortly after our arrival, a number of water-carts came up and I was able to have a long drink, as well as re-fill my bottle. Only then could I swallow the bully and biscuit of which I was in great need.

Our platoon officer presently appeared on the scene, and suggested that we might like to hear what he could tell us of the news. Of course, we all crowded eagerly round, for this was the first opportunity we had had of hearing anything at all about the battle in which we were soon to take part. His account, however— though I have no reason to believe that we were being deliberately misled—was a travesty of the truth. He said that the long-expected German attack had opened the previous morning with great vigour on a seventy-mile front, but that so far the enemy had been held everywhere without gaining a yard, except on the sector opposite to which we were now standing; here they had broken through to the depth of a mile on a two-mile front. This gap, he said, we were now called upon to fill, and a counter-attack which the Scots Guards, supported by the Coldstream, were to launch in the morning was expected to restore the line to its former position.

All this was very encouraging, and perhaps it was as well that we did not know how very far it was from the actual facts. The true story is now, of course, well-known. The German attack, far from being held, had entirely shattered our defences over a very wide area, and the whole Fifth Army, out-numbered and unsupported, was even then in rapid retreat to the south of us. It was the worst crisis since Mons. The point to which we had been rushed was of vital importance, since it covered Arras, and with Arras the whole front up to Belgium. In the south there was, if need be, room for manœuvre, but northwards the British line dared not risk a substantial retirement, for we stood almost literally with our backs to the sea. Should the enemy succeed in breaking through here, nothing could save the Channel ports and the Allied forces would be cut into two isolated sections. The task of the Third Army, of which we were a part, was therefore not only to meet and throw back direct attacks, but at the same time to swing our line on Arras as a pivot, so as to preserve some sort of alignment with General Gough's retreating troops and prevent the Germans from getting round our southern flank.

About all this, however, we were in complete ignorance at the time, and our officer's story had the effect of making us think that things were not as serious as we had feared, though it was evident that we were in for a bad time. Obviously, if the German attack had failed at first they would not accept defeat without further efforts.

The officer went on to say that we were to move into the line at midnight, and that we had better try to get some sleep first, as he could see that we were all very tired after our trying journey. Hot tea and fresh rations were then served out, for which, especially the tea, we were very glad, and we made various necessary adjustments to our equipment. All superfluous articles were crammed into our packs, which were then loaded into the supply lorries to be taken back to Headquarters—wherever they might be.

.   .   .   .   .   .

By this time night had fallen and the scene from the rising ground on which we lay increased in awesomeness as the darkness deepened. We seemed to be on the fringe of the fighting area, and out of shell-fire range; it was impossible to guess how far away the enemy might be—probably then at least five or six miles—but since the ground appeared to slope more or less regularly towards the east a wide panorama of the battle lay open before us, and in the dark the effect was that it was very much nearer. It was a fine, clear night, and a moon five days from the full rode high in the cloudless sky. Westward, the last faint flush of sunset lingered on the horizon and a few stars pierced the glory of the moon's radiance ; the air, though cold now, held in its perfume the promise of summer warmth. It was a night such as comes but rarely in early spring.

But its beauty was entirely shattered and annihilated by the man-made hell which raged in front of us. Out of the darkness came the never-ceasing roar of hundreds of guns, thudding upon the ears like physical blows, while the curtain of night was slashed continually by their lightning-like flashes. The solid ground beneath our feet quivered with the thundering roll of explosions, and, like an undercurrent of pizzicato in the tremendous orchestration, distant machine-guns cracked and rattled. Some distance away several buildings were burning furiously, sending lurid clouds of smoke across the landscape, through which the ghostly light of star-shells played to and fro. The imagination of a Dante could scarcely conceive a scene more grand and terrible ; it was like looking into the mouth of Hell itself, and one would hardly have been surprised to read in letters of fire : " All hope abandon, ye who enter here ! "

However, I was very tired and did not spend much time in watching the spectacle, fascinating though it was, but spread my waterproof sheet on the ground and, wrapping my greatcoat round me, slept prosaically for a couple of hours, despite the uproar.

About midnight we fell in and marched off by platoons towards the line. The distance we had to cover was not great, but the march occupied us about two hours, owing to the congested state of the road. It was only a narrow country lane at best, and was thronged with vehicles and men, in darkness except for the moon, and the two streams of traffic going in opposite directions frequently became tangled. Great guns drawn by tractors on caterpillar wheels passed us at times, filling the whole width of the road and crowding us ignominiously into the ditch, while bodies of troops, Staff cars, ammunition limbers and supply lorries constantly clattered past. Once or twice we heard a Jerry aeroplane drone overhead, fired at with tracer bullets and shells, and some British machines returning from a raid could be distinguished by lights on their wings. We passed through a ruined village, which was probably Boisleux, looking weird and spectral in the moonlight, and then through Hamelincourt. Of the identity of the latter there could be no doubt, for the name was on a large board at the roadside near the first cottages. Our destination was about a mile farther on—as far as I can now judge on the map, a point about 500 yards north of a line drawn between Hamelincourt and St. Leger, and nearly facing " Judas Copse."

Here we came to a new trench, which had been marked out and already excavated to a depth of perhaps two feet ; we quickly sorted ourselves out along its length and commenced digging. This we continued to do until dawn, working hard, for although we were all tired we realised the necessity of making the trench deep enough to stand in. We did not know how far away the enemy might be or how soon we might have to repel an attack. (No further mention had been made of going over the top in the morning.) When daylight made it dangerous to risk attention by throwing earth over the parapet, we stopped work, having by that time constructed quite a neat and serviceable line, complete with fire-bays and traverses. We were still apparently some distance from the enemy, whose exact position no one seemed to know, for it changed almost from hour to hour. The Verey lights before dawn had seemed to indicate that we were near the apex of a salient, for they gleamed in a wide semi-circle reaching well round on either hand, though this, we knew, might be deceptive. No hostile shells troubled us during the day, which was cloudless and quite hot for the time of year, and there was nothing to do but stay quietly under cover in the trench. We tried to get some sleep, squatting on the floor of the trench, but it was impossible to do more than doze for a few minutes at a time, for only a few dozen yards away a battery of big guns kept up a heavy fire all day, the concussion from which would have aroused the Seven Sleepers.

· · · · · ·

Rations came up soon after dark, and not long afterwards we received orders to move to a new position lower down the slope which descended into a shallow valley between Judas Copse and Ervillers. We had just climbed out of the trench in readiness to start thither, when the "S.O.S." signal, a series of red and green rockets, went up in front, indicating an enemy attack, and the artillery of both sides opened up vigorously. Consequently, we were halted to await developments, and listened to the progress of the raid—there was little to see, but much to hear—from the comparative security of the trench. After a strong bombardment for about half-an-hour, the raiders were apparently driven back (or, perhaps, it was only a wind-up) and everything became quiet again—as quiet as the line ever was in those clamorous days—so we proceeded to carry out our orders. Descending the slope from our former position, we came to a stretch of comparatively level ground about a thousand yards nearer to Ervillers, bordering a road which ran north-eastwards, and proceeded to mark out a new trench astride this road. We found ourselves immediately in front of a collection of Nissen huts, evidently a Rest Camp of some sort, which had been abandoned in a hurry ; one or two men who slipped away on a scrounging expedition reported that the stock in the Y.M.C.A. canteen had been left behind. It seemed obvious, from this, that our officer's story of a one-mile advance by the enemy must be wide of the truth, for Rest Camps would hardly have been built less than four or five miles behind the front line, probably much further back, and the retreat must have been somewhat precipitate.

But we wasted little time in speculation, and the cigarettes and chocolate which lay open for the taking in the huts might have been—for all the good they were to us—a dozen miles away, for the new line must be finished before dawn, and it was already near midnight. The ground was chalky and hard to dig, especially as we were not allowed to take off our greatcoats or equipment for the purpose, but by the alternate use of picks and shovels we managed to construct quite passable protection for ourselves by the time daylight came.

The next day passed without major incident; the enemy were probably aware by now that fresh troops had been brought up to the area, and were re-grouping before making a new onslaught. For our part, we had strict instructions to keep under cover, and no movement outside the trench was allowed during the day, as, for all we knew, we might be under direct observation from German outposts on the far side of the valley. Our new line ran through meadows roughly between Judas Copse and Ervillers, the latter village being partly hidden among trees about a mile to our right. In front of the trench, the ground rose slightly, so that a clear-cut skyline terminated our view only about a hundred yards ahead, and about half-a-mile behind us was a road bordered by poplar trees which ran down into Ervillers. The lane across which our trench ran came from this road, passed the "Rest Camp" and disappeared over the rise in front of us. On our right front we had a clear view across gently-sloping fields down to the little river Sensée, which ran roughly north from in front of Ervillers, and beyond which the ground rose gradually into a long ridge between Mory and St. Leger. (I did not, of course, know any of these names at the time, but traced them out on the map afterwards; and also, some months later, during the final advance, I passed over the same ground again.) The ridge was treeless and open, rather like one of the Sussex Downs, and just beyond the summit the enemy or our own retiring troops had set fire to a large dump, which sent up clouds of smoke all day, with an intermittent pyrotechnic display of exploding rockets and Verey lights in many different colours.

The weather continued as it had been since the beginning of the offensive, fine and cloudless, with a slight mist in the early morning which quickly cleared as the sun rose. In the middle of the day it was quite hot. The Germans had had all the luck on their side so far, or else their meteorological forecasting was far in advance of ours, for conditions were ideal for a big-scale offensive. From our point of view, although our physical state would have been even more uncomfortable, we would have welcomed a steady, continuous downpour of rain, such as greeted *our* offensive at Passchendaele, to bog down the enemy tanks and give time to bring up our reserves ; but for the time being the "Clerk of the Weather" was apparently in German pay!

Although that day we saw nothing of the enemy and no shells fell anywhere near us, there was no possibility of rest, for we were " standing-to " continuously in expectation of the attack which did not come. By this time, we were all suffering from the prolonged lack of sleep, and tempers were getting frayed. No one—at least, no one among the rank-and-file—knew how far away the Germans were, but we knew that contact could not be long delayed. During the evening, soon after dark, we had just recommenced digging with a view to further improving the trench, when a fierce cannonading broke out, heralding a German attack in force on the positions ahead of us. The enemy was still apparently unaware of our line, for we were not shelled at all, though the main road behind us was heavily bombarded and many of the poplar trees were brought crashing to the ground. In front, beyond the crest of the rising ground, the fire for a time reached barrage intensity. It was then that, for the first time, I witnessed a direct demonstration of the prestige of the Guards and the evident respect in which they were held by the so-called " Infantry of the Line." The forward posts ahead of us were held by troops of the " Blankshires," and soon after the attack opened a crowd of them were apparently seized with panic, for they came pouring over the ridge towards us. One of our officers, revolver in hand, stepped out into the road in front of them and challenged them. The foremost men gave the name of their regiment, and then shouted that " Jerry was coming ! "

" Who are you ? " they demanded.

" Coldstream Guards," replied the officer.

" Blimey ! are the Guards here ! " was the exclamation, in tones of unmistakable surprise and reassurance. " We thought there was no one behind." And such was the confidence inspired by the presence of the Guards that, without hesitation, they turned back and the attack was beaten off.

．　　．　　．　　．　　．

A parenthetic word may not be out of place here, in praise of the soldier's main comfort and support in the field—Tobacco. We were inveterate and unrepentant Slaves of the Weed; it was our constant companion and solace, at once a luxury and a necessity. In quiet times, in the line or out of it, our intervals of leisure were made more enjoyable and periods of boredom less irksome by it; but it was in times of great mental and physical stress like this that we knew its full value. Tired bodies and strained minds were alike soothed by its influence, and it remains a mystery to me how the few non-smokers in our ranks managed to exist without it. Occasionally, when in the line, there was a free " issue " of cigarettes, mostly provided, I believe, by public or private charity through official channels; the packets bore names which were strange to me, both before that time and since, such as " Trumpeter," " Red Hussar," " Oros," " Ruby Queen," etc., and they varied considerably in quality. But for the most part, we had to rely on our own purchases in the canteen, and always, before going into the line, we would fill our pockets and haversacks with as many as we had room for, or our purses would " run to," sometimes even stuffing them (illegally) into gas-mask cases and ammunition pouches.

On this occasion, however, we had been rushed to the front without warning, so that most of us were very " short," though on the third day there was a small issue of " Ruby Queens."

Whenever the shelling became violent, the first thing one thought of doing was to light a fag, and all down the trench during a night " alert " one might see the little red pin-points glowing, carefully shielded in cupped hands. With nerves stretched to their utmost tension, without sleep, warmth or adequate food, and almost ready to drop from exhaustion, tobacco was an inexpressible comfort; I am sure that we would rather at any time go short in rations than in fags, however inferior the brand. A cigarette (or pipe) between our lips seemed in some way to give us a hold on ourselves, and helped us to carry on sometimes in conditions which otherwise might have been unendurable.

.   .   .   .   .

Although the attack was soon driven back on the sector immediately in front of us, on our right it made more progress. Advancing down the valley under heavy fire, the Germans broke through the forward posts, and reached to within a hundred yards of the British line. But they got no further, for the 2nd Irish Guards, who were on our right flank, left their trenches and rushed forward to meet the enemy at the point of the bayonet. The " Micks " drove the enemy back for some distance, but were unable to prevent him from keeping his footing in the valley and digging in. Much of this we could see from our post, in the bright light of a nearly-full moon.

After a time the artillery fire died down, and the remainder of the night was comparatively quiet. About midnight we received orders to leave our present position and move about a hundred and fifty yards to the left, on the other side of the road though still in part of the same line of trenches. The reason for this was not given, and we spent the rest of the night with pick and shovel, trying to improve our defences.

I was tired—dear God, how tired I was! We all were. During the past three days and nights none of us had slept at all, and all the time we had been feverishly digging or else tensely alert. My limbs felt like aching cotton-wool, my eyes smarted, and if I sat for a moment on the fire-step or leaned against the wall of the trench it was a real physical effort to keep awake. I felt I could barter my soul for a few hours of uninterrupted slumber. and I remember looking back with longing at the deserted huts of the Rest Camp behind us: now that the attacks have ceased, I thought with wild unreason, why don't they let us sleep in them by relays! But there was no rest for any of us, of course, for the lull could only be temporary and none knew when the enemy might come on again.

. . . . . .

Next morning, when the rations were distributed after the dawn stand-to, we were pleasantly surprised to find that there was a tot of rum for each man, to warm us after the cold night, but it was very weak and there was only about a tablespoonful each. Even this was invigorating, however, and when the sun rose we soon got warm. The tea which we made over small fires lighted on the floor of the trench also helped considerably, but the rum, inadequate though it was, was a god-send. There were certain comfortable, self-righteous Stigginses in England at that time who made a great fuss in the papers about the iniquity of supplying alcohol to the troops in the Line; one good lady from my own home-town, I remember, was virtuously indignant because (she declared) " our boys are being drugged " and wanted to have the rum issue stopped. I should like these people to have spent just *one* night in the trenches, under the same conditions as us, and see whether they would then have refused the meagre stimulant which we (sometimes) got ! In any case, the size of the "ration" which reached us (via the Q.M. stores and intermediate channels) was never large enough to corrupt the morals of a louse; nevertheless, I think that the incidence of sickness, both physical and mental, in the Line would have been much higher without it.

The day began as bright and clear as ever, but a little later clouds began to form, and towards evening rain fell. About ten in the morning the artillery commenced a heavy bombardment of the positions in the valley which the enemy had occupied during the night and where they had successfully dug themselves in. For about an hour the air above us was filled with the screaming of shells, and hundreds of explosions shot bursts of smoke and soil into the air from the apparently empty fields ahead. There was no hostile reply, and at last the firing died down—rather to our surprise, for we had supposed that it was the preliminary to a counter-attack.

It seemed remarkable to me, both then and on other occasions, that wild birds appeared to take very little notice of gun-fire; they seemed to be quite indifferent to the turmoil around, and the shrill screeching of the shells passing overhead left them unperturbed. A few yards in front of our trench a lark had her nest in the long grass, and during all of the fiercest part of the bombardment I saw her winging her way upward in full song and returning to the nest quite undisturbed.

Once, during the morning, a British aeroplane swooped

suddenly out of the clouds and—apparently taking us for Germans
—loosed a couple of bombs at the trench, one of which exploded
less than a dozen yards from the parapet behind which I was
standing. I happened to glance up at the moment, and saw the
bombs leave the machine, which was probably not more than fifty
feet from the ground, but curiously enough I did not at first connect
the explosions with the aeroplane, but thought they were shell-
bursts, especially as the plane bore R.F.C. markings. It was not
an uncommon sight, in those days before wireless communication,
to see British planes drop messages behind the lines to the artillery
and occasionally to front-line posts.

Soon after mid-day a certain amount of stir was apparent in
the enemy's lines on the ridge across the valley; figures could
plainly be seen moving about in the open, and Ervillers was
subjected to a heavy dose of shelling, to which our guns replied.
Something was obviously going to happen. Before long the
attack opened in earnest. We were in a curious position: overlooking the valley from our trench, we had an excellent view of
the attack along nearly the whole length of the ridge opposite
Ervillers, half-right from our position, yet we were apparently
unnoticed by the enemy, for no attempt was made to shell our
trench. Soon random machine-gun bullets were flying about
around us, but by keeping in the shelter of the traverses we were
fairly safe from them, but the distance was too great for us to
give any effective help to the defenders by rifle-fire. The attack
seemed to be developing in a direction diagonal to our line, and
immediately in front of us there was no sign of any movement.
Whether they were actually aware of the existence of our trench
is difficult to say. Our aeroplanes held so complete a command
of the air that no enemy plane had been seen since we arrived, but
I can hardly believe that we were not visible from the ridge behind
which they assembled. In any case, they seemed not to be
advancing in our direction, but rather trying to work round the
far side of the village—tactics which, if successful, might have the
effect of outflanking us and place us in danger of being surrounded.

We could see, as if from a favoured position at "Manœuvres,"
the Germans swarming over the top of the ridge and pouring down
the slope in what looked like countless thousands; they were not
in their favourite mass-formations, bunched together shoulder to
shoulder in solid waves of assault, but spread out in "open order,"
and at that distance, in their grey uniforms, they looked like a
multitudinous army of ants. Shells burst among the scattered
figures in scores, but seemed to make little impression on them;
they came on through the hail of death as though invulnerable,
until one noticed that many of the black dots on the hillside had
ceased to move. Their own guns were deluging Ervillers and its
neighbourhood with high-explosives, and their range gradually
lengthened as the attacking troops pressed forward on the far side

of the village. Before long they were nearly in our rear, though still about two miles away, and it was becoming obvious that our position would soon become untenable and that we should have to retire very shortly if we were to avoid being encircled. But in the meantime, as we had received no orders to the contrary, there was nothing we could do but "stay put" and watch the battle impotently. The resistance of our troops around Ervillers was stern and determined; Lewis-guns and rifles were blazing madly, quick-firing guns and mortars spat death at the on-coming Bosche, while low-flying aeroplanes swept down the valley a few feet from the ground, pouring machine-gun bullets into them. But nevertheless, we could see, from our vantage point, the advancing tide' creep more and more round our distant right flank.

It was now about five o'clock, and a counter-attack was launched from Ervillers, but I was unable to watch its progress, for at that moment our immunity ended and a heavy bombardment by big shells opened with devastating suddenness on our trench—from our own guns. Rumour of a much later date suggested as a reason for this tragic error that the airman who bombed us a few hours earlier had reported that the position was already in German hands; also it was stated that, in accordance with orders which never reached us, we were supposed to have retired westwards before dawn that morning. Whatever may have been the truth—and such mistakes were not uncommon in times of confusion like this—it seemed to us as if we were being subjected to the concentrated fire of the whole British artillery! Our officers tried repeatedly to get through to the batteries by field-telephone, but either the lines were cut or the gunners thought it was a ruse of the enemy, for the shelling continued with unabated fury.

Huge shells screamed down on all sides of us with appalling roar and devastation, tons of soil spouted upwards in every direction, and the huts of the Rest Camp were flung about like houses of cards. I saw eighty-foot-long wooden huts lifted bodily a score of feet into the air, disintegrating as they went, and nissen huts flying like paper before the wind. Hardly any of us expected to escape with our lives; we crouched on the floor of the trench, expecting every minute to be our last. I know I was convinced that this was the end, and although I was "scared stiff," I don't think I felt afraid to die—there was no time to be conscious of any kind of emotion—but I remember vaguely thinking that this meant rest at last, and wondering in a detached sort of way how they would receive the news at home. It is difficult to describe one's feeling "in extremis." I think my chief desire was to get it over as quickly as possible.

After a while—it is impossible to say how long: it seemed like hours, though it was probably no more than ten minutes; time had ceased to count—as the fire showed no signs of slackening, orders were passed along from mouth to mouth to move to the left.

Crouching as low as possible, crawling over smoking heaps of debris and dead bodies, and falling flat every now and then, we stumbled along the trench, but there was no escaping the barrage. At last, as no good purpose could be served by holding on, and it looked as though the Battalion would be practically wiped out by our own guns without doing a ha'porth of harm to the enemy—I was told afterwards that our Company had more than thirty men killed in that ten minutes—an officer jumped up on the parados and shouted to us to run for it.

We scrambled out and ignominiously ran for all we were worth, shells bursting everywhere among us. Burdened with great-coat and rifle, and weak with exhaustion, we could not make very good speed even with almost certain death at our heels, and I was soon so winded that I could hardly struggle along. My feet seemed to weigh tons, and for a few minutes the feeling was exactly like one gets in a nightmare—a desperate struggle to run, without being able to move at more than a snail's pace. Pure funk, of course. Then an indescribable feeling of disgust for the whole show swept over me, and I slowed to a deliberate walk, not caring whether I got through or not. A few more paces, an enormous explosion close at hand, and — nothing . . . .

. . . .

My memories of what followed are not very clear. Trying to look back, most of it is mixed up in a haze of dizziness and fatigue, a jumble of vague impressions, among which it is sometimes difficult to decide which are facts and which are merely the hallucinations of exhaustion. I do not think I was unconscious for long, probably not more than a few minutes, and the first thing of which I was aware was brandy being forced between my lips and a feeling of annoyance as the sharp edge of the flask grated on my teeth. I seem to remember someone saying something about " . . . . one of the new men," but I felt too sick to take much notice ; as my mind cleared a little, I found I was lying in a shell-hole into which I had apparently fallen or been dragged, and the stretcher-bearer whose flask I had been biting said, "You'll be all right, chum ; wait here a bit and then get off up the road to the First Aid Post toute suite." Then he hurried away, and I was alone.

I suppose the shelling had ceased in the immediate neighbour-hood, and there was no sign of the Battalion, but I was too dazed to take much notice of my surroundings. I sat in the shell-hole for a time, until the ground stopped swaying around me, and then, not knowing where I was going and hardly what I was doing, but with a fixed conviction that I had to find the Aid Post, I got to my feet and stumbled towards the road. I was probably suffering from slight shell-shock or the effects of blast, for at first everything was confused and I did not seem to be clear about what had happened ; I only knew, as one knows in dreams, that I had to go along this road. I can only have gone a short distance, however, when a fresh wave of dizziness overcame me and I slid into a ditch or trench alongside. I had a vague impression that the ditch was lined by troops, but if they were really there or if I only imagined them, they took no notice of me, and when I felt better I scrambled out and went on again, walking unsteadily in the middle of the road, although it was again being shelled fairly heavily—for I had reached the point where shells were almost a matter of indifference and I hardly cared what happened.

I must have missed death by inches many times, and had got a good distance farther when faintness forced me to stop again, fortunately close to a small shelter in the bank, in which there was a Red Cross man. He gave me another dose of brandy, which revived me considerably, and then noticed blood on my left hand. On investigation, he found that I had a wound in the forearm, probably caused by a small shell-splinter as I came up the road, or perhaps earlier; I have no memory of being hit. It was apparently quite slight, little more than a deep cut, and it was not giving me any pain, for the flesh around it seemed to be numbed. He bound it up, and seemed reluctant to allow me to go on alone; but he could not leave his post and there was no one to send with me, so after I had rested for a few minutes he gave me general directions for finding the Dressing Station and told me te enquire again from the driver of an ambulance at the top of the rise. I was now feeling much stronger and the shelling had stopped, so I thanked him and set off. If ever there was a "Good Samaritan," that anonymous Red Cross man was one! He even pressed a piece of bread from his rations upon me. Of course, I never saw him again.

Following his directions, I found the ambulance about half-a-mile farther on, at a cross-roads, and the driver told me to take a turning to the left for Hamelincourt. Following the small Red Cross flags stuck in the bank as a guide, I came at last to the village half-an-hour later, passing several dead bodies by the roadside who, because they lay tidily under the bank, I concluded were men who had died of their wounds on the way to hospital; for at a time like this, men who did not survive to reach the aid-post had to be unfeelingly "dumped," so as to release the stretchers for other cases. My way led past the churchyard, which was in a gruesome condition; tombstones were thrown about in all directions, graves churned up and violently-exhumed coffins and their contents scattered. It was not a spot in which to linger. At last I saw a building flying the Red Cross flag, which I took to be the Dressing Station, but as I approached it I found it to be in ruins and deserted, and in the middle of the gateway there was a man lying dead, face downwards on the ground, with the Cross of Geneva on his arm!

It was getting dusk, and the place was not—to say the least—

a pleasant spot in which to pass the night alone. I was just turning away, feeling rather hopeless and uncertain in which direction to go, when I heard voices and saw an officer and an N.C.O. coming round the corner of the building—apparently the only living beings in that God-forsaken village. I immediately went up to them and said I was looking for the Dressing Station ; could they direct me? The officer replied that the Station had been moved that day, owing to the shelling, but he did not know where it had gone. He advised me to go back for about half-a-mile, and then turn to the right, when I would come to a trench and probably find someone to direct me.

Looking back, I am inclined to wonder if he may have taken me for a straggler or even a deserter, for the road led back towards the line and in the opposite direction from that in which we eventually located the Aid Post. If so, I can hardly blame him, for he may not have noticed my bandaged arm in the dusk, and my dirty, unshaven and haggard appearance would scarcely inspire confidence. But I may be doing him an injustice ; he may have been as ignorant of my proper route as I was, and he did not question me in any way.

However, such an idea did not occur to me at the time, so I saluted and turned back, past the cemetery and the corpses, until I reached the turning indicated. There I soon found the trench, which was manned, but here again I was doomed to disappointment, for no one had any idea of the location of the Dressing Station. But just at that moment several other "walking-wounded" men came along, on the same quest as myself, and after a short confab. among ourselves, we decided to return to Hamelincourt and push on beyond the village. At any rate, it was, as far as we could make out, in the general direction of the rear. I was immensely relieved to fall in with company, for I was entirely ignorant of the lie of the land, and might easily have wandered towards the enemy's lines in the darkness. As I learned afterwards, it was lucky that we did decide to get beyond Hamelincourt without delay, for the village was in German hands two or three hours later.

None of us knew much about the geography of the surrounding country, and the only guidance we had was the light of the star-shells which, as we knew they must indicate the approximate position of the battle-front, we were careful to keep behind us. It was not long before we reached the village again, and had made our way to the other side. Darkness had now fallen, and it was raining, but the diffused light of the moon behind the clouds enabled us to see the road. The Germans were again shelling the place, though fortunately not heavily, for we could make but slow progress, and one or two of our party were wounded in the legs and had to be helped along. Several times we had to dive hurriedly into the ditch to avoid shell-bursts, from which we had some narrow escapes.

I remember very little distinctly about the journey after we left Hamelincourt, except that it seemed interminably long. Actually, I believe, we were about four hours on the road—a painful ordeal for those of us who could only limp and, indeed, trying enough for all of us. My own wound was beginning to throb a bit, as the numbness wore off, but it was no more of a handicap, in itself, than a bad toothache might have been. I have a vague recollection at one time of crossing a railway by way of a level-crossing—probably near Moyenville—after which, for some reason which I have forgotten, we left the road and struck across open country. No more shells bothered us. As far as my memory serves, we kept on the move all the time, but it seems hardly possible that we did not halt occasionally for a rest, weak and exhausted as we all were—the whole journey was like walking in one's sleep, and I remember nothing clearly. We passed a battery of guns standing in the open, and not long afterwards found ourselves on a road which was crowded with traffic. Here we soon obtained information as to the whereabouts of the Dressing Station, and about an hour later reached our goal in the village of Ayette.

The ambulance station was crowded with wounded men who were pouring in in a continual stream, and they were packing up for a further retirement, so that had we been delayed an hour longer we should probably have missed them again. I was profoundly grateful for the bowl of hot tea which was given me on arrival and which tasted better than anything I ever drank, and shortly afterwards my arm was again dressed. The orderly who attended to me said that he had been going hard all day, and had only had time to eat a piece of bread since morning. I had the good fortune, thanks to a kindly Sergeant, of obtaining a place on the floor in one of the first ambulances to leave after my arrival, and was soon away to the C.C.S.

Owing to the congested state of the roads—a further retirement was made during the night and Ayette was abandoned before morning—progress was slow and we were frequently held up by traffic-jams. Before we had gone far a German aeroplane appeared overhead and dropped a couple of bombs at the slow-moving stream of traffic, which must have been plainly visible in the bright moonlight, for the sky was now clear again. Both, fortunately, missed their mark, though one of them fell close enough to our car to rock it with the blast of the explosion. Not long after this we reached a part of the road which was less crowded, and got along more quickly. I fell into an uneasy doze, crouching on the floor of the car and holding on by the leg of one of the stretcher racks, and was roused after an indefinite time by our arrival at the C.C.S., a group of marquees and huts near Beaumetz, alongside the Arras-Doullens main road. Its official title was "Casualty Clearing Station No. 43."

On alighting, we were given more tea and some bread-and-butter, after which we (that is, the walking cases) lined up in a queue for particulars to be noted as to name, regiment, wounds, length of service and—inevitably, but, as far as I could see, quite irrelevantly—religion, all of which were entered on a card which was then attached to our person with string, as though we were so much labelled luggage. We were not treated as "luggage" in any other respect, though, for everyone was most considerate and cheerful—really wonderfully so, indeed, considering how frightfully busy they all were, with hundreds of wounded continually pouring in. I take off my hat in sincere appreciation to the R.A.M.C., the Red Cross, Battalion stretcher-bearers, and all who help the casualties in war ; theirs was a devotion to duty beyond all praise and much too seldom recognised.

The floor of each marquee, dimly lighted by oil lamps, was covered with stretchers laid on the ground in rows, and the minor cases, like myself, filed past the Reception Officer's table in a never-ending stream. Most of the bad cases on the stretchers endured their sufferings with stoical calm, but many were groaning quietly and now and again one would cry out. The atmosphere was heavy with the smell of blood and disinfectant.

My wound was examined by a doctor and bound up afresh, after which I received an anti-tetanus injection. Then, the time by now being about four a.m., as many of us as could get near lay down on the floor around the stove in one of the huts and went to sleep.

.   .   .   .   .

About six-thirty we were roused with the news that a hospital train was expected at any moment. I felt greatly refreshed by the rest, short though it had been—it was, in fact, the first time I had slept for four days—and my first task was to despatch a "field-card" which I happened to have in my pocket from a post box in the camp, to let them know at home that I was wounded and on my way to Base, for I knew they would be anxious for news. As a matter of fact, about three weeks after getting my card they received an official notice stating that I was "missing."

All that day, and intermittently for several days afterwards, whenever my attention wandered or my mind relaxed for a moment, I could hear the scream of shells coming towards me. This was a plain case of hallucination, for we were miles beyond artillery range ; I don't know what the medical or psychological name for it would be, but it was more than a mere memory—I could actually *hear* the shrill whistle, and several times had to take a firm grip on myself to stop me from ducking instinctively. But after a few days the illusion faded.

A railway line ran along the rear of the C.C.S., and we waited all the morning for the expected train, but it failed to put in an appearance. We could see, towards noon, shrapnel bursting over the ridges on the eastern horizon several miles away, and gathered from this that the Germans had advanced again during the night; it was reported that the railway line had been closed to traffic owing to the possible danger of long-range shelling. The C.C.S. was already preparing for removal, and in the afternoon we were evacuated in ambulance cars to Doullens. The only incident during the journey was when the ambulance I was in skidded and nearly overturned in the ditch. We passed streams of refugees going in the same direction, women, old men, children, some pushing perambulators or handcarts loaded with all they could save from their abandoned homes, some with only a bundle done up in a sheet or old table cloth, and some carrying babies. As they trudged doggedly along with an air of weary hopelessness, they were an eloquent comment on the "honour and glory" of War!

On arrival at Doullens, we were taken to a large building on the summit of a steep hill, evidently once a school or convent and now a temporary hospital. The pressure of wounded was so great that there was not room for nearly all of them inside the building, and hundreds of stretchers were laid in rows in the spacious court-yard. Fortunately, the weather was dry; what would have happened to all those helpless cases in a downpour I cannot imagine.

I did not know it until very much later, of course, but on that very day a conference was taking place in Doullens between the Commanders-in-chief of the Allied Armies, which resulted, with swift unanimity, in the appointment of Marshal Foch as Supreme Generalissimo on the Western Front.

Our stay at the "Convent" was short—just time enough to have some tea and for a fresh batch of papers to be filled up—and we were then re-embarked in the ambulances and taken to the railway station. By this time darkness had fallen and there was a brilliant moon. The train was not yet due, so we pulled up in the station yard and remained in the cars. We had not been there long when an aircraft of the enemy raided the town and dropped six or seven bombs in quick succession, to the accompaniment of wild shrieks and a stampede for cover on the part of the crowd of civilians gathered round the cars. The bombs, though aimed at the station, fortunately missed their mark and exploded in a field on the further side of the line. The aeroplane then made off at great speed before the anti-aircraft gunners could get the range, and shortly afterwards our car was drawn under a bridge for greater protection in case it should return, but nothing further happened. After a wait of about an hour and a half, the train came into the station ; loading-up took in all about two hours, and it was well past midnight before we were at last on the move.

The journey was slow, of course, but the coaches were well warmed and I dozed for a good part of the way. The route to the coast took us through St. Pol, where the long-range bombardment was still continuing intermittently, and Boulogne was reached about noon. There, it was not long before I came safely to anchor at last, in a hospital camp near Wimille, on the high ground to the north of the town. That night, in a real bed, I very thankfully enjoyed my first decent sleep since leaving Tincques.

BEHIND THE LINE

I COUNTED myself extremely lucky to have come out of the battle not only with my life, but without serious injury, though I could hardly feel proud of the part I had played in the tremendous struggle. In hard fact, my contribution towards meeting the German attack seemed to have amounted to precisely nothing! I had spent some days and nights helping to dig trenches, out of which we had been blown, not by the enemy but by our own guns ; and now I was down the line again—without, so far as I could see, having hindered Jerry's advance in the slightest degree. Even the hurt I had sustained—though this, of course, was not a matter for personal regret—was trifling compared with most war-injuries, and I often felt a bit of a fraud to be walking about with my arm in a sling, like a real "wounded hero," while so many of my comrades were still in the thick of it.

But I am afraid thoughts of my company or late companions did not trouble me much—at first. I had been with them only two days before we were rushed into the line, and after that the time was too full of tension for the formation of personal ties and relationships. I have but the vaguest recollections of the men in even my own section, and I cannot remember (if I ever knew them) the name of a single officer or man in the Company at that time. They were all complete strangers to me, and by the time I rejoined the Company its personnel had been almost completely changed.

The last few days, brief though they had been in actual duration, had tried my powers of endurance severely. I do not claim, of course, for a moment, that I had had a worse time than many a thousand other men—quite the contrary, in fact—but the prolonged nervous strain and lack of sleep, the bombardment and "shell-shock" (or whatever it was) had combined to take a sharp, though temporary, toll of my physical resistance, and my nerves were in a state often described as "jangled." This short taste of real "active warfare" had made my previous experiences seem almost negligible by comparison.

But any qualms of "conscience" which I may have felt about my failure (as I saw it) to withstand the test of battle, were at first outweighed by my thankful appreciation of the present respite. The wound in my arm gave me little discomfort ; the M.O. put three stitches in it, and it did not heal up for several weeks, but I only had to wear a sling for a short time. (I got rid of the sling as soon as possible, because it made me feel self-consciously conspicuous.) The neural illusions of the sound of shells, to which I have already referred, soon disappeared, and after a few days the feeling of extreme fatigue and physical exhaustion wore off. On Active Service one seized such interludes of rest like unexpected reprieves, made all the more enjoyable by contrast with what had gone before, and without worrying over-much about what might follow. I was ready to go back to the line when the authorities considered me fit to go, but in the meantime I felt no urge deliberately to hasten the day! It was, I felt, a matter which was out of my own hands, so why worry? None the less—strange though it may sound in the circumstances—the events since the 21st of March had jerked my mind out of the temporary phase of "defeatism" to which I have already alluded, and opened my eyes to the reality of the German peril.

"It made me wonder if, after all, I was looking at the war in the right light . . . . The question worried me a good deal, but I am satisfied in my own mind, and when I go back to the line I shall go confident in the justice of our cause and the righteousness of our aims. God works in an unexplainable way, and I believe that He is using this most horrible instrument of war to work His purpose of freeing the world. . . Above all other ' war-aims,' I am here to secure the safety of my home, so that it shall be *mine* and not Germany's in the future, and that the future generations shall not have to go through it all again. . . . I don't honestly think I should want to be out of the Army now, on the same conditions as before I joined up—I shouldn't feel comfortable." (More quotations from my letters.)

The time I spent in hospital and convalescent camp was, in general, very easy and pleasant; but, like most enjoyable periods, it was comparatively lacking in incident—at least, the kind of incident that makes interesting reading—so this chapter will be mainly a brief series of notes, cataloguing my movements and leading up to my return to "duty," and to the more dramatic events of the "Big Push."

.   .   .   .   .

No. 7 Convalescent Camp was situated on the cliff-top between Boulogne and Wimereux. In normal times it was, as its name indicated, a camp for "convalescents," but owing to the great rush of casualties due to the great battle now raging, it was being used as an auxilliary hospital for the less serious cases. It was one of a number of similar camps spread over the surrounding district, and was composed of wooden huts and tents, arranged in the usual geometrical order. The population of "No. 7" was at that time, I think, round about fifteen hundred men, who were divided into ten "companies"; I was placed in "B" Company, one of the hut-dwelling sections. We considered ourselves to be very comfortably lodged, for at first we slept on iron hospital beds, though before long the camp became so crowded that the bedsteads had to be folded up and we laid our mattresses on the floor, in order to accommodate more men. Still, it was luxury to have even mattresses! The huts, of the standard "W.D." type, held between twenty-five and thirty men; and between them were sandbag-roofed shelters sunk a foot or two below ground level, in which we were supposed to take refuge during air-raids; but they were in bad repair (many with several inches of water on the floor) and I seldom saw them used.

When we arrived, we were first ushered into a large "recreation hut" to have our injuries attended to, and gathered round the stove while awaiting our turn. Presently the voice of a newspaper boy was heard in the distance, calling "Eenglish paperz!" and there was a general exodus. We had all come from the battle-area, but—apart from verbal reports and rumours—we knew nothing about what had happened in the line during the past week except our own very limited personal experience. After a chase round the camp, I managed to secure a paper, and, returning to the hut, was able to form some idea of the tremendous events in which I had recently taken part. It was not cheerful reading. The line had apparently been broken along an immense front, from south of Arras to St. Quentin, and the British and French were in rapid retreat towards Amiens. All the hard-won Somme battle-field, which had cost months of fighting and scores of thousands of lives to win, had been lost again in two or three days. The Russian collapse had released thousands of German troops, who were now hurling themselves with renewed fury upon the crumbling bulwarks of the West. It almost seemed as if the Allies' cause was in final eclipse — but nobody seemed unduly alarmed and everyone, especially those who had come from the battle-area, was confident that the enemy would be stopped.

The camp routine was very easy, and we had plenty of time to ourselves. Every morning we attended at one of the large recreation-huts to have our wounds re-dressed, during which operation an orchestra usually played—whether with the object of nerving us for the ordeal, or of drowning our cries of pain, I cannot say! On certain days of the week, when it was fine, there was a "route-march" for those who were fit to attend, though this term was merely a formal name for a pleasant country walk, in a rough semblance of military formation, along the inland lanes, sometimes as far as Wimille or St. Martin, at others following the cliff-edge past the Napoleon Column—whence the shores of England could be seen on a clear day—or down into Boulogne and around the old Citadel and the Cathedral of Notre Dame. All that district, where more than a centruy ago the "Grande Armée" had been encamped for the invasion of England, now presented a very varied panorama of races. The hospital-camps contained men from almost all parts of the British Isles, Canada, Australia, New Zealand and South Africa; and close at hand were camps of

Hindoos, Portuguese, Chinese, Negroes and West Indians, as well as French and Belgian troops. A short distance away there was a prison-camp of Germans.

The surrounding country was more varied and picturesque than any I had hitherto struck since leaving England, quite unlike the bare swelling rise-and-fall of the Picardy landscape, with its arrow-straight roads and angular fields. Here there were hills and little valleys, green and tree-shaded, with rippling streams in the hollows and lanes that wound in and out between hedgerows, just like Kent ; the fields were white with daisies and the woods bright with the first fresh green of Spring. The most noticeable difference from the countryside across the Channel was the absence of oak-trees—I don't think I saw a single specimen while I was overseas.

Within the Camp, ample amusement was provided for us by several large huts under the auspices of various "war-charity" organisations. The Red Cross maintained a large concert-hall, in which there were frequent variety shows or orchestral concerts, some of which were very good ; among others, I remember seeing excellent shows by the 29th Division Concert Party and Miss Lena Ashwell's Party. The Y.M.C.A., besides providing several recreation huts with all conveniences for reading, writing, playing chess and billiards, etc., also ran a cinema in which free shows were given on two or three nights every week ; there was a large "Expeditionary Force Canteen," in which many essential articles could be purchased as well as food—most useful to men who, like myself, had come down the line with no more than the contents of our pockets. And there was also a well-stocked lending-library, of which I made full use.

We soldiers of the B.E.F. were wonderfully well served by these voluntary organisations—Red Cross, Church Army, Catholic Club, Salvation Army, Free Churches, etc., which—although they were run by sectarian bodies (except the Red Cross)—were by no means confined to their co-religionists and in which religion was never obtruded. Particularly ubiquitous in France was the Y.M.C.A., to which (as to all of them) we owed a debt of gratitude which can never be adequately repaid. It might well be said that wherever there were troops, there also was the Y.M.C.A., with its canteen, its cheerfulness and its never-ending effort to bring some at least of the comforts of civilisation into our existence. It was to be found close to the firing-line as well as at the Base, and the "Y.M." was the social centre of every village or camp where British troops were quartered, were it only a tent or a room in a shell-blasted building ; its popular "sing-songs" will long be remembered by all who took part in them. Sometimes, too, on railway platforms in the chilly hours of dawn, or at the roadside as we came wearily out of the trenches after a spell in the line, we would be greeted by a little band of indefatigable workers in their light-khaki uniforms, who distributed hot cocoa or coffee and biscuits among us. Good old "Y.M."!

Besides the amenities of the Camp, one of its drawbacks should also be mentioned—on the principle that "there is a fly in every ointment." Our "fly" was "Country Dancing." Where the idea originated, I have no notion, probably in the mind of some æsthetic spinster or Brigadier with a bee in his bonnet, but it was seized upon by the Camp authorities and made into a compulsory parade for the more able-bodied convalescents. So, on certain occasions, a number of us from each Company were marched to one of the large huts, where we solemnly clumped, in our Army boots, through the complicated manœuvres of several Old-English Country Dances, under the direction of some (no doubt, well-meaning) elderly ladies and accompanied by a tinkling piano, much to the amusement of the onlookers and our own embarrassed discomfort. What these corybantic displays were expected to achieve, I do not know—perhaps to make us eager to escape back to the front!—but fortunately the idea fizzled out after a few practices.

The other occupants of my hut were a cheery crowd, and I made several good friends during my stay. Four of them, who with myself occupied the beds at one end of the hut, I remember particularly: a man of the East Surreys, who before joining-up had superintended a Church Army hut at Shoreham; a Royal Engineers sapper; a tall, broad-shouldered Boer from Cape Town, who had fought against the British in the South African War; and a Welsh lad, not yet nineteen, wounded in the head. "Lights-out" was often the signal for some wild ragging, in which pillows, "biscuits," balls of screwed-up paper, and anything else handy flew from side to side with reckless and hilarious abandon. When I eventually left the Camp at short notice, I left my watch, which had broken down, to be posted home by the "East Surrey" man, with whom I had formed a close friendship. The watch reached home safely, but I never saw or heard of any of my friends again; I do not even remember their names—such was the way with many chance friendships in the Army.

Air-raid warnings were frequent at Boulogne; the signal was the firing of a gun down near the harbour, followed by a pandemonium of sirens, bells, and engine whistles, impossible to sleep through. On only one occasion while I was there, however, was there a raid, when I was awakened in the small hours by heavy gun-fire, and went out of the hut to find searchlights sweeping the sky in all directions and a barrage of anti-aircraft shells bursting overhead. The planes droned round for a long time, and at last dropped a number of bombs near the harbour, though I think without doing much damage. It was necessary to keep under cover in the huts while this was going on, for shrapnel and spent bullets were falling around, and they were a greater danger than bombs in our high and exposed area, which, being a clearly defined hospital district, was never (so far as I know) bombed.

The German advance in Picardy slowed down and finally stopped in the first few days of April, when the British and French succeeded in forming a new line east of Amiens. With the failure of their great attempt to smash the Allies in one tremendous blow, Germany's last hope of winning the war had vanished, though this was by no means clear to us at the time—or, perhaps, to them either. They had come near to success for a few days, but in the end all they had achieved was to recapture a broad stretch of territory which they themselves had devastated in their retreat of a year earlier, and over which they were unable to bring up supplies and reinforcements quickly enough to maintain their pressure. And, although far outnumbered, the British resistance had proved to be unbreakable.

One more bid for a decision was made, however, when, on April 9th, they attacked in great force in the valley of the Lys, south-east of Armentieres. For a time the position was very critical, and it looked as though they would succeed in driving through to the coast. At Boulogne all preparations were made to evacuate the Base, including the wounded, to England if that should happen. We could hear the guns, particularly at night, coming nearer (as it seemed) hour by hour. But it was largely due to the 31st Division (including the 4th Guards Brigade), which was rushed to the scene of action around Merville and the Foret de Nieppe, that the enemy's plan was frustrated. Sir Douglas Haig, in an official despatch afterwards, singled out the 31st Division by saying that it had "saved the existence of the British Army."

When I had been six weeks at Boulogne my wound was nearly healed, and at the usual weekly inspection on May 13th I fully expected to be marked for return to duty. But the Doctor, who, by a coincidence, was none other than the former Medical Officer of the Household Battalion—the recognition had been mutual— surprised me by asking if I had any more sore places on my limbs similar to those he had treated me for in January. I had to admit that I had one or two small ones, and on examination he seemed to regard them more seriously than I did, for he promptly ordered me to another hospital, "under observation" for some unspecified form of skin disorder. As it turned out, the suspicion was entirely groundless, and the places healed up quite quickly under treatment, but it sufficed to give me a most delightful fortnight's holiday by the sea. I left Boulogne, in company with several others, by ambulance that afternoon, and, after a pleasant ride through the country, arrived at the 25th General Hospital at Plage d'Hardelot about 3.15.

．　．　．　．　．　．

Plage d'Hardelot is a seaside resort about six miles south of Boulogne; it was then quite a tiny place, somewhat off the beaten track, and in peace-time was probably a very select watering-place for the wealthy, for it consisted of little more than a row of quaint chalets and bungalows facing the sea, the rococo peaks and gables of which formed a fantastic skyline when viewed from the sands; most of them were shuttered and empty, however, and there were very few civilians left in the place. A paved promenade followed the sea-wall for about half-a-mile, from the centre of which a flight of steps descended to the sea, while behind the houses were the Dunes—low, irregularly-shaped sandhills whose outlines were softened by a few trees and shrubs and dry reedy grass. To the north the promenade was bounded by a little stream, the Becque, which ran into the sea at this point, and at the other end a small Casino, as bizarre as the chalets, jutted out over the sands. This latter was now a Soldiers' Club, run by the Church Army and the C.E.M.S.—a rather incongruous metamorphosis!

The Hospital itself was about two hundred yards from the shore. Its Headquarters were in the "Hotel d'Hardelot," the only considerable building in the place, but it also included several of the surrounding bungalows and a large number of temporary wooden huts and tents. My ward was in one of the huts, a large light and airy room in which there were twenty-six beds, each with a locker for personal belongings, a stove and a table in the centre. At the far end an opening, screened by a curtain, led to the Ward Sister's room and the small kitchen, and beyond was the room in which the daily dressings were performed. There were curtains at the windows and a table-cover on the centre table, on which there was always a bowl of wild flowers, as well as in vases on each locker. It looked really civilised, and my bed, with its spring-mattress, blankets, white sheets and pillow, seemed positive luxury after months of sleeping on the floor. We took our meals—only two or three of us in the ward were "bed-patients"—in three large inter-connecting marquees a short distance away, in which the tables were actually covered with real damask cloths!

The Hospital Staff—doctors, Sisters and orderlies—were all Australian; and, as far as I was concerned, they were all of them "top-hole." It was my good fortune that three times while I was in France I was, for short periods, in the hands of Overseas Red Cross—American at Tréport, Australian at Hardelot and—much later—at Abbéville—and each time I was favourably impressed by the organisation as compared with our own. It was not that the personnel of the English Red Cross were not every bit as splendid as any other, but in British hospitals there was always a devotion to rigid routine and red-tape that was somehow lacking or better disguised in the others, without any obvious loss of efficiency. Those in authority did not show so much consciousness of their "rank," but talked to us and treated us as equals, and the atmosphere in these hospitals was altogether more free-and-easy, more human and home-like. One felt that one was a human being, and not merely a "case."

The Sister in charge of "M1" Ward was a typical example. She was young (about thirty, I should think) and good-looking, and kept us all in order by the quiet friendliness of her manner. We all idolised her, of course, but she had no favourites, and treated us all with an impersonal "camaraderie" which compelled respect. I used to enjoy helping her in various small jobs about the Ward, such as assisting in dressing the wounds of one of the bed-patients and making his bed, and she sometimes left me in charge of the medicines while she was off-duty. Since no-one died, I presume I always gave the right dose to the right men!

The fortnight I spent at Hardelot was a wonderful time of perfect Spring weather and complete rest. Apart from the daily "dressings" and an inspection of the Ward by the Matron in the morning, we usually had the day to ourselves, and I spent most of my time on the sands. It was so hot that we needed no more clothing than shirt and blue "hospital" trousers, and I soon became very sunburned. We awoke in the morning with the sun streaming into the Ward and the intoxicating air coming in at the open windows like a breath of paradise, making me feel glad to be alive. A wash and breakfast, then "dressings," and the Ward was tidied-up ready for inspection. Presently the Matron sailed in and walked round, with a cheerful word for each of us as we stood by our beds ; and then we would go down to the beach, purchasing on the way large juicy oranges from a woman at the gate (who, incidentally, knew how to charge for them!)

Below the promenade, the sands stretched far and wide when the tide was out, and I spent many an idyllic hour wandering by the water's edge or lying at full length on the sand, reading in the sun. My letters home became almost lyrical in my whole-hearted enjoyment of the holiday, and I might be accused of sentimental exaggeration if I quoted from them. But, indeed, this seemed to be the one supremely golden moment life had held for me since I came to France. I was aware, with a new intensity and unfailing delight, of the small things around me—the sparkling water, the fleecy cloudlets, the scent of the sea ; tiny crabs, delicate fronds of seaweed, dainty shells ; the scudding flecks of sea-foam on the wet sands—all had a beauty and significance for me which was the greater, perhaps, because of their complete contrast from the filth and squalour of war.

There was, indeed, little to remind us, at Hardelot, of the war—in daylight. Occasionally we would see a silver airship patrolling up and down the coast, on the look-out for submarines, and once a squadron of Bosche reconnaissance planes passed overhead, so high as to be almost invisible.

But at night there were several air-raids on Boulogne, only a few miles distant, and the attacking planes usually buzzed over our heads for some while, trying to penetrate the barrage. We had few apprehensions on our own account, for there were no military works of importance in the neighbourhood, and we used to stand outside the Ward and watch the gun-fire over Boulogne until the raiders had been driven off. Then, feeling loath to go back to bed, we would stand about in the warm scented night, talking, until perhaps two or three o'clock—unless the Sister came along, when we would scuttle back to the Ward and pretend to be asleep, like schoolboys.

The worst of these raids was the notorious one on Whit-Sunday, May 19th. In addition to Boulogne, London and Etaples were simultaneously attacked—it was London's last raid of the war, and at Etaples a hospital was badly bombed. For three hours the Gothas circled over our heads, vainly trying to reach Boulogne, but were repeatedly driven back by terrific bursts of gun-fire. Time after time, with a concerted roar of engines, they hurled themselves at the town, but each time a cloud of bursting shrapnel forced them to retreat. They tried attacking from one direction after another with the whole squadron, and from several different points at once with individual planes (at least, that is how it seemed to us) but without success. At last—mysteriously, and almost as if the gunners had said in disgust, "Let them *drop* their bloody bombs and have done with it!"—the guns with one accord stopped firing completely, the planes darted in, dropped all their bombs with a series of crashes which shook the ground even at Hardelot, and made off.

At Etaples, where we could see the shrapnel bursting in the distance, the struggle was over sooner, but terrible damage was done to the hospital on which some of the bombs fell. One of the men from the bombed buildings was brought to Hardelot next day and occupied the next bed to mine. He told me that, in his opinion, the disaster had been entirely unintentional. The aeroplane containing the leader of the raiding squadron had been brought down and its occupants captured ; my informant said that the German Kapitan was taken to the hospital to see the damage he had wrought, and was genuinely horrified. He showed them the map by which he had flown, and the site of the hospital was plainly marked (in German) "military works." It was a fact that this particular hospital was entirely surrounded by training camps and store depots, as I saw for myself some time afterwards, so there may be some truth in the Kapitan's story. Our own airmen always expressed respect for their opponents, whose courage and chivalry on many occasions was only matched by their own, and I believe that, despite propaganda stories, it was never definitely proved that they deliberately attacked a hospital. Indeed, in a night raid on a crowded Base town it is difficult to see how such tragic errors could be avoided. The real blame lay with the authorities, for failing to segregate the wounded in clearly-defined hospital areas, like Hardelot, well away from "legitimate" targets.

Much to my regret, the doctor certified me fit for Convalescent Camp at the end of a fortnight, and indeed I had no grounds for questioning his judgment. I still wore a bandage on my wounded arm, which was not entirely healed, but physically I felt fitter than for months past, and the complete rest and civilised surroundings of the hospital had done "wonders" for my nerves. I left Hardelot on the following afternoon, and a short motor ride brought me to No. 10 Convalescent Camp, near Ecault, about three miles away.

.   .   .   .   .   .

The Con. Camp was situated about midway between two hamlets, Ecault and Equihen, on the slopes of a small valley running parallel to the sea and separated from it by a plateau and cliffs about half-a-mile to the west. The head of the valley was occupied by the Camp parade-ground, which also did duty as a football field on occasion, and was surrounded by a large number of huts for the "convalescents" and the Headquarters offices, dining huts, recreation huts, etc. The present population of the Camp, however, was much too great for the existing permanent accommodation, and hundreds of bell-tents had been pitched along both sides of the valley to hold the additional Companies. I was in one of these, "Z" Company, and shared a tent with only four others, so that we were not overcrowded, though, of course, not so comfortable as in Hospital. A small stream bubbled out of the ground just below the parade-ground and followed a bend in the valley beyond the camp to the sea, through a break in the cliff. The ground on which the camp stood was for the most part open turf, but lower down the brook ran through deep grasses and over-arching trees, with many flowers and ferns, while the landward slopes were crowned with foliage.

There was more restriction about life in the camp than there had been in Hospital, but the duties were light and, for the most part, pleasant. There were parades in the morning, mostly of a physical-training nature, and a few fatigues at various times, but on the whole we led an easy life. The most popular of the "compulsory" duties was the Bathing Parade, which took place every fine afternoon and which everyone who could, even if they were otherwise exempt, attended. We marched to the sea, towel and bathing-slips in hand, and undressed on the beach in a canvas enclosure ; the water was warm and shallow, and I always looked forward to these half-hours of splashing in the sunshine with great enjoyment, even though I could not swim.

I did not expect to be at the Con. Camp for longer than two or three days, but shortly after I arrived the Sergeant-Major in charge of "Z" Company offered a temporary "appointment on the Staff" to me and another man, and we were not unwilling to take on the job, since it meant at least a fortnight in the Camp. I was at first inclined to think the work—that of "sanitary orderlies"—was somewhat beneath my "dignity" as a Guardsman (!), but I had long since ceased to be particular. Indeed, we took a real pride in the conscientious performance of our duties, and scrubbed the ablution benches until the inspecting officer remarked that he had never seen the place so clean. Anyhow, the "work" took only about an hour each morning, and we were "ex officio" exempt from parades—though, as I said, we always volunteered for Bathing Parade.

Little that is worthy of special note occurred during my stay at No. 10 Con. Camp. The weather remained fine for the most part, and there was an air-raid on Boulogne nearly every night. Once a parachute flare was dropped directly over the Camp and we fully expected bombs to follow, but the brilliant light apparently showed up the Red Cross markings and nothing happened. There were several good variety shows by various military troupes, and I particularly remember a well-acted scene from "Julius Cæsar," given by (I think) the H.A.C. Party. It was a real treat to hear Shakespeare's language spoken, after months of Army talk.

．　　　．　　　．　　　．　　　．　　　．

As soon as my fortnight's "Staff job" came to an end, I was marked out and, with a number of others, travelled by car to St. Martin's Rest Camp, high up on the cliffs above Boulogne. We were there for two days, under canvas, and on June 16th entrained at Boulogne station for Harfleur. We travelled, of course, in cattle trucks, but were not uncomfortably crowded, and the journey was without incident until we reached Abbéville about dusk. Some little distance beyond the station the train pulled up on a siding, and it appeared that we were going to remain there for some time. Abbéville was one of the most important rail junctions in the British area, and men working on the line told us that it had been bombed regularly every night for some time past, so we prepared for an exciting night.

Our expectations were realised, for not long after dark the German planes were signalled. They circled about over the town for some time, followed by searchlights and a heavy barrage of shells, while from several points machine-guns sent streams of tracer bullets into the darkness. At last they swept down upon the station. The first bomb was incendiary and set the station building ablaze, and by the light of the flames the Germans began to place their bombs methodically. To us, crouching under the cover of the trucks, the explosions seemed to be coming nearer with every burst, but fortunately the airmen exhausted their supply of ammunition before they reached us. After a time they departed, though one plane seemed to be cut off by the barrage to the west of the town, and buzzed around for a long time, trying to get through. About an hour later our train got up steam and we were soon under way, but we pulled up once in a cutting, apparently to avoid another plane which seemed to be following us.

Our route took us, early next morning, close to Amiens, which at that time was within shell-fire range. We could see shrapnel bursting over the firing line to the eastwards, and the ground on both sides of the railway was pitted with shell-holes or bomb-craters. We felt relieved when that particular stretch of line was cleared, for it is a peculiarly helpless feeling to be packed in a train while under shell-fire.

However, the enemy took no notice of us on this occasion, and we reached Harfleur without further adventure about seven p.m. that evening. After a meal at the Y.M.C.A., for which they firmly refused to accept payment, we split up into our respective units, and I reported to the Base Depôt of the Guards Division.

I was there for a little more than a week—presumably while a sufficient number of casualties and other "spare parts" were collected to make up a train-load for the 4th Guards Brigade. Nothing of special interest occurred at Harfleur, and the routine was much the same as on other similar occasions — gas drill, inspections, parades for the replacement of deficiencies in kit (in my case it amounted practically to a complete new outfit), etc. "Spit-and-polish," "wind-up" and the general air of regimentalism was much more marked at the Base than in the line, and the place was "lousy" with senior N.C.O.'s who had "dug themselves in" on various pretexts to avoid being sent to the front. I don't think I was altogether sorry when, on June 25th, a large party of ex-casualties marched into Havre, to entrain for the line, or wherever our Battalion happened to be situated.

It was very hot, and most of us were out of practice with full marching order, so that we were not sorry when the station was reached. The train, however, did not leave until four-fifteen, nearly four hours after we boarded it, and we killed time as best we could, wandering round the station in search of cigarettes and chocolate. There was only one small canteen, a temporary movable affair, within bounds, and it was closed when we arrived; when it opened presently, such a dense crowd converged on its small counter that it had to be hurriedly closed again, to avoid being overturned in the crush. I and others who were in the front row were squeezed so tightly against the counter by those behind us that we found it impossible either to pick up our purchases or to get at our pockets and take out our money!

An all-night journey brought us to Doullens at six-thirty in the morning, and here we left the train and were taken to a rest-camp close at hand. We only stayed for a few hours, but the interval enabled some of us to take a stroll round the town. There seemed to be far fewer people in Doullens now than when I was there last March, and, of course, the hospitals and store depôts had long since been moved away, for the town was now comparatively near to the line ; business was practically at a standstill and the streets were deserted, though there did not appear to be much damage. But I was pleased to discover in the course of my walk a small shop where they had a stock of English novels in paper covers, of which I immediately bought two or three.

We re-entrained at two o'clock, and, after a short run, reached a station near Saulty, which was the "rail-head" of that area ; from there, we marched to La Cauchie, near which we found the Battalion encamped.

V

WITH THE 3rd BATTALION

MY arrival caused some surprise in No. 2 Company, for it appeared that after the bombardment near Ervillers in March my name had been posted among the "missing" and it was assumed that I was either dead or a prisoner. Indeed, I and one other man—not yet re-joined—were apparently the only survivors of the section to which I had been attached during that eventful week, and the personnel of the whole Company was almost entirely different. From what one or another told me, mostly at second-hand, it seems that during the night on which I was taken down the line the Batt. retired to a new position near Ayette, and next day a shell had landed right in the midst of the Section, killing or wounding all but one of them.

I had already, a few days earlier at the Base, met my fellow-survivor, who had told me that shortly before this happened, a parcel from home had arrived for me, and as it was believed I had been killed the contents were shared among my erstwhile comrades. I am glad to think that, before they "went west" they enjoyed a last smoke from the fags it contained, for very few of us had any left on the previous day.

The Battalion—or what was left of it—was now encamped among scattered trees between Humbercamps and La Cauchie, about a kilometre from the latter. We were nowhere near up to full strength, and the whole Brigade occupied little more space than would have been required for a complete Battalion; for after the "March Do" (as it was popularly called), they had been rushed north to meet the German attack in the Lys valley and had suffered badly at Merville. Indeed, after this battle neither the 3rd Coldstream nor the 4th Grenadier Guards could muster the equivalent of two full Companies each, and for some time they had been formed into a "composite" battalion. Since then, withdrawn from the line, small drafts and a trickle of returning casualties had slightly improved the position, and the Battalions had resumed their separate identity, but they were still too weak to form a fighting force. The 4th Guards Brigade was now in "G.H.Q. Reserve," unattached to a Division, and formed a depot from which to recruit the Guards Division as occasion required. Our immediate business in the La Cauchie area was to construct a reserve system of defences between Bavincourt and Beaumetz, along the main Doullens-Arras highway.

The camp was in a pleasant situation, and except for the scattered copse in which we lay the surrounding country was intensively cultivated. I was rather surprised to see how many peasants there were still working on the land, which was scarcely out of shell-fire range. One might often see them, only a short distance from the camp, patiently filling in a new shell-hole and replanting their crops. An observation balloon which floated overhead about half-a-mile away was methodically shelled with shrapnel each time it went up.

Our tents were "dug-in" about two feet below ground level, as a partial protection against possible shells or bombing, though we were not troubled in that way while I was there. But the tents, in that midsummer weather, became almost unbearably stuffy at night, when we were all inside, and several times after "Lights-out" I crept through a hole in the hedge which marked the camp boundary, and slept in the open field beyond. Once, however, I slept so soundly that even "Reveille" did not wake me, and the first I knew was two of our fellows, who had been searching for me, shaking my shoulder with the news that it only wanted ten minutes to Parade-time! They had collected my breakfast, and I bolted it as I had a lightning shave, rubbed my brasses and arranged my kit for inspection, and "fell in" just in time! After that I always slept in the tent.

Each morning we paraded at seven-fifteen, and marched across country to the scene of our labours, which was some distance away from the camp and quite near to the C.C.S. at Beaumetz to which I had been brought in March. To each Company was assigned a definite daily task—a certain length of trench to dig or barbed-wire entanglement to construct—and each platoon returned to camp independently as soon as its allotted "piece-work" was completed. The trench-system we were constructing ran through flourishing cornfields, in which the grain stood nearly breast-high and was sprinkled with a brilliant display of poppies, cornflowers and mignonette. It seemed almost an act of desecration to slash it down and tear open the good brown earth. We had usually finished work by mid-day, though this was dependent, of course, on the energy with which we worked and the nature of the soil, and if we were lucky we might get a lift for part of the way by jumping a passing lorry; otherwise, we had a walk of several kilos over the fields. In the afternoons we usually "got down to it" until tea-time, after which we were free to go where we would.

The nearest civilian habitation was the little hamlet of Humbercamps, about three or four hundred yards away, but it was very poor and practically destitute of interest. About half-an-hour's walking distance in the direction of the line, however, was the village of Pommier, where there was a Y.M.C.A. tent, in which one could usually buy biscuits or chocolate, and occasionally other things; but the place was frequently under shell-fire, so, though we often went there, we had to go circumspectly. La Cauchie, which was nearer to us on the north (and safer), had no attractions.

Apart from trench-digging, there were few parades or duties, except for a twenty-four-hour Headquarters guard, which was mounted every morning, though I was only on it once while we were at this camp. It was quite "cushy," however, for there were only two two-hour spells on sentry for each man, and we got extra rations. The rest of the time, although we had, of course, to remain in the "guard-room" fully dressed in case the guard should be turned out, gave us ample opportunity for reading, writing, talking or otherwise amusing ourselves. Our rations at this time were extremely good, probably because we were so much under strength, and we hardly needed to resort to the Canteen for extra food—though we usually did !

On Sundays we did no digging, but there was a Church Parade in the morning, for which we had to "posh up" very thoroughly—brasses shining, boots polished, trousers creased, as though we were on "King's Guard." Our Padre, however, who was broad-minded for an Army Chaplain and quite a good sort, did not believe in applying compulsion in religious matters, and as often as possible made the service a voluntary one. Although the attendance was naturally not so large at these times, the service and the singing always seemed to me to be much more sincere and hearty. One "can't make a man sober by Act of Parliament," still less can one make him religious by compelling him to attend a formal service once a week and punishing him if his buttons don't shine ! That, at least, is how I saw it at the time, and, as I remarked (with doubtful truth), "the Army system doesn't aim at making a decent, honest man out of its raw material, only a *smart* man. Religion in the Army is only a concession to public opinion."

On my second Sunday in camp, after tea, there was a Baths Parade. In the Army, "cleanliness" ranked, not next to but ahead of "godliness" in importance, though on Active Service both were more honoured in the breach than in the observance ! The Bath House (so called) was at Saulty, about an hour's march away —a wooden hut from the roof of which a number of pipes oozed a thin trickle of warm water, under which we stood in our "birthday-suits" and washed as well as we could. It was refreshing, if nothing more, though by the time we reached camp again, after the return journey, we were pretty well covered with dust and perspiration again.

At Humbercamps we were about five or six miles behind the Front line, but it was a quiet sector at that time and the Germans appeared to have few long-range guns in the neighbourhood, for no shells landed nearer to us than Pommier, about a mile away. Sometimes at night, however, we could hear heavy barrage-fire to the north, where raids were of fairly frequent occurrence. Close to the camp—within two or three hundred yards—there was a large ammunition dump, where hundreds of huge shells were stored beneath light wooden shelters and camouflage, in the charge of a detachment of West Indian troops. One morning, just before dawn, we were awakened by a great uproar and the crash of bombs; poking my head out of the tent, I was just in time to see two German planes, very low down, dart swiftly across the camp in the direction of the line. They had bombed the dump, and although they had missed their main objective, they had succeeded in setting fire to some cordite, which was blazing fiercely. Clouds of smoke arose and the red glare increased rapidly; we fully expected to see the whole dump go up at any moment. But hardly had the aeroplanes vanished than the B.W.I. were out of their tents and racing down the road at top speed towards the fire. Their prompt action had the blaze under control in a few minutes, and the situation was saved. My estimation of coloured troops was considerably enhanced by this display of courage.

Soon after I rejoined the Battalion rumours began to circulate among us to the effect that the Allies were soon to take the offensive on this part of the front. Civilians (who always seemed to be better informed on "secret" matters than we were) told us definitely that there was to be a big attack in two or three weeks—that was why dumps of shells and other stores were being accumulated in the vicinity! Consequently, we were very much surprised when, in the first week of July, it was officially announced that the Brigade was to move back, right out of the war-zone altogether, and that we were to remain out of the line for a considerable time. It seems that, as a result of their part in the actions of March and April, and their consequent heavy losses, the Brigade had been awarded what was known as "King's Rest"—a period of about three months at the Base, for recuperation and reinforcement. Our luck was decidedly in; and I—although I had only recently rejoined the Battalion—was to share in the good fortune!

Therefore, (on July 9th we struck camp and marched (nothing loath) in column-of-route to the rail-head, starting about 11 a.m. It took us about two hours, heavily ladened in very warm weather, to reach Mondicourt, where we bivouacked at the rail-side and had dinner. The train arrived about two o'clock, and we boarded the cattle-trucks of which it was composed and settled ourselves in very contentedly; in the knowledge that we were on our way to the coast, not even a Pullman car could have seemed more luxurious than the hot and crowded truck, and everyone was in high spirits.

After an uneventful and comparatively rapid journey, we arrived at Eu, near Le Treport, about ten-thirty in the evening, and unloaded both ourselves and the Brigade stores. A drink of tea was provided from the field-cookers which accompanied us, and we made a meal of the rations we carried with us.

Shortly afterwards we started on the march to our new quarters. This was the most trying part of the journey for most of us, for we had to carry full kit for some twelve kilometres, and we were already none too fresh, after the heat of the crowded trucks. For my own part, the soles of my feet had become very tender, almost raw, from some cause which is still a mystery to me, so that it was very painful to walk. However, pride forbade that I should fall out, so I hobbled along with the rest, though at times it was like walking on red-hot iron. The road seemed unending and the kilometre-stones very far between, but at last we reached our journey's end about half-past two in the morning, and were very thankful to find that the tents had been erected beforehand and everything was ready for us. It did not take us long to turn in, and we slept until ten o'clock, without rocking.

.   .   .   .   .   .

At Criel Plage, a little sea-side resort between Treport and Dieppe, we were in a district not previously occupied by British troops. Our camp was pitched on a westward-facing hillside, close to the sea, where the lines of tents and other temporary structures stood on a fairly gentle slope of short green turf. At the foot of the hill ran a road leading to Criel (as distinct from the " Plage ") and a small stream, beyond which rose a low ridge known as " Mont Jolibois." The Plage consisted of an hotel and about a dozen houses around a little bay, but the " town " of Criel was a more pretentious place, and boasted a number of shops, a multitude of estaminets, a church and a cinema. It was about five minutes walk from the camp. The nearest large towns, Dieppe and Le Treport, were out of bounds to us, but we could, and we did, visit Criel as often as we liked when not on duty.

When we first arrived, we were given very strict instructions that not only was the name of the place not to be mentioned in letters, but that we were not to describe the kind of scenery or hint that we were on the sea-coast. But this rule was soon relaxed or allowed to lapse, and, re-reading the letters I wrote from there, I cannot believe that before long my parents had not at least a general idea of where we were, despite the censorship. No objection was made by the authorities when I wrote for bathing slips to be sent from home, or spoke of learning to swim.

The country was then at the height of its summer beauty, and there was a profusion of wild flowers everywhere, unspoiled by the depredations of peace-time holiday-makers. The fields were starred with marguerites, the woods and hedgerows full of anemones, columbine and wild geranium, and patches of poppies and cornflowers made splashes of brilliant colour among the yellowing corn. The sea was within two minutes of the camp, and we looked forward to unlimited opportunities for bathing. It seemed almost too good to be true.

Because of the sloping ground on which the tents were pitched, and in order to provide more headroom inside, we soon began to excavate the floor of the tents to a depth of about a foot, and this gave rise to the idea of making gardens around them. The idea caught on, and the officers encouraged it, and soon after duties every day each tent would be surrounded by a knot of willing gardeners, digging, transplanting wild flowers, watering and tending the small plots, until the bare ground "blossomed like a rose." Some of the effects achieved were really fine, the Coldstream Star, the Tudor rose, the Irish shamrock and the Grenadiers' badge, etc., being reproduced in plants of different colours.

Once we were settled in the new camp the daily routine was a nearer approach to ordinary barrack life in England than I had yet experienced on this side of the Channel, though there was less formality and the programme was more varied and lighter than at Windsor. There was usually a Battalion Parade in the mornings, on the level ground above the tent-lines, or frequently a route march, though sometimes these were superseded by fatigues, either in our own camp or at a Convalescent Camp on the cliffs in the direction of Le Treport. A Camp Guard and Picket was mounted daily with the appropriate ceremonial, and of course we had to keep our brasses, etc., shining as in England, but on the whole we had a very easy time.

Although we were the first British troops in the neighbourhood of the Plage, there was a Battalion of Belgian infantry stationed at Criel, and a large number of Americans in the vicinity. The uniform of the "Doughboys" was becoming increasingly common in France by this time and, indeed, we became more familiar with it and with the distinguishing marks of its ranks than with those of the French Army, whom we seldom saw in this area.

One of the advantages of being back with the Battalion was that one could get fairly regular pay. Previous to re-joining, I had only been able to draw any cash at all on two occasions (once at Boulogne and once at Ecault—twenty francs in all) and had had to rely almost entirely on supplies from home, which were frequently delayed by my changes of address. Of course, we were never at any time paid the full amount due, but the arrears went to our credit on the regimental books, so that I had the "satisfaction" of knowing that a substantial sum was accumulating for me to draw during my first "leave;" but that longed-for event was extremely uncertain, and in the meantime I was often "on the rocks." At Criel, however, there was a Pay-parade every week, ten or fifteen francs each time, though that did not go far in a French village. There was a Canteen in the camp, which supplied most of our immediate necessaries such as cigarettes, chocolate and cleaning materials for persons or equipment, at a cheap rate—for instance, "Players" were ten for 2½d.—but supplies were sometimes erratic and they were often out of stock for days together. One could buy much more in Criel, but there prices were very high, owing probably to the presence of American troops, who always had much more money to spend than we did.

About this time I was receiving, at frequent intervals, a whole budget of letters which had been posted to me during the previous March and which had not been delivered because of my separation from the Battalion. All were marked "Missing," and it speaks well for the conscientious perserverance of the Army Post Office that the envelopes were covered, back and front, with re-directions. Naturally, the news contained in them was somewhat stale, but even old letters did not come amiss to us in France. One of these was a four-months-old letter from Arthur Brookes, enclosing an even earlier one which he had written in January, but which had been returned to him because I had gone into hospital (at Treport). When I wrote from Criel in reply to these, I was surprised to receive, almost immediately afterwards, another letter from him, this time an up-to-date one. It appears that, after hearing nothing from each other for more than six months, we had both written on the same day !

I also received back a letter which I had written months before to a friend in Salonika; before it reached him he had sailed for England, and the letter had been sent back from the Balkans, and after weeks of wandering from depot to depot in England and France had finally been returned to me as undeliverable. About this time, too, a cousin of mine in the R.N. wrote to say that his boat had put into Le Havre recently and, knowing that the Guards Base Depot was at Harfleur, he had made his way thither on the chance of seeing me; unfortunately I had left for the Front two days earlier.

Not long after we arrived, a "School for Young Officers" was established adjacent to the camp, and we were often formed into squads on which they practiced the art of conducting a Parade, under the instruction of our own Sergeants. As may be imagined, there was a good deal of amusement to be gleaned from this kind of work, for the "Young Officers" were novices and frequently managed to tie us up in knots. I remember one occasion, when we were extended in line opposite the Canteen tent, that the officer in charge gave the order, "Quick March" and then forgot what to do next. We marched straight on, until brought up by the wall of the marquee, and the files opposite the entrance continued right up to the bar, where they stood marking time expectantly, until the Sergeant dashed up and gave the "About Turn!" These "Young Officers," who had only just received their commissions, were under canvas in a camp of their own adjoining ours, and they were evidently a gay crowd, for sounds of revelry could be heard coming from their quarters until long past midnight each night.

The "Country Dance" craze, which I mentioned earlier at Boulogne, had spread even to Criel, and several times we suffered instruction in this gentle art, as part of the physical-training parade. It was extremely popular and a cause of endless amusement, in which we all joined heartily, none more so than our Company

Officer, Captain Briggs. One of the " star turns " was a dance known as the "St. Pol Two-step," which was performed en masse and which I described at the time as a mixture of the " Military Two-step " and the " Cake Walk." During these displays we often had an audience of Belgian officers, who were highly amused by the antics of " ces pauvres Anglais," evidently thinking us not a little mad !

Sea bathing was a constant source of pleasure when off duty. There was no restriction on our indulgence in this kind of amusement, and we were often in the water on fine days. We would undress in the tents and go down to the sea wearing overcoats over our bathing slips. The shore was rocky, but just opposite the Plage was a fair-sized strip of sand which afforded a convenient splashing-point for those of us—the great majority—who were non-swimmers. A strong cross-current made it dangerous for any but strong swimmers to venture far out to sea, and one man was nearly drowned while trying to swim round to the next break in the cliff.

In Criel there were several shops which professed to take photographs, and I was rash enough to have my portrait taken, in fulfilment of a long-standing promise to my parents. The " studio " was the back-yard behind a postcard shop, and the picture which emerged from the camera was badly out of focus and extremely weird. No one would have recognised me—I hope!

Sometimes Capt. Briggs took the Company into the woods on Mont Jolibois and there, seated on the banks of a shady lane, gave informal talks on matters ostensibly connected with military routine, the subject having been chosen by ourselves beforehand ; but more often than not, these "lectures" developed into a most entertaining exchange of reminiscences between the Captain and the Sergeant of my Platoon, relating to the time when they had both been privates together. Capt. Briggs was immensely popular in the Company and, although a stickler for discipline, was never unfair and treated us in a frank, straightforward manner. In dealing with delinquents he "knew all the answers," but he was always ready to acknowledge our point of view—which, having been in the ranks himself, he could often appreciate almost as well as we could. It was said—though perhaps not reliably—that he had distinguished himself in action, and had been given the choice between a decoration and a commission.

Our Padre, too, whom I have already mentioned, was well liked. He was always ready to talk to any of us on grounds of mutual respect and equality, and held somewhat independent views on the subject of compulsory Church Parades. Whenever he could, he persuaded the C.O. to make attendance at these services voluntary, and, owing largely to his personality and enthusiasm, they attracted increasing numbers, until the "church" tent became almost too small to hold the congregations. When at Criel he started a series of Sunday-evening "Talks" on religious subjects, followed by a general discussion, when there were often so many interested listeners that the tent became uncomfortably crowded, and the subjects were afterwards debated among ourselves at considerable length, at any rate by the occupants of my tent.

There were several short spells of wet weather during August, and at least one severe thunderstorm, but at other times it was extremely hot, and on such occasions the tents, which furnished the only available shade in the camp, became almost unbearable when the sun was beating down on the canvas. On one of these occasions the pumping engine which supplied the camp with water broke down, and we had to fetch what little we could from the stream in the valley, and use it very sparingly. It was only possible to get enough for drinking and shaving ; to wash, we had to go down to the beach. At this time, too, insects were a great nuisance. Apart from lice, from which even here we were not entirely free, ants swarmed in the tents ; they ran over us at night, and it was almost impossible to keep them out of our food. And in the grasslands surrounding the camp there was a plague of horse-flies, large greyish-brown insects which fastened themselves upon any exposed portion of our anatomy and gorged themselves on our blood. They produced lumps similar to wasp-stings, which were intensely irritating, and we had orders that whatever we were doing—even in the midst of a movement on ceremonial parade—we were to knock away any fly which attempted to settle. Of course, on such formal occasions the flies were—to judge from the ragged performance of drill movements—specially aggressive !

During the latter part of the month we did a good deal of practice in ceremonial drill, such as the "March Past" and "Trooping the Colour." In view of the very encouraging news now coming from the front, it is not altogether surprising that the rumour went round that this was in preparation for a great "Peace Day" review in Hyde Park !

But many things were yet to happen before that day dawned.

Our expected three-months stay at Criel was, however, brought to an abrupt close at the end of seven weeks. The tide had turned at last on the Western Front, and the Allies were everywhere taking the offensive. Following the great advances made by the French and Americans on the Marne, the British line began to move forward, and the "Big Push" in Picardy was opened by the Guards Division (among others) on August 21st at Moyenville, in the course of which they suffered heavy casualties, for the German resistance was very determined at first. An order for reinforcements was sent to Criel, in consequence of which a large draft, which comprised nearly the whole of the personnel of the Battalion with the exception of a nucleus of Headquarters Staff and a few "old sweats," was detailed to leave for the Front, to fill the gaps in the other two Coldstream battalions. Drafts from the other two battalions in the Brigade, the 2nd Irish and 4th Grenadier Guards, also left at the same time.

We bade a reluctant farewell to the sea and to the peace of Criel, packed our kit overnight and turned in early. Reveille sounded at 2.15 on the morning of the 26th, and after we had drawn our day's rations from the cook-house and breakfasted by candle-light, we fell in and marched away from the camp some time before dawn. The column was headed by the band, and was accompanied by nearly all the officers and men who were remaining behind. At Le Treport we boarded the train which awaited us, and the Y.M.C.A. served out hot cocoa. Captain Briggs shook hands with each of us, and seemed genuinely sorry that he was not coming with us; the Padre went along the carriages ladened with magazines and papers, which he distributed among us with reiterated good wishes. At 6.15 the guard's whistle blew and the train steamed out, amid the farewell cheers of those left behind and the strains of the band playing "Good-bye-ee."

The journey was uneventful. We reached Abbéville at nine o'clock, and remained there until half-past seven in the evening : after a slow journey lasting all night, we arrived at Saulty about 10.30 next morning, and left the train. A short march brought us to Berles-au-Bois, where we camped for the night in a wood outside the village. Next day we paraded in the village street, and two officers, representing the 1st and 2nd Coldstream Battalions, selected the men for their respective units by each choosing a man alternately. I was one of those picked for the 1st Battalion, and about eleven o'clock we set off for Adinfer, near which the Battalion was resting in and around some old gun-pits.

THE "BIG PUSH"

THIS latest transfer, from the 3rd Battalion to the 1st Battalion of the Coldstream Guards, was a definite turning-point in my Army life, and the beginning of a period of more settled allegiance than I had yet known. Hitherto, I had been moved from one unit to another at rather short intervals, and had hardly remained with any one Battalion for long enough to become in any real sense a part of it. Now, however, I was to be a member, not only of the same Battalion, but also of the same Company and Platoon, for more than a year—until, in fact, the end of my military service.

My Company in the 1st Coldstream was No. 2, before long to become one of the most celebrated Companies in the Guards Division—not, I hasten to add, solely on account of my presence!— as I shall tell in its proper place ; and I was posted to No. 6 Platoon. In command of the Company at that time was Capt. C. H. Frisby—of whom also I shall have more to say hereafter— and the Sergeant of 6 Platoon was, to my surprise and pleasure, none other than ex-Corporal-of-Horse Reed, who had been in charge of my Platoon in No. 1 Company, Household Batt., in the far-off Windsor days.

At Adinfer Wood we were—or seemed to be—right out of touch with civilisation. The surrounding country on all sides was a wilderness of shell-holes and abandoned trenches, splintered tree-trunks and houses levelled to their foundations. The nearest villages were Ransart and Monchy-au-Bois (the latter is not to be confused with Monchy-le-Preux, near Arras, where I had spent part of the previous winter), but both places were battered entirely out of recognition as human habitations, though at Monchy the Y.M.C.A. had established a temporary canteen (which seldom had anything to sell). There were, of course, no civilians within miles.

The Battalion was camped in and around some empty gun-pits, and lived under light canvas bivouacs, on open ground, for we were out of artillery range. We had no newspapers and very few letters, and consequently, though so near to the war, had very little idea of how it was going. At night we could hear an occasional enemy plane buzzing overhead, but by day our airmen held undisputed command of the air, and every day the sound of the guns seemed to be farther away. A few hundred yards from the camp was a "forward-zone" prisoners-of-war cage, an area of ground surrounded by a high barbed-wire fence, in which newly-captured men were concentrated before being moved further back ; we used to barter cigarettes for medal ribbons or cap-badges with the occupants, who all seemed pleased to be captured. Every night the day's arrivals were taken back to the rear, but by morning the cage was usually full again.

When I joined them the Battalion was out of the line "resting," but with the arrival of the reinforcements from Criel it was obvious that we should soon move forwards to follow up the advance and "keep the ball rolling" with a new attack. In the great offensive which had begun a week ago, the Guards Division had entirely broken the line which the Germans had established after our retirement in March, which in this area had run just west of Ayette, and had recaptured all the ground from which we had been driven on that occasion. The forward battalions of the Division were already somewhere in the neighbourhood of St. Leger, but there had been some heavy fighting during the advance and it was evident that the Germans were determined to sell their positions dearly.

The failure, after such immense efforts, of the "Kaiser's Battle" (now that it was unsuccessful, they were calling it "Ludendorff's Battle"!) and the fact that, despite their reverses, the Allies were able so soon to attack in great force, was already having an effect on German morale, but they were still far from admitting defeat and were resisting desperately. If the pressure could be kept up, they might be forced back to the Hindenburg Line, but they believed that that redoubtable obstacle would resist all attacks. To us, also, the strength of the Line was almost legendary, and we did not expect to be in a position to threaten it seriously for many months to come.

.   .   .   .   .   .

But the final advance to victory, as it unfolded, was amazingly swift. In June the enemy had been farther forward than they had been at any time since the Battle of the Marne in 1914 ; four months later they had been hurled out of France altogether, and were suing for peace. To us who took part in the advance, no less than to people at home, the daily record of successes was incredible. After years of trench-warfare—when every gain of a few yards of worthless mud had only been made at the cost of thousands of lives—when even these meagre prizes were more often than not snatched back again immediately afterwards—when the long meandering black line across the map of France seemed as fixed and immutable a feature of geography as the coast-line itself—when life to the soldier had become an alternation of spells "in the line" and "out on rest," and danger, mud, filth, weariness of mind and body were things inseparable from mere existence, with no more permanent prospect of relief than a "Blighty one"— it is hardly to be wondered at, that we scarcely believed our own senses as, day after day, the advance went on, and, day after day, the black line on the map swept forward beyond places which for years had been to us only unattainable names.

But the Big Push was no miracle. Its spectacular events were the result of long preparation, and were, in fact, the direct outcome of the disasters of the Spring. Though we had been far from realising it at the time, the series of great attacks which had commenced with the Battle of Picardy in March and had continued until the end of June, had been the last desperate efforts of an almost exhausted enemy to force a victory before the American armies could be landed to reinforce the Allies. They knew that against these fresh millions they had no chance, but they had thought that the British and French were even more exhausted and "war-weary" than their own people, and that a tremendous blow would drive us out of the war and leave them free to deal with the new adversary on more equal terms. But, to their chagrin, the Allies reeled but ultimately defeated every onslaught ; nothing could break their lines, thinly though they were held, and every day in which the Germans wasted their strength in vain assaults saw the power of their opponents growing. At last, broken and demoralised, they could go on no longer, and that was the "psychological moment" for which General Foch, the newly-appointed Supreme Allied Commander, had been waiting.

The first of the famous series of "Hammer-blows" fell at Chateau-Thierry, on the Marne, hard on the heels of the last German attack in this same region, and was swiftly followed by others north and east. The enemy resisted strongly, but his line was too long and he had no reserves. The great bulge between Amiens and Rheims wilted and collapsed, and the line surged forward. Then came the turn of the British, and from Arras to the Somme they pressed forward irresistibly. Further attacks in the north, in the Argonne and beyond Verdun gave the enemy no rest, and made it impossible for him to concentrate his shrinking forces in any one area. After the breaking of the Hindenburg Line at the end of September, the issue was no longer in doubt ; Germany had no more strength to hinder our victory, though her troops continued to put up a brave fight to the last against hopeless odds. The final surrender was inevitable after the beginning of October.

That, at any rate, is how history and the people at home saw it. We, who seldom saw a newspaper and who were so close to the actual events as often to be unable to "see the wood for the trees," were—in the earlier stages, anyhow—not so sure of the inevitability of victory. We felt that there must be "a catch in it" somewhere. Presently we should come up against a new line and the old conditions would be re-established — it seemed impossible that the Germans, who had always found a means of frustrating our attacks or of rendering them barren, would allow themselves to be beaten! There must be some subtle scheme behind all this retreating, just as there was after the Battle of the Somme. And in the meantime shell-fire was just as unpleasant.

.   .   .   .   .

I am not attempting, however, to write a History of the " Hundred Days " ; my task is merely to set down an account of such events as actually affected me, an infinitesimal individual among the millions who took part in this, the biggest campaign in the history of the world, in which the units were whole armies and the field of battle was continents and seas, mountains and deserts and forests. For not only in France and Flanders, but in Italy, Serbia, Roumania, Palestine and Mesopotamia, the armies of the Allied Powers were advancing, and all contributed to the final victory.

Four days after I joined the Battalion, on Sunday, September 1st, orders came through that we were to move forward in readiness for a new attack, and we were told to be prepared for an early start on the following morning. We assembled our kit and turned in " all standing," so that after an early breakfast it took only a few minutes to buckle on our equipment and fall in on the road near the gun-pits, in full marching order, at six o'clock. The morning was fine and cloudless, and as soon as the sun got up it became very warm. We were none of us eager to go, for we knew well enough what lay ahead, but the brightness of the sunshine and the invigorating freshness of the morning breeze raised our spirits, and we swung along cheerfully enough, with snatches of song and whistling. The first stage of the march lasted about four hours, during which we halted for the regulation ten minutes in each hour and fell-out at the side of the road. By some freak of acoustics, the sound of the guns was at first curiously muffled and they seemed far less loud than their distance would lead one to expect. We passed by the villages of Adinfer and Boiry, and after crossing the Arras-Bapaume railway near the original British front line, we reached Hamelincourt. On the further side of the village we halted and fell out ; an old trench ran through fields on both sides of the road, and in this we soon constructed rough shelters with wood and corrugated-iron scrounged in the neighbour-hood, and settled in as comfortably as possible for the afternoon. A hot meal was forthcoming, for the field-cookers were accompany-ing the march. The sky clouded over soon after we had dinner and several heavy showers fell, making us glad of our temporary roofs, but the sun was shining again before long.

About five o'clock we were instructed to adjust our equipment from " full pack " to " fighting order," the principal difference of which was that in the latter the pack was discarded and the smaller haversack, which usually hung at our left side, was fastened in its place on our shoulders. The packs, containing most of our personal belongings and spare change of clothing, were then loaded into a lorry to be taken back to Battalion H.Q. until such time as we should come out of the line again ; we were then issued with an extra bandolier of rifle-ammunition, two Mills hand-grenades and a smoke-bomb apiece, and each man had to carry either a shovel or a pick in addition to his rifle. These impedimenta disposed more or less gracefully about our persons, with much clanking and profane expostulation, we were ready to resume the march.

We passed Judas Farm, of which nothing but a heap of bricks and a signpost remained, and reached the outskirts of St. Leger about sunset. Here, on the summit of the ridge between the village and Mory, we bivouacked for the night in some old artillery shelters. We were now in the midst of the guns, and the uproar was sufficient to prevent anyone getting much sleep. One huge naval gun, in particular, about a hundred yards away, fired regularly every few minutes throughout the night with a shattering roar and a blinding flash, the concussion from which brought down showers of grit upon us every time. Otherwise, the night passed without incident. Though we were told by gunners that the area had been heavily bombed from the air on each of several preceding nights, on this occasion the planes stopped away and the enemy's guns also were silent, at least so far as counter-battery fire was concerned.

The ridge upon which we were encamped was the one which I mentioned in Chapter 3 as facing us across the valley of the Sensee beyond Ervillers, on which the Germans had massed for their attack on March 25th, when we could see them swarming down the slope towards us. The fact that we were now back there, and still some distance short of our forward troops, brought home to me the magnitude of the advance that was now in full swing. The "Push," however, in this part of the front was only beginning, and the Hindenburg Line, the real core of the enemy's defence, was still miles ahead. The attack in which we were to take part next day was intended to bring us a good deal nearer to this formidable obstacle, though it was expected that the Germans would strongly contest any attempt to break into even the outworks of their famous "Line."

Some time before daybreak the guns around us increased their fire to barrage intensity, and for about half-an-hour the uproar was terrific. Our rations for the day, with the addition of some chocolate and a lemon each, had been issued overnight, and shortly after dawn we had breakfast, tea being served from the field-kitchens. Afterwards, from various sources, we learned something of the day's programme, at least so far as the Brigade was concerned. At 5.20, the time when the barrage had opened, the 2nd Scots had gone over the top from their positions between Ecoust and Vaulx-Vraucourt ; they were to push on behind the barrage to Lagnicourt, about a mile ahead. This objective attained and consolidated — according to schedule, by 11.30 a.m. — our

Battalion was to go through their lines and press on as far as possible until definitely held up by the enemy's resistance. That was all I was able to discover, for although we knew that the action was to be on a wide front, we were not told anything about the plans for other sectors.

Consequently, about nine o'clock we moved off, to follow up the troops who had "kicked off." For some distance we marched by platoons over open country, and an hour later halted in a trench on the near side of a valley, from the opposite slopes of which the attack had been launched. There was a quantity of abandoned German rifles and ammunition lying about, and our officers had some difficulty in preventing the men from loading themselves up with "souvenirs," all of which would have been useless encumbrances on the march and very much in the way during an attack. Indeed, during the last months of the war the craze for mementoes of any kind was widespread throughout all ranks, and everyone wanted to possess some articles which they could claim had been "captured" from the enemy: badges, medal-ribbons, pieces of equipment, bullets, army biscuits, even an old letter picked up in an abandoned trench—anything that had belonged to a German. The man who was lucky enough to find a German revolver could obtain a good price for it from one of our officers. I think even field-guns would have been appropriated if there had been the slightest chance of getting them home!

By this time the artillery fire had died down almost to silence, and on either side of us we could see the guns being rushed forward. This made it clear that considerable progress had been made, but it was with surprise and excitement that we learned a little later that there had been no opposition, and that the "Jocks" had gone well beyond their objective without a casualty save those caused by our own shells.

"Jerry" had retired during the night!

This altered the whole scheme of attack, of course, and our officers had no choice but to await further orders. We moved across the valley to some dugouts, evidently of German construction, just under the ridge from which the Scots had "kicked off" that morning, and made ourselves comfortable. The cookers were still following, so we had dinner and rested for about an hour. Fresh instructions having arrived from Headquarters, the march was then resumed, and we entered what had been No-man's-land only a few hours previously.

There were remarkably few signs of conflict. We passed the bodies of two Jocks near the starting-point; one of them showed no visible sign of injury and it was difficult to believe that he was not alive and leaning back against the bank watching us through half-closed eyes. The ground of course was pitted thickly with shell-holes, but that was the same in all the country we had covered since yesterday morning. Farther on, we came upon several

German corpses in a group, probably some of an unfortunate rear-guard left behind until the last moment to maintain the illusion that the position was still being held in force. In another place—grim relic, more impressive to me even than the dead bodies—I noticed a single, isolated human foot, newly severed and still clad in sock and boot. There was no sign of its owner, nor any means of knowing whether it had belonged to a German or to one of our own men. By this time—I hoped—whoever he is, he is well on his way to Blighty.

The artillery had now entirely ceased firing, and the sun shone brilliantly over the silent fields which had so lately been swept by a tornado of destruction. Hitherto, we had marched in "artillery formation," the four platoons of the Company forming the angles of a diamond and separated by about a hundred yards from each other; but now, so peaceful was the scene, we closed up and marched in "column-of-route," as though we had been a dozen miles behind the line. It was an exhilarating experience, after trench warfare, to be moving freely over open ground in pursuit of a retreating enemy. Every step, in our imagination, seemed to bring Blighty nearer!

Soon we began to meet men coming back, singly or in twos and threes—runners, stretcher-bearers, walking-wounded, etc.—and all brought the same amazing tale: "We can't find Jerry. He's gone —— right off the map!" Gunners, too, when asked why the guns were not firing, said (though in rather more "flowery" language): "What's the use of firing? There's nothing to shoot at!"

On we marched, and on, excitement rising to fever-heat, and still the uncanny stillness persisted, until we almost began to believe that the war had ended and that the barrage had literally blown the German army over the Rhine. It was the queerest "attack" most of us had ever imagined. A few aeroplanes buzzed around at times, low down and obviously searching the ground, and away in the distance two or three tall columns of smoke indicated burning dumps, but not a machine-gun, not a rifle, broke the almost Sabbath calm, and the sunlit air was full of the song of birds. As we came out on the high ground near Lagnicourt, a wide panorama over miles of open country spread before us, and only the ruined village in the hollow and the scarred ground reminded us that we were not taking part in a "Field-day" at Windsor.

Presently we reached the road which runs between Lagnicourt and Morchies, and here we were ordered to halt. The enemy had at last been located in Moeuvres and along the Canal du Nord—the Hindenburg Line itself! he had given up nearly all the forward defences without a fight! According to the altered plans, we were to go no farther that day, so we fell out and set to work constructing quarters for the night. These had, of necessity, to be improvised, for every village, every single building or barn, in all that region was wrecked beyond habitation. The Germans had seen to it that the country we re-occupied was a desert, not so much during their present retreat, for there would hardly have been time for so much calculated destruction, but much earlier, during their evacuation in 1917. There were a number of unroofed sand-bagged shelters along the side of the road, and these we severally appropriated ; they were little more than depressions in the ground, but were better than sleeping altogether in the open. I and two other men of 6 Platoon, Summers and " Dusty " Smith, joined in occupation of a hole in the bank about six feet square, and after staking out our claim we went prospecting.

By good luck, some little distance away we found an unoccupied trench which was elaborately revetted and fitted with corrugated-zinc shelters. After a careful search for explosive " booby-traps " —Jerry was fond of arranging pleasantries of that sort for his successors—we lost no time in stripping the roofs from some of the shelters and carting the material back to our bivouac, where we soon had quite a passable habitation. Having spread the news of our find to the rest of the Company, the trench was very soon stripped of everything portable it contained.

After finishing our " house-building " we wandered down into Lagnicourt in search of water, for our flasks had been emptied long since and we were feeling decidedly dry. But there we were not so lucky ; there was only one well in the place which had been certified as fit for drinking by the M.O., and at that one we found a long queue lined up with dixies, water-bottles and tin hats. We had to take our turn at the end of the line, and long before we reached the well it was dry. However, before long the water-carts came up from the rear, so it was " san fairy an."

Lagnicourt was in a terrible mess. There was not a house or cottage which was more than a burnt-out shell, many were just heaps of unrecognisable rubble, and the streets were strewn with wreckage of the most gruesome kind. In one place a waggon, with horses and driver, lay a heap of indescribable fragments, where a shell had burst upon it, and there were dead horses everywhere. They were not all recently dead, either, for one which lay beside the road by which we reached the village advertised its presence by such a powerful odour of decay that we were obliged to make a wide detour to windward.

By the time we returned to " camp " it was nearly dark, and a " gas-guard," for which I " clicked," was detailed. I was fortunate, however, in being picked for the first relief, from nine to ten o'clock, which meant that I was able to get a good uninterrupted sleep before my next turn on sentry. Hostile aeroplanes were active for a time during the first part of the night, and dropped bombs on the guns some distance behind us ; otherwise, apart from a moderate amount of gun-fire from our batteries, the night was quiet.

When we turned in we noticed a queer, unpleasant smell in our bivouac, like decaying vegetables, but being very tired and used to smells by this time, we ignored it and went to sleep. Several times during the night we were disturbed by the scampering of rats, and no wonder—for next morning I happened to see what looked like the corner of a dirty blanket sticking up from the ground, and on investigation we found that we had been sleeping almost on top of a dead German, buried about a foot below the surface.

.   .   .   .   .   .

Reveille sounded at five-thirty, and breakfast appeared about half-an-hour later. Shortly afterwards the Battalion formed up and we resumed the march, going as before in column-of-route and by easy stages. Striking across country, for the most part along artillery tracks in an easterly direction, we passed another valley, and on the summit of the opposite rise came to a road. Following this for a short distance, we reached a slight hollow in which a transport depot was being formed. It was by now nearly mid-day and the order to halt was given, so throwing off our equipment a short distance from the road we applied ourselves to the business of dinner. We were evidently approaching the new line at last, for over our heads floated an observation balloon, and several others were visible on either hand. About every ten minutes a long-range shrapnel shell burst high above us in a vain effort to hit the balloon.

The weather was still fine and sunny, with a slight haze high up in the sky, and aircraft of both sides were very busy. We watched squadrons of British machines manoeuvring at various heights and sweeping to and fro across the German lines apparently with impunity, though constantly followed by the black bursts of anti-aircraft fire. German anti-aircraft shells produced billows of jet-black smoke, whilst British ones formed round white cloudlets. Occasionally a Bosche plane appeared overhead at a great height, but it was quickly chased off by our patrolling machines every time it showed up. There was no doubt that we held command of the air, for enemy planes hardly dared to approach the line during daylight.

Later, orders were received that we were to remain in that area for the night. The 1st Coldstream was the supporting battalion of the Brigade, and we were to relieve the 2nd Scots Guards in the line the following night. Captain Frisby thereupon took possession of an old trench about a hundred yards forward along the road, as billets for No. 2 Coy., and we proceeded to make ourselves at home. The trench was, I believe, a part of the old British front line, as it had been before the German advance in March, and was naturally not in very good repair, but we soon made it reasonably habitable. Our position, as far as I can now identify it, was about halfway along a straight line between Pronville and Boursies, and in front of us a rise of ground screened us from the enemy positions along the Canal du Nord and—what was more important—we were not under observation from Bourlon Hill. This latter eminence, the scene of bloody operations by the Guards Division in 1917, dominated the whole countryside, and had been visible to us from far behind Lagnicourt. For the next three weeks it was a source of constant uneasiness to us, for every movement in the British lines over a wide area must have been visible from its summit, and it was one of the main bulwarks of the German defence of the road to Cambrai.

By the time we had finished the construction of our bivouacs in the trench it was getting towards evening, and as we were not yet in the line—that is, not in the front line or the support line—there were no sentries to be posted other than a look-out for possible gas, from which duty I was exempt on this occasion. About half-past six a violent cannonading broke out some distance to the southward and lasted for half an hour. We were told that in that direction the advance had not progressed so far on the previous day, and that an attack was being made with the object of bringing this sector into line with the rest of the front.

During the evening Sergeant Reed and the senior Corporal caught a bird, which they proceeded to cook for supper. They told me that it was a young partridge—a description which, though I am no poultry expert, seemed to me to be "wishful thinking!" But as it is not tactful to question the omniscience of N.C.O.'s, in natural history no less than in other matters, I agreed; but my acquiescence was not rewarded with more than a sniff of the undoubtedly appetising odour of its cooking.

. . . . . .

The advance, in this area at any rate, was by now definitely held up. The Germans had reached the supposed security of the Hindenburg Line, the deep belt of super-modern fortifications based on the Canal du Nord, and it was evident that only a very big effort would dislodge them from this, their last and strongest organised line of defence. They would hang on desperately here, if only because a breach in the famous " Line " would have disastrous political repercussions on the morale of the German people, who had been taught to regard it as a symbol of the invincibility of the Reich. However, we had no doubt that the effort would be made, or that it would be successful.

In that belief, though—as appeared from later information—the people at home did not all share our optimism. It is said that Mr. Lloyd George and the War Cabinet endeavoured to persuade Sir Douglas Haig to delay the attack until the Spring, being afraid, seemingly, of the effect an abortive attempt might have on the morale of the Army and the nation. Haig, however, was of the opinion that the German defence could be broken by an immediate drive, before they had time to recover from the recent defeats, and that by resolute action the war could be ended before the Winter. Consequently, preparations were at once begun, and the result abundantly justified his optimism.

In the meantime, we reverted more or less to the " normal " conditions of trench warfare, though with the instinctive feeling that it was only a temporary pause—for of course we knew nothing of the plans and intentions of the High Command. On September 5th, the 3rd Grenadiers held the front line around Moeuvres in our sector, with the 2nd Scots in support. We, the 1st Coldstreams, were in reserve, and were to relieve the Jocks that night.

The day passed without much incident. The road in front of our trench was shelled intermittently at long range, but only one shell fell anywhere near us. The weather was fine, though the sky was partially obscured by low, broken masses of cloud, and it continued to be very warm for the time of the year. During the afternoon we saw a German observation balloon brought down in flames by a British airman, but hardly had it disappeared when, out of the clouds overhead darted a German plane, bent on reprisals, and made a swift dart at the balloon which hung above us. The observers dropped out immediately and floated safely to earth in parachutes, while the ground-crews began frantically to wind the balloon in; but the great sausage was doomed. Sweeping round it in fantastic and daring gyrations, the Bosche poured a stream of incendiary bullets into the envelope as fast as his machine-gun could pump them out. Our Lewis-gunners on the ground took up the tale, and the air was full of the whine of bullets. The anti-aircraft batteries also fired at the intrepid invader, but the shells necessarily burst so low that they were as dangerous to the balloon as to the aeroplane, and indeed distributed their shrapnel so indiscriminately that they put the wind up us. We retreated hurriedly into the shelter of the trench and got underneath our tin hats. One man was wounded slightly in the head by a splinter, and retired to the dressing-station in good spirits—I believe he got back to Blighty on the strength of it ! But all their efforts were unavailing, for soon a small patch of red appeared on the side of the balloon, and opened out swiftly like a great scarlet flower, until in a few seconds the ill-fated monster sank slowly to earth, a roaring mass of flames.

Seeing that he was successful, Herr Fritz wasted no time but darted away to the next balloon about a mile to the north, and brought that one down also, while at the same time another Fokker attacked and destroyed the one on the other side of us. Feeling, no doubt, thoroughly satisfied with themselves, the two machines then sailed away complacently together, supremely regardless of the following cloud of shrapnel. Soon after they had disappeared over their own lines, a British plane came tearing along with the fussy, important air of a policeman arriving after a street accident. We greeted it with ironical cheers.

About seven o'clock in the evening we received orders to move off, so we collected our kit and fell in on the open ground in front of the trench. Heavy clouds had been rolling up from the south-west, and before we were ready to start, a sharp thunderstorm burst upon us. Rain came down in torrents and ran in streams over our equipment, penetrated our clothing and left us thoroughly soaked and bedraggled. The storm did not last long, however, and just as we moved off the setting sun broke through a rift in the clouds, spreading a perfect double rainbow over the eastern sky.

We marched down the road for a short distance and then turned off along a light-railway track which led to the left. After following this for some time it brought us, at about nightfall, to the crest of the ridge overlooking the valley of the Canal, and we then struck across country in semi-darkness. Progress here was slow and difficult, for the ground was full of shell-holes, mostly old and overgrown, and was littered with quantities of rusty and tangled barbed-wire, over which we picked our way in the murk with much stumbling and cursing. We were now in part of the trench system which the Germans had held after their counter-attack in December, 1917, and after about an hour's scrambling and tearing of clothes we reached the present Support Line. We clambered in and took over from the 2nd Scots, who filed away, nothing loath, into the darkness.

No. 6 Platoon was at first assigned quarters in a large dugout on the right of our sector, fairly clean and fitted with wire bunks; but we had scarcely settled in, congratulating ourselves on our luck, when some Artillery officers appeared and laid claim to the place. There was a prolonged parley, and Sergeant Reed sent a messenger to Battalion H.Q. for instructions. He returned with our Platoon-officer, but unfortunately the Artillerymen overbore the latter by their superior rank and we had to turn out. Another dugout was found for us on the extreme left of the line, in a trench which seemed not to have been occupied by our troops previously; it was very dirty and uncomfortable compared with the one we had left. But when we had turned out a large quantity of German rubbish and had tidied up a bit, we were not at all badly off. Indeed, we were in luck's way to have a dugout at all, instead of having to live in the open trench, like some of the other platoons.

.   .   .   .   .

There was little of sufficient interest or importance to record during the next day. We followed the usual routine of trench life, and, being under direct observation from Bourlon Hill, which was immediately opposite us across the Canal, we had strict orders to show ourselves in the open air as little as possible. Indeed, except for the inevitable spells of sentry-go on the fire-step outside the dugout entrance, we were kept underground nearly all day. Our position was on a slope overlooking Moeuvres, which at that time was still in German hands, and although we suffered little from direct fire, we had several times to resort to our gas-masks when gas-shells landed in the vicinity. Down in the valley there was almost continuous restlessness, where patrols of either side were constantly trying to capture advance posts in and around the village.

During the morning our Platoon-officer, Mr. Willock-Pollen, came along to inspect the quarters he had secured for us after our " ejectment " the previous night, and brought with him a recent copy of the " Times " which he had just received from home. He said he thought we might like to read the latest news of the advance; but the real reason for his consideration on this occasion was apparent when we found that the paper also contained an announcement of his own engagement, an event which had taken place during his recent leave. He received our congratulations with an appropriate mixture of pride and embarrassment.

A little later, while visiting the latrine, I took the opportunity of exploring an unoccupied part of the trench beyond our post, and came upon a number of pamphlets and maps printed in German, showing the daily extent of the Allies' advance since August 21st; they were evidently propaganda broadcast with the object of impressing on the Germans the futility of continuing the war. We had several times watched this being done—sometimes the leaflets were dropped from a plane flying over the enemy lines, and at others, when the wind was favourable, small balloons would be sent up which, by a mechanical device, released a shower of pamphlets at regular intervals. I took a handful of them back to the dugout, where they were eagerly seized upon as "souvenirs," though Sgt. Reed reprimanded me for wandering away from the post.

We were told during the day that an attack was planned for the following morning, in which we were to take a leading part, but night brought the not-unwelcome news that it had been cancelled.

.   .   .   .   .   .

It may be interesting, perhaps, to attempt to describe the events of that one night in some detail, and see how much of the atmosphere of a typical " quiet " night in the trenches I can recapture in retrospect. Not that there is much to tell, in point of incident—if there was, it would not have been a " quiet " night— but it may serve to exemplify conditions in the trenches during normal times when there was no particular " stunt " on, typical of many such another night I had spent in the line at different times and places ; and in describing my own feelings—very inadequately and unskilfully, it is true—I believe I am putting into words more or less what the majority of men thought and felt in similar circumstances, though they might not always own to it.

About half an hour after sunset, as it begins to grow dusk, we turn out and line the trench on each side of the post, with loaded rifles and fixed bayonets. This is the evening " Stand-to " and lasts for an hour, until darkness has fallen completely, for dusk and dawn are the times when, theoretically, there is most danger of an

G

attack. Actually, however, it is the time when we feel safest from disturbances of that kind, for "Jerry" undoubtedly knows all about this invariable daily routine (he observes the same ritual himself), so that if he has aggressive intentions it is unlikely that the first move would be made at a time when we are known to be thoroughly prepared. Still—one never knows, and we keep our eyes skinned. We stand about in the trench, nursing our rifles and talking, and as the dusk deepens some of us get up on the firestep and peer out across No-man's-land at the tangled wire and grass-grown shell-holes, secure in the knowledge that we cannot now be seen from the lines opposite. One has to be wary, though, for occasionally there is a sharp rattling splutter as a machine-gun traverses at random, and we duck below the parapet while the fugitive bullets whine harmlessly overhead. A light mist gathers in the valley and the Verey lights begin their nightly dance. They are nearly all sent up from the other side, and as Jerry has an apparently-unlimited store of them we are content to let him provide nearly all the illumination that is needed.

The Orderly Officer for the day comes along to see that the post is properly manned and to receive the Sergeant's report, and presently the order to "Stand-down" is passed back. Thereupon, with the exception of the sentry on duty, we all file down into the dugout and get out our rations. There is a brazier made from an old biscuit tin filled with glowing coke at the bottom of the steps ; most of the smoke escapes up the shaft into the open air as through a chimney, but quite enough remains below to make our eyes smart and run as we boil water in our mess-tins and make tea. My supper consists of the residue of a tin of bully, a piece of bread and some broken bits of Army biscuit, helped down with a little of my jealously hoarded ration of butter. The tea is a success, despite the tendency of tea-leaves to float on the surface; it is well sweetened and its warmth is very comforting.

The low, oblong dugout is like the interior of a huge coffin buried thirty feet underground; the air is stuffy with damp and the frowsty smell of humanity, while the smoke from the brazier, to which our cigarettes and pipes add their quota, makes a haze through which the glimmering of half a dozen candle-ends struggles gallantly but ineffectually. There is a babel of voices and a clatter of equipment and rifles. Conversation is discursive and trivial, for the most part, but generally good-humoured and often humorous, though the language would hardly pass muster in a drawing-room. There might be arguments—wordy, repetitive and leading nowhere —and a good deal of blasphemously-expressed grousing, but it all amounts to very little. Three or four men are squatting on the ground in a group, playing "nap" with a dirty pack of cards; one or two are trying to read, or catching lice in the seams of their tunics. Someone starts to sing, and others join in: the songs are usually popular ballads or music-hall hits, among which the

favourite seem to be such sentimental ditties as " Sweet Adeline "
or " It's only a Beautiful Picture," rendered with exaggerated
feeling.   Or it might be one of those lugubrious satirical "classics"
which poke fun at ourselves and the "windiness" which we all feel
but do not acknowledge :

> " I want to go home,
> I want to go home,
> I don't want to go in the trenches no more,
> Where there's bullets and whizz-bangs and shrapnel
>   galore;
>
> Put me over the sea,
> Where the Alleman can't get at me—
> Oh, my !   I don't want to die,
> I want to go ho-o-o-me ! "

or else:

> " Send out the Army and the Navy,
>   Send out the rank and file,
> Send out the good old Territorials—
>   They'll face the danger with a smile.
>
> Send out the boys of the Old Brigade
>   Who made old England free;
> Send out my brother, my sister or my mother,
>   But *for God's sake! don't send me!* "

Presently there is a call down the entrance shaft, of
" Rations ! " and two or three men of a fatigue party clatter down
the dugout steps and deposit sandbags containing supplies for the
next day. We crowd eagerly round the Sergeant as he distributes
the mail that accompanies them, calling each name aloud and
throwing the letter or package to its owner. There are several for
me: the Sergeant calls, " Noakes, coming over ! "—" Noakes,
here's another ! "—" Noakes, you lucky b——! "—" Christ
Almighty still they come ! "—with friendly groans and chaffing
from the others. There are a couple of newspapers and a magazine
for me as well, and I am at once beseiged by requests for a rever-
sionary interest in these, for reading matter is very scarce, and
before they are completely worn out they will have passed through
dozens of hands and will have been read from cover to cover,
advertisements included. I retire to my " bed " with my letters,
and for a short space my surroundings fade into the background
as I abandon myself to memories of home.

Then, as " it takes me " for sentry-duty soon after midnight,
I turn in for a short sleep. We are not allowed to undress, of
course, or even to remove our boots, but I pile my equipment
against the wall in the way which experience has taught me makes
the least knobbly pillow and, with the facility of those days which

I have often envied since, I am quickly asleep. It seems as if I have hardly lapsed into unconsciousness, though, when I feel the Sergeant shaking my shoulder, telling me that it is time to take my place on the fire-step. All around are slumbering forms, snoring or muttering in their sleep, or turning over with an impatient sigh, dimly visible in the red glow of the brazier. Half-asleep, cold and hardly sure whether I am awake or still dreaming, I huddle on my equipment and tin hat, pick up my rifle and stumble up the dugout steps. At the top the chill night air, after the stuffiness below, shocks me awake like a cold douche. The man I am relieving, with a sleepy " Good-night," disappears into the dugout, and I am alone.

I get up on the fire-step and peer around. The night is very dark, and I can see only a few yards ahead. Overhead, a few stars show through rents in the clouds and a breeze blows coldly. There is very little firing, although every ten seconds or so a flash on the horizon shows that the artillery is awake. Each night, from soon after dusk until about midnight, the guns shell the back areas and cross-roads in the hope of impeding the supply of rations and munitions to the trenches, but it is now one o'clock and things are quiet. Down in the valley below, the Verey lights curve upwards at intervals, but their light makes very little difference to the darkness where I am. A sudden rattle announces a machine-gun, and there is an isolated rifle-shot or two.

As I lean my elbows on the damp sandbags and look across towards the invisible horizon, my thoughts return to the letters I have just received, and I wonder if they are all asleep at home, or if, like me, they are watching flashes in the sky, from a distant air-raid on London. My home !—how well and in what detail I remember it. Scenes of other days flash through my mind, days before I knew anything of war, so long ago in retrospect that they are almost like recollections of a previous incarnation ! My mind drifts to the early days of the war, to my unsuccessful efforts to enlist (would that they had remained unsuccessful, I think!), to the now-incredible enthusiasm of my first days in the Army. . . . Windsor and recruit-training. . . . the draft . . . .Arras, the H.B. . . . . the " March do " . . . . I try to visualise the end of the war and my return home, but there imagination fails me; it seems almost impossible that the war should ever end, that there should ever come a time when the old life can be taken up again and I shall live in comfort and safety once more. Now that it has me firmly in its grip, it seems as if only a miracle could make the military machine loose its hold on me. My mind refuses to envisage any more permanent release than an almost impossibly wonderful vision of " Leave."

A sudden outburst of machine-gun fire from in front brings me back to reality with a jerk. A fusilade of rifle-shots joins in, some of which whine away high over my head. More machine-guns rattle furiously and Verey lights shoot into the air. What is it?—a raid? If so, they are sure to put down a barrage on the Support line. I watch tensely for the "S.O.S.," but there are no coloured lights among the flares, and gradually the shooting dies down. I heave a sigh of relief. Only someone in the front line got the wind up!

Wind-up—yes; probably some sentry in a forward post has caught sight of an enemy patrol in No-man's-land and opened fire —or perhaps they attacked him! This reminds me of stories which have been going round lately, of German snipers who have lain hidden between our lines, to creep out in the darkness and attack sentries in isolated posts. I begin to lose hold on my imagination, and the dim shapes of the tumbled ground in front take on new and sinister forms. That dark lump a few yards away—is it still in the same place? I feel sure that it has moved since I last looked that way—not only which, but its shape has changed—it is creeping, creeping towards me! I strain my eyes into the darkness, hardly daring to breathe, and am just about to fire, when a Verey light goes up and I realise that there is nothing there but a hummock of rank grass.

Frightened of shadows! That's a nice way to go on! There is a sudden gust of wind, and something—perhaps a loose strand of wire or an empty tin—makes a distinct scraping sound, like someone moving cautiously over rough ground. I grip my rifle again and strain my ears, every nerve and muscle taut as I wait for a repetition of the noise, but the seconds pass and nothing happens. I give myself a shake and turn up the collar of my tunic against the grave-like chill of the wind. This won't do! Mustn't get the wind up over nothing. It is very lonely, though—if only I had a companion! I almost wish we were in the front line instead of in support, for there are always two sentries on duty together in the front-line posts. Indeed, what is the use of single sentries in the line? If anyone got near enough to attack me—if, for instance, they got into the trench farther along, where it is unguarded between the posts, and came at me suddenly round the corner of the traverse —how could I give the alarm quickly enough to the others? They are probably all asleep down there, anyway. How cosy and companionable it must be in the dugout! Its black entrance near the end of the fire-step looks friendly and home-like, and if I step down into the trench for a moment I can smell the warm smoky air coming up from below. How is the time going? Only half-past one?—my watch must have stopped: I seem to have been here for several hours already! No, it's still ticking.

Boom! Boom!—hullo, the guns are waking up. Crash! Crash! That's all right—well over. So long as they don't come any nearer, the sound of the shells is almost a relief. Crash! Crash! They are firing at the batteries behind me. It is hard luck on the gunners, of course; but to us of the "P.B.I." it always appears more seemly that the guns of both sides should fire at each other, rather than at us!

A big bombing aeroplane passes high overhead on its way to some distant target far behind the fighting-front. It is invisible, but I can hear the laboured " zoog—zoog—zoog " of its engines as they drag their heavy load of bombs apparently with difficulty across the stars, and I can see the red pin-points of light from bursting shells that follow it. Gradually the sound dies away in the distance, and there is a renewed outbreak of firing in the valley. Confound the fellows! Why can't they keep quiet! They'll stir up some serious trouble between them, if they don't look out. For I cannot avoid a foolish and half-superstitious feeling that the brute-beast, War, is sleeping and might be awakened by too much noise.

Crack—whish—Crash! They are firing at the trenches now. I saw the flash of that gun on Bourlon Hill. They can fire point-blank at us from there by direct observation. Crack—wheeEEE—CRUMP! That one was not far away! Crack—Crash! Another, farther off that time. I don't think they are after this part of the trench after all; probably the communication-trench farther down . . .

So the long two hours drag slowly on, in alternate spells of boredom and spasms of "wind-up." It is cold, with the hopeless chill of the "dead hours," and my feet are like ice. I try several times to warm them by stamping on the duckboards, but without much success, and put my rifle down for a moment while I do a hasty "cabby-flap." Oh! for a fire, a hot drink and a soft bed!— but that is dreaming of the impossible. My eyes are heavy with the sleep which I know I must not give way to, and smart with straining them into the darkness. My limbs feel numbed and my mouth is dry. I would give a great deal to be able to smoke, but dare not while on sentry, lest an officer should come along.

At long last my relief appears—late, of course (or so I think!) —and, after a brief word of greeting, I am free to retire thankfully into the dugout, for a couple of hours' sleep before " Stand-to " at dawn.

The following day was comparatively uneventful. The front was quiet, with only a normal amount of shelling, and until evening the weather was brilliantly fine and quite hot. There was little to do except lounge about in the more sheltered parts of the trench or in the dugout during most of the day. We were to go back " in Reserve " that night, and our relief arrived unusually early— about eight-thirty, just after the evening " Stand-down."

" Handing-over " a position in the line was always a somewhat slow and confused operation, for certain formalities had to be performed by the N.C.O.'s, the position of the bomb-store indicated, any points where snipers were troublesome or which were specially overlooked by the enemy in daylight, etc., pointed out to the incoming troops ; and section-corporals had to collect their men in readiness to move back—all in darkness and without noise. There was an air of agitation and impatience, and everyone was eager to be gone. " For Christ's sake, get a move on ! " could be heard muttered on all sides ; now that release was at hand, everyone was windy, with the unspoken fear lest something should happen at the last moment —just as the bravest man, on his way back to go on leave, would jump at the sound of a rifle or dive for cover if a shell exploded a hundred yards away ! The trench, for the moment, is crowded with men, both ours and the relieving troops, and would be a particularly vulnerable target, should the enemy chance to open fire.

But this time all was well, and at last we climbed out of the trench and started back, one platoon at a time. There was no communication trench, and we had to go, as we had come, over open ground. Each party was led by a " guide "—one of our own men who had been over the same route previously by daylight and was supposed to know the way—but No. 6 Platoon had not gone far before our guide confessed that he had completely lost himself. Not unnaturally, our comments were unrestrained, both to the unfortunate guide and to each other, and for what seemed like hours we wandered about in a long string, hanging up in wire, falling into shell-holes, tripping over stones, and cursing the war, the Germans, the guide and things in general. Presently we wandered unwittingly in front of a battery of field-guns, which announced its presence by firing over our heads, nearly knocking us over with the unexpected concussion, deafening us with the explosions, and half-blinding us with the flash. Then, indeed, the air turned blue for several yards around !

At length, by dint of repeated enquiries, Mr. Willock-Pollen, who was apparently the only man among us with any remnants of temper left, managed to land us on the right track—a light-railway track, to be exact—and before long we came out on the road not far from our previous camping-place. Here we halted by the roadside, and some Y.M.C.A. people served out a welcome snack of cocoa and biscuits while we waited for the rest of the Battalion to come up.

In about half-an-hour all the platoons had arrived at the rendezvous, and the march was resumed in column-of-route. We reached Lagnicourt about midnight, heralded by two big shells which burst just ahead of us, and passing through the village we mounted the rise beyond. Here, on the crest of the ridge, alongside the Lagnicourt-Noreuil road, we found our " billets," a trench provided nominally with bivouacs for our use—but so " nominal " was the accommodation that it took us some time and no little labour to furnish shelter for everyone. When at last we wrapped our greatcoats round us and settled down, even bomb-dropping in the neighbourhood did not suffice to prevent us from sleeping soundly.

. . . . . .

For a whole glorious week we were " on rest," camping there in the trench between Lagnicourt and Noreuil, and the days, though not lacking in hard work—for " rest " must be understood in the technical Army sense — passed all too quickly. Parades, field-training, bad weather and some very tiring fatigues were all taken in our stride, with the minimum of grousing, for we were " out of the line " for the time being, and could breathe freely once more. As one always did on Active Service, we made the most of the respite, thinking neither of the past nor of the future, but getting the utmost out of the present, despite the fact that we were in the midst of desolate country and miles from civilisation.

Indeed, the utter devastation of all this territory was appalling. For nearly two years it had been an almost constant battlefield, ever since the Germans had evacuated it after the Battle of the Somme. During their retreat at that time the enemy had made it a desert by deliberate and systematic destruction, not only destroying the buildings but even cutting down the trees and uprooting the shrubs. Since then, the ground had been ploughed and re-ploughed by shell-fire and advancing and retreating armies, until not a bush or scarcely a blade of grass remained to conceal the bareness of the tumbled and poisoned earth. The villages were heaps of rubble and broken bits of brickwork, and it was only when one came upon garden flowers growing wild in unexpected corners among the debris that one realised that here had once been carefully-tended gardens and flourishing human homes.

And the dead lay everywhere, for there were so many corpses and our advance had been so recent that the burial-squads had hardly commenced their gruesome task ; even on our hill-top there was always a faint smell of putrefaction. One came upon bodies in collapsed trenches, in ditches or shell-holes, sun-dried and horrible, and all more or less rifled for " souvenirs "—for most men became callous with use, and a belt or a jack-knife, a good pair pair of boots or a revolver, were of more value to a living Englishman than to a dead German. The ground was strewn with broken rifles, ammunition, shell-cases, mouldy equipment, rusty bayonets, and all the jetsam of a retreating army. Salvage corps were busily engaged in collecting all this debris into dumps, which were surrounded with barbed-wire and carefully guarded—we, during our stay in the district, had to provide a nightly guard on one which was near our camping-place—but I failed to imagine that anyone would want to steal such useless rubbish, or what use it could be for any purpose when salvaged.

Arms drill, bombing practice, kit- and rifle-inspections kept us busy during most of the day, and as we had recovered our packs and their contents, we were expected to keep our brasses shining—no easy task when living in a muddy trench. An order was even made that our trousers were to be kept creased ! Our billets were semi-underground, being burrows constructed by roofing over sections of the trench, which was very narrow, so that there was seldom room for more than one man in each "bivouac." My "home" was about six feet long by two feet wide, just long enough to lie down in, and I roofed it with a sheet of corrugated-zinc covered with a layer of earth to keep the warmth in. It was the nearest thing to a grave, in size and position, I have ever lived in! In the walls of the trench on either side I scraped ledges to hold my small kit, food, etc., and spread my ground-sheet on the floor to keep out the damp. When I had made up my bed of blankets and greatcoat, with my pack for a pillow, and dropped a piece of sacking over the entrance, it was quite a cosy little "bug-hutch" in the light of a candle. Strange, how little constituted comfort on Active Service! My two pals, "Dusty" and Summers, occupied similar constructions "next door."

Being below ground-level, however, had its disadvantages, and after one experience of a heavy thunder-shower, which nearly flooded me out, I found it necessary to dig a large hole outside to carry off the water—with only partial success. There were several miniature cloudbursts during the week, against the worst of which we had little effective shelter. One night I was doing duty as a member of the guard on a salvage dump, and being off sentry had "got down to it," when a heavy rain-storm broke over us; the canvas tent which formed the roof of the "guard-room" had been loosely fixed and sagged in places, and the water collected in a bulge just over my head. The weight soon proved too much for the fastenings, the pegs tore free, and the whole cascade poured full upon me, waking me up very thoroughly and literally washing me out of bed!

The nearest village, other than Lagnicourt, was Noreuil, down in the valley on the other side of our ridge. A railway passed through it which was methodically shelled in a lazy fashion every morning and evening by a long-range gun in the vicinity of Bourlon Hill. We went there one day for a bath in an improvised bath-house, and a change of underwear. Welcome though the bath was, it was not so necessary as the clean clothes. One of the things which surprised me at the front was that, despite the often filthy conditions in which we lived, we were seldom bodily dirty. Often, coming out of the line after two or three weeks, looking like tramps and "bearded like the pard," on taking our clothes off our skin would be white as milk, except for hands and faces. The reason was, of course, that strenuous work caused us to sweat profusely and frequently, and every particle of dirt on our bodies was soaked into our clothes. These, indeed, became unspeakably stale and smelly, but our bodies were clean.

Cut off in the midst of desolation from contact with civilisation, we had little news of the outside world, other than letters and occasional newspapers from home, though these were not very frequently forthcoming. Capt. Frisby, realising how little we knew about the progress of the war, would sometimes call the Company together for an informal "lecture," in order to give us an outline of the latest events. I remember the thrill he gave us one evening, when he told us that the Americans and French had succeeded in wiping out the St. Mihiel Salient. This sharp dent in the Allied line south-east of Verdun had been so familiar and unchanging a feature of the war-map for nearly four years that its disappearance seemed a sure portent of the coming of peace.

During our week's "rest" a further stage in the approach to the Hindenburg Line was effected by a British advance to the south of our area, which resulted in the capture of Havrincourt, thus bringing the line into a favourable strategic position for the big attack which no one doubted would soon take place. Another operation of the same kind we were able to witness ourselves. We were sitting on the ground at the summit of the ridge, whence a wide view of the line in the direction of the Canal was open, and the Captain was explaining the method of a new form of attack behind a barrage of smoke-bombs. Glancing at his watch, he said, "You will soon see an example of what I have been describing. An attack is being made this evening, over there in front; it is now almost zero-hour." We sprang to our feet and strained our eyes in the direction of the line, and there, sure enough, far away below Bourlon Hill, a line of tiny white puffs appeared, which rapidly swelled and coalesced until they formed a continuous wall of dense smoke, while at the same time the distant guns awoke into the rolling thunder of Barrage-fire. This was an attack by the 57th Division, and resulted in the capture of Moeuvres. It was a thrilling and most interesting demonstration—when seen from a safe distance!

.   .   .   .   .   .

On Sunday, September 15th, our "rest" came to an end, and in the evening we started off for the line again. While we waited for the order to move off, drawn up at the side of the road, the 2nd Battalion marched in from the trenches, dirty, unshaven and weary as we had been a week ago, to take over our vacated "billets," which—muddy holes though they were—we relinquished with reluctance. We marched through Lagnicourt and followed the road to the crest of the ridge overlooking the Canal, but then, instead of turning to the left towards our previous sector near Moeuvres, we turned right and descended the slope diagonally, over open country. It was now dark, but a moon approaching the full was shining brilliantly from a cloudless sky, so we had no difficulty this time in finding our way. The night was exceptionally quiet and there was very little gun-fire, though the landscape was so brightly illuminated by the moonlight that it was hard to believe that we could not be seen from the enemy's lines as we wound down the hillside. However, we were not molested in any way and, after following vaguely defined cart-tracks for some distance, we struck a sunken road, in the left bank of which we passed the entrances to several dugouts. This road brought us at last to the Cambrai-Bapaume main highway on the outskirts of Boursies, and we turned towards the village; but about fifty yards beyond what had been the first cottages we left the road and followed a narrow path through the ruins. After threading our way in single file through a maze of devastated houses, gardens and orchards, we reached another road leading to Demicourt, and crossing it, an artillery track led us past the village to the entrance to the trenches a short distance to the north.

The hardest part of the journey came after we entered the communication-trench. Walking along a trench as a member of a large party was an exhausting experience under the best conditions in the dark. It may be thought that nothing could be easier than to follow each other in single file along the duckboards—as simple as "follow-my-leader"—but in practice it was not so. "The speed of a column is that of its slowest member," but the leading files, anxious to get to their destination, were apt to forget this and hurry along too quickly; owing to the way in which the trench wound continually around sharp corners and traverses, it was seldom that one could see more than one or two of the men one was following, and it was absolutely necessary to keep in touch in order to avoid taking a wrong turning. If one stopped for a moment, to shift one's rifle or to ease a cutting pack-strap, it was easy to lose sight of the man in front. And there were frequent obstacles to negotiate on the way, such as slack wire under foot in which one tripped up, sagging telephone wires overhead which caught in the piling-swivel of one's rifle, unexpected holes in the duckboards or places where the trench had been damaged by a shell. It was an unwritten law that the leading men should pass back word of each obstacle as it was encountered, but it frequently happened that the warning was transmitted much more quickly than we moved, and would be forgotten by the time the obstacle in question was reached. A man half-way along the column would receive the word, "Step up" or "Wire overhead," and would keep a sharp lookout for a few moments, and then, when reaching the point referred to about ten minutes later, would fall over the step or be half-throttled by the wire. Each mishap would delay the files behind for a few seconds, and they would accelerate their pace in order to catch up, whereupon would come frenzied appeals from the rear to "Go easy in front, for Christ's sake!" Thus, we would be pounding along at a killing pace, with our heavy equipment swinging and clattering, stumbling and cursing in the darkness as far as our breath allowed, sweating profusely, longing for a rest or a drink, but unable to stop for a "breather" until our destination was reached.

On this occasion, we came to a breathless halt in a trench known as "Walsh Support," and had hardly taken over from the men we were relieving when we were greeted by a short but vicious whizz-bang strafe ; the shells pitched all round the trench, but as far as I know none fell inside and no one was injured. At first we were told that there was no shelter available for No. 6 Platoon, so we prepared to make the best of it in the open trench, but presently Captain Frisby, mindful as always of his men's comfort, came along and soon found room for us in a dugout which had been appropriated by Company H.Q. Staff—much to their disgust, when they had to make room for thirty more men in what had promised to be luxuriously spacious quarters.

I "clicked" for gas-guard that night, and my second spell on sentry came to an end at Stand-down, just after sunrise. My relief brought me a message from the Sergeant, ordering me to report at once to my Section-commander. On doing so, I found that the section had been detailed to proceed immediately to the front line, where there was an important post which the two platoons on duty were not sufficiently strong to hold in addition to their own sector. Hastily cramming down some breakfast of "sandbag" ham and tepid tea, eight of us, with a Sergeant and a Corporal, set off and picked our way carefully along the communication-trench, which was so damaged that in places it was necessary to wriggle along on our stomachs in order to avoid being seen by the enemy. ("'An army marches on its stomach '—I'll say it does! " remarked Bill Everton, who was crawling in front of me.) We had hardly reached our post when a violent bombardment broke out on the right, and for half-an-hour we stood-to in expectation of an attack, but at length it died down without apparent result.

The trenches we were in were part of the old German front-line system of 1917, the outworks of the Hindenburgh Line, and as we held part of these positions on the near side of the Canal and the enemy were in others, both sides were often rather uncomfortably placed, and were exposed to enfilade fire at many points. The post held by my section was at the junction of what we called "Goat Trench" with another old trench which ran directly into the German lines not very far away. Of course, this sap had been blocked midway between the two armies, but there was always a strong likelihood that it might be used as cover for a bombing raid against our post, and our sojourn there was necessarily a time of frequent alarms and "wind-up."

Of the enemy's lines nothing could be seen from where we were, for they were hidden from us by a slight rise in the ground immediately in front; we knew that No-man's-land could here be only narrow, for hand-grenades were occasionally thrown which fell short of our parapet by only twenty or thirty yards. A frequent cause of annoyance came from snipers, and on the night following our arrival one of them established himself in such a position on our right flank, across a slight dip in the ground, that he could fire right down our trench and we were obliged to post our sentries in the old sap itself. Another enterprising gentleman managed to get behind us and concealed himself in the tumbled ground; he blazed away at us from the rear for several hours, until someone spotted his hiding-place and settled him. It was by no means a healthy and restful spot !

There was a small dugout close by, no more than a single straight shaft of about ten steps under the parados, which led nowhere but which was useful as cover whenever one or two of us could snatch a few minutes sleep sitting on the steps—I noticed that the Sergeant and the Corporal made good use of it !—but the entrance faced the wrong way and during a strafe it was almost more dangerous than the open trench, for a direct hit on the single entrance would bury its occupants alive.

But there was little chance of sleep for anyone, particularly at night, for we were all constantly on the alert and the best we could do was to snatch an occasional brief and uneasy doze while sitting on the fire-step. The next day was quiet, and the only diversions were occasioned by the before-mentioned snipers, and a few trench-mortar bombs which burst in the vicinity at intervals, though not near enough to cause us much uneasiness. (In the light of the Germans' subsequent attempt to attack, it is probable that they were trying to clear a path through our wire.) Another local British attack had been planned for the following morning, in which our Battalion was to take part, the object of which was to advance our line to the Canal bank as a jumping-off place for the big offensive. At five o'clock in the evening, however, the Germans launched an assault in force upon Moeuvres, to the accompaniment of a heavy bombardment, and succeeded in recapturing the village. Although we were not included in the area of this battle, the set-back apparently deranged the plans, and we were informed a little later that our " show " was cancelled.

During the earlier part of that night there was bright moonlight, and the planes were busy. We watched a German aeroplane brought down by one of our machines in the focus of a dozen searchlights concentrated upon it, and glittering like a falling star as it fluttered to earth. Soon, however, heaped ramparts of inky clouds overspread the sky and a thunderstorm rolled up from the south-west. The lightning was very vivid but there was no rain, and about midnight the sky cleared again.

It was just after one a.m., I had finished a spell on sentry and was sitting on the fire-step (almost the only difference, here, between being on sentry and being off duty was that one could sit down during the latter—one was almost equally on the " qui-vive " all the time) when another storm burst suddenly upon us.

It was almost tropical in intensity, one of the most violent I have ever experienced. The lightning seemed to blaze continuously, streaking the inky-black sky in all directions like many-tributaried rivers on a map, while the ground trembled under the crashing onslaught of the thunder, drowning every other sound. It may have been imagination, but most of us could swear that the air smelt sulphurous, and that the electric discharges spread a violet glow around. Several men confessed afterwards that they had truly thought it was the end of the world !

Very soon the rain came, not in drops but in cascades, sweeping down in mighty gusts that rapidly flooded the trench. But for the fact that the ground sloped slightly towards an un-occupied hollow, our position would have soon become untenable; as it was, we crouched upon the fire-step in the downpour, knees drawn up under our chins, under the utterly inadequate protection of our ground-sheets, while a veritable river swept past us along the floor of the trench. We were speedily soaked to the skin. All artillery fire ceased, and I could imagine the " strafe-makers " frantically baling out their gun-pits. The storm lasted for only about half an hour, but it left both us and our surroundings in a thoroughly sodden state. Nevertheless, it put an end for the time being to all fear of a bombing raid by way of the old sap, the possibility of which had kept us all " bobbing," so we were not seriously concerned about our damp condition.

After a miserable night, the morning dawned bright and clear, and the early autumn sun soon dried our clothes. In every hollow of the trench floor pools of water remained, and we hastened to collect as much of possible in our mess tins, regardless of the risk from possible gas-contamination. After some trouble with damp sticks we managed to light a fire and make some tea. Hitherto, although we had plenty of tea and sugar, water had been one of our chief deficiencies, so that the storm was not without its compensations. It was remarkable how quickly the hot drink, followed by a cigarette restored our spirits, irritable and short-tempered as we all felt after the sleepless night in wet clothes; very soon jokes were beginning to pass, and we extracted some comfort from the thought of Jerry's much less enviable plight in the low-lying valley of the Canal.

The morning passed without incident, but about half-past three in the afternoon the German guns opened a vigorous bombardment of the artillery immediately behind us, which lasted about an hour. We had been listening to the salvos of heavy shells screeching over our heads, and were congratulating ourselves that it was only what the newspapers call " an artillery duel," when the fire suddenly redoubled in intensity, now directed on us and the Support line, while the front line was also plastered with whizz-bangs and trench-mortar bombs.

The barrage appeared to be general all along the line, and an attack was evidently in progress, but our artillery put down such a strong counter-bombardment that no assault developed in our sector. We spent a nerve-destroying time, however, for what seemed like several hours (from later accounts, it seems to have been only about thirty minutes !) crouching on the bottom of the trench and burying our noses in the mud, while the shells ripped and tore at the parapet above us; all the time tensely waiting for the first sign of a lengthening of the range of the barrage, which would probably mean that the German infantry were close behind. The uproar was so deafening that we were obliged to " speak " in signs, and we lay under a continual rain of debris; the man next to me received a violent whack on his steel helmet from a splinter, but was not hurt. During the height of the bombardment a British aeroplane swept backwards and forwards along the front of our line, close to the ground, and raked the enemy with machine-gun fire. It may have been this, as well as the counter-barrage from the guns, which prevented an attack from developing on our sector.

At last, about six o'clock or thereabouts, the enemy's fire slackened and finally ceased, though for some time our own guns kept up a retaliatory strafe on the German lines. When a messenger finally got through from Company H.Q. he was able to report that the Battalion's front was intact, and I afterwards learned that there had been only three casualties in the whole Battalion—a most remarkable fact, considering the violence of the bombardment.

The rest of the evening was fairly quiet on our front, though an hour or two later heavy shelling could be heard some distance to our right. The Germans were trying to launch an attack on the 3rd Division, which held the sector adjoining the Guards' line, but they were unable to reach their objective and were driven back with heavy losses, mainly because a Coldstream Lewis-gun team posted on a slight rise was able to enfilade them as they advanced, with devastating effect.

About half-past eleven the Battalion was relieved by the 2nd Scots Guards, and after several inexplicable delays we handed over " Windy Corner " to the care of a section of the Jocks, and filed off without reluctance to the rear. The trenches through which we had to pass were considerably damaged in many places by the storm and the bombardment, and in one place we had to climb out in order to get round a fallen German plane which had crashed on the parapet—probably the one we had seen brought down the previous night.

Just as we emerged from the trench into the Demicourt Road, we saw another plane destroyed in a similar manner. The method seemed to be: as soon as the plane was picked up by a searchlight, all the beams in the neighbourhood, sometimes a dozen or more, were focussed upon it, so that the pilot was dazzled by the glare whichever way he turned; then a British plane would speed up, and from the darkness outside the ring of searchlights would pepper it with machine-gun bullets, to which the German aviator, blinded by the intense light, was unable to reply effectively. The plane we watched was soon disabled and began to fall. As it neared the ground it released all its bombs in a rapid series of detonations and then crashed.

We tramped wearily through Demicourt to Boursies, where, to the west of the village, we reached the Brigade reserve area, and the various Platoons dispersed under their own guides to their allotted billets. No. 6 was at first led for nearly a mile along an old trench, until it was discovered that we were going in the wrong direction. Retracing our steps, we came to a sunken road, on the opposite side of which we plodded doggedly along another trench, grousing and grumbling continually as we stumbled along—until presently a salvo of big shells burst around us and put fresh life into our aching legs, and we finished the rest of the journey in record time !

Our quarters turned out to be a half-finished dugout of German construction, the entrance to which was a steep slope of smooth timber instead of steps. Some of us, taken by surprise, descended very rapidly in a recumbent position, picking up a number of splinters on the way ! (Getting out again called for almost Alpine activity.) Down below, about thirty feet underground, the dugout was in a very rough state, only partly excavated and the floor strewn with boulders ; there were two adjoining chambers, each with its own shaft to the surface and communicating by what was so far only a small tunnel just big enough to crawl through, but even so there was not nearly room enough to accommodate us all with ease, and we could not stretch out properly without putting our feet into each other's faces. But at least it was dry and comparatively warm, so we did not worry about the discomfort.

.   .   .   .   .   .

We remained in this area, the Brigade Reserve Line, for eight days, during which we had an easy time. There were few fatigues, and no duties beyond gas-guard at the dugout entrance. After only three days in the line, we had not hoped for so long a respite, and rumours circulated that the Battalion was shortly going farther back still—to civilisation and "canteen-land," in fact ! But the event showed that, on the contrary, we were being rested because we were to be one of the spearheads in the coming attack, "storm-troops" in the assault on the Hindenburg Line, though we were not, of course, told this until the last moment. The day following our return from "Windy Corner" the Headquarters Staff of No. 4 Coy. was moved from the dugout it had occupied in the sunken road previously mentioned, and, on account of the unfinished and crowded state of our quarters and our comparative isolation from the rest of the Company, we were invited to move thither, which we did with alacrity.

Our new home was a fine roomy dugout some thirty-five or forty feet below ground-level, where we were comfortably secure from any but the heaviest shells, and it consisted of two large compartments with three entrances For reasons of warmth and "candle-power" we only occupied one of the rooms, though even so we were not overcrowded. We were in the midst of the guns, and at times were treated to very heavy bursts of shelling, during which we retreated to our burrow like so many rabbits. Two or three of the men, loudly expressing their contempt for the somewhat fuggy security underground and their preference for fresh air, took possession of a half-ruined sandbag shelter outside our "front door," but about midnight on the first night a shell exploded nearly on top of their abode, and they returned to the fold again very hurriedly —not without a good deal of chaffing !

Our rations came up every night and were quite generous in quantity. They consisted, in the main, of bully, ham, bread, butter, tea and jam. Instead of the rum-ration, we often got an allowance of oatmeal (which was not nearly so popular !) and I soon became an adept in the art of making porridge—or "bergoo," in Army parlance. One of our principal difficulties was the supply of water, which we had to fetch for ourselves from a distance, for all purposes. There was an excellent "water-point" about a mile away, but it could be reached only across open fields which were often under heavy shell-fire, so that each journey was a somewhat hazardous adventure. We took turns daily in fetching the supply for the dugout, usually going in pairs at well-spaced intervals, and had some narrow escapes.

The mail also was delivered with admirable regularity, and several of us received food-parcels from home, the contents of which were always shared and provided a very welcome variety in our diet. Newspapers and magazines, too, were passed round from one to another, until they fell to pieces from sheer use, for we had plenty of time for reading but insufficient means, and also ample opportunity for writing letters. Often the evenings would be enlivened by an impromptu concert, when our candle-lit subterranean abode would ring with popular choruses, sentimental ballads and even operatic arias ; two men in the Platoon were comedians in the Battalion Concert Party, and frequently kept us in roars of laughter by their impersonations of Cockney charwomen.

The sunken road into which the entrances of the dugout opened was surrounded on all sides by the heavy guns of the artillery, and offered a good target for the counter-battery fire of the German gunners, who could look down on the whole area from Bourlon Hill. At times we were deluged with shells, though, safe in the friendly depths of the dugout, we could afford to treat them with contempt. Even at that depth, however, some of the largest shells, particularly those known as "armour-piercing," would make the walls rock when they exploded directly overhead, and in one instance even brought down part of our roof.

One night there was an alarm of gas, and we were ordered out to line the adjacent trench, wearing our respirators. A slight smell of "pineapple" gas was perceptible, but it was not strong enough to be harmful, and I suspect that a chance gas-shell had been made the pretext for a trial turn-out, though had there been a serious bombardment with gas the trench would have been much the safest place, for our dugout was not then protected against this form of attack. While we stood on the fire-step waiting for the order to stand-down, a German aeroplane dropped a number of bombs on a near-by battery, one of which fell too near to us to be pleasant. Next day, the Royal Engineers fitted the entrances to the dugout with gas-proof curtains.

Efforts to increase the demoralisation of the enemy troops continued at every opportunity, and we frequently watched propaganda leaflets being scattered from aeroplanes or balloons, in the way I have described. No means was neglected of impressing on the Germans the extent and rapidity of the Allies' advance and the hopelessness of holding out against us. Soon, rumours of the coming assault on the Hindenburg Line began to circulate, and before long it was definitely known that a big attempt was about to be made to force the passage of the Canal du Nord. Every night fresh guns were brought up, until the country fairly bristled with them, standing almost wheel to wheel, silent as yet for the most part and covered with tarpaulins and green branches. Some of the bigger ones, so the gunners told us, were intended to bombard Cambrai itself, more than twenty kilometres away. The darkness resounded every night with the clanking of "female" tanks, bringing up ammunition and other stores, R.E.'s swarmed everywhere, and the air was thick with rumours. Nevertheless, the date and time of "zero-hour" remained a profound secret.

On the 24th I was one of a party which marched out, in the morning, to a point about a mile behind Boursies, carrying picks and shovels for the purpose—so it was said—of clearing the ground for the construction of a new Divisional Headquarters, in anticipation of the coming advance. The scene of our operations was near a newly-commenced dugout on the edge of a large open space, in the middle of which, about a hundred and fifty yards from where we were working, stood a battery of heavy guns, uncamouflaged and unprotected by earthworks, and firing at intervals. Close to the guns were piles of big shells, similarly exposed.

Away over the eastern horizon a German sausage-balloon, small and remote, could be plainly seen, and it was soon evident that its occupants could see us no less plainly. We had not been long at work when a shell burst in the field behind the battery, and shortly afterwards another fell short of the guns and nearer to us. Then, having got the range and before we had time to realise what was happening, a salvo of eight or nine shells burst right among the guns themselves. Neither the guns nor the dumps of shells appeared to be directly hit, but a number of boxes of cordite were set on fire and burned spasmodically in fitful bursts of intense flame.

The gunners, aware of the danger, worked desperately and at no little risk to themselves, to drag the incandescent boxes away from the vicinity of the shells, but the heat of the flames became too great. More and more cordite flared up, and at last they were forced to abandon the guns and make for safety. Only just in time. Hardly had the last man reached a ditch on the far side of the field when — with a mighty, rending crash which defies description—the shell-dump blew up.

I was directly facing the explosion, and I stood " rooted to the ground," while an immense fan of black smoke shot upward for a hundred feet or more, carrying with it soil, wheels, planks and wreckage of every kind. It was only a shout of warning from my neighbour which made me realise that the spectacular catastrophe held a personal menace, and I flung myself down under the meagre shelter of a low bank just as the debris came thundering down all round us. It was almost by a miracle that only three of our party were injured by the tons of falling metal, and neither of those seriously. A large piece of steel, almost red-hot, buried itself in the ground within a few feet of me, and several small fragments rattled like hailstones on my tin hat and all around.

A few minutes later another pile of shells went up with equal violence, but this time we were better prepared, and had taken cover in the entrance to the half-constructed dugout close by. The three injured men were carried off on stretchers, and the rest of us completed the job we had come to do without further excitement.

VICTORY

NEXT day we were told officially that the great attack on the Hindenburg Line, now in visible preparation, was to begin on the morning of September 27th—two days hence—and that we, the 1st Coldstream Guards, were to take a leading part. More than this, to No. 2 Company had been assigned the honour of "opening the ball" for the Battalion—that is to say, we were to be the first to advance against the enemy's positions on what was described to us as the most vital point of the whole battle, the crossing of the Canal du Nord, on the punctual success of which the hope of an early end to the war depended. No doubt we were suitably impressed, but I doubt if we fully appreciated the "honour," for the first waves of the assault would obviously have no picnic!

The offensive, indeed, was to be on a scale hitherto unapproached in the history of war. All the Allies on the Western Front were to be involved, along the whole five-hundred-mile line from the sea to the Rhine, and the onslaught in Picardy was only one of four simultaneous thrusts—in Flanders, Champagne and the Argonne as well—which, it was hoped, by bringing into action the maximum strength of all the Allies at the same moment, would shatter the already-tottering confidence of the Germans and bring them to their knees in final surrender. It was a bold plan, for failure might be almost as bad as a German victory, but it was splendidly organised and brilliantly carried out, and—as all the world knows—resulted in complete success.

In the area west of Cambrai, where the 3rd Army (which included the Guards Division) was to attack, the enemy were at their strongest, aided by the supposed impregnable obstacle of the Hindenburg Line, and it was recognised that this would be the crucial point of the whole scheme. Indeed, the Germans themselves were fully alive to its importance, as captured official documents proved, and it was evident that they were prepared to put up a very stubborn defence—if they could. They knew that if they were beaten here, they had no chance of stopping the Allies' advance, much less of winning the war. An Army Order, which was found in a trench which was over-run during our attack, and which was subsequently translated and circulated, is significant in its desperate attempt to minimise previous British successes and its evident nervousness for the future :—

"Until now, for military reasons, we have permitted the English to occupy some devastated enemy territory. In the rear-guard battles we have inflicted heavy losses upon them.

But now that we occupy very strong defensive positions, it is necessary to yield not another inch. The English seek here to obtain the decision, and the 14th Corps occupies one of the most important sectors of the line. Remember that you defend your firesides, your families, your beloved Fatherland; and think what would happen if the war, and with it the enemy hordes, should be carried to the territory of our dear Fatherland."

But the wider aspects of the great battle were not explained to us at the time. As far as we were concerned, it was an attempt to clear the German fortifications on the near side of the Canal du Nord, to cross the Canal and make a frontal attack on the main Hindenburg Line, which lay along the rising ground beyond. This was in itself a quite formidable enough task, for the Germans had had ample time in which to consolidate their positions, which were supposed to be the " ne plus ultra " of military defensive science. Cambrai was only a few kilometres away, and beyond that was open country which had been untouched by war since 1914.

A relief-map had been constructed on a shelving bank by the roadside, and we gathered round it, a Company at a time, while an officer explained the plan of attack. The Canal was indicated by a white tape, and the various roads, trenches and other features were marked out with coloured stones. It was considered that the Canal, though dry in this area (it had been in course of construction at the beginning of the war), was too formidable a barrier along most of its length to be crossed in face of the enemy, so we were to storm it on a narrow front of only about a hundred and fifty yards, from the " Lock " to just north of " Mouse Post," a broken-down bridge on the road leading to Graincourt.

At " zero-hour "—as usual—kept secret until the last moment No. 2 Company was to leave the assembly trenches in two waves of two platoons each, separated by about fifty yards, and, following the barrage, would rush the German front line trenches and push on to the Canal bank. Here, near the broken bridge, we were to descend into the Canal bed, cross it and climb the opposite bank, and then take " Steve Post " at the cross-roads. Re-assembling there, we were to advance without delay to the main Line, and after taking the double line of trenches of which it was composed were to consolidate and repel any counter-attacks which might be made. This was scheduled to take about three hours, and completed our share of the business. The second main wave would then go through our lines, to link up with the Canadians, who it was hoped would by this time be coming down from behind Bourlon Hill; in the words of our officer-instructor, we should " just sit down and watch the whole British Army go through the gap we had made." Then we should go home to breakfast !

It sounded quite simple and easy, the way he told it, but we were not deceived. Obviously, it could hardly be other than a desperate and hazardous venture for those taking part, and I don't suppose there was one among us who did not feel that he would be lucky if he was still alive in two days' time. Of course, no one gave voice to his feelings, but there was a noticeable air of gravity as we dispersed after the "lecture." Nevertheless, the "sing-song" in the dugout that night, though it may have been a case of "whistling to keep our hearts up," lacked little of its usual boisterousness.

Next day was devoted to preparing our kit, drawing extra ammunition, rations, etc., and to writing letters in which we could say little of real significance. The mail came up during the afternoon and many of us received the satisfaction of a last message from home. For some it was, in the most literal and tragic sense, the "Last Post."

At dusk we moved off along the sunken road, past the dead and stinking horse at the cross-roads, through Boursies and Demicourt, and so to the trenches. About an hour's tramp over the duckboards brought us to the dugout which had been allotted to us for the remainder of the night; the entrance had been half blocked by a direct hit, and we were very much cramped for room inside, but made ourselves fairly comfortable. A tot of rum, weak but very welcome, helped in some measure to keep out the cold, and we made the most of what remained of the day's rations before snatching an hour or two of uneasy sleep. During the night the guns kept up a normal amount of desultory firing, but there was nothing to indicate that anything unusual was afoot. The German lines were very quiet.

Major-General Sir F. Maurice, K.C.M.G., C.B., in his book, "The Last Four Months," says: "The British attacks were timed to begin in the early morning of September 27th, and on the evening before a great bombardment opened on a thirty-mile front, from a point about two miles north-west of St. Quentin, as far as the Sensée River north-west of Cambrai." While I can hardly presume to contradict the gallant General, I can only assume, either that silent and invisible shells were used for this strafe, or that I was deaf, blind and unconscious at the time; for, as I mentioned above, I have no memory of any unusual shelling until shortly before the attack started. Gen. Maurice, with characteristic British modesty, also does not mention the Guards; he infers that most of the work on this part of the front was done by Canadian corps!

"A History of the Great War," by H. C. O'Neill, also mentions this inexplicable preliminary bombardment, while Major Carey and Capt. Scott, in "An Outline History of the Great War," say in addition: "At dawn *in mist and rain* the 3rd and 1st Armies attacked . . ." To the best of my recollection, there was no rain—on the contrary, the sun shone most of the day!

About half-past four we scrambled out, stiff and cramped, into the cold air and crept along the trench to our appointed "jumping-off" place. This was only a short distance away, and lining the trench we stood under the parapet and awaited the coming of "zero-hour." It was still dark, for the sun was not due to rise for two hours yet, though in the east there was a slight suspicion of greyness and the stars were beginning to fade there. The guns had ceased firing altogether, and only an isolated shot or spasmodic rattle of a machine-gun at rare intervals broke the stillness that hung over No-man's-land like the breathless hush before a storm. A faint breeze now and again raised a chilly rustle in the grasses beyond the parapet, like a half-suppressed sigh.

We waited in silence, each man occupied with his own thoughts and no doubt wrestling with his own secret fears. I think that half-hour was probably the worst I have ever spent. Slowly and inexorably the minutes passed, second by second, and the time approached which might be the end of everything for me. The suppressed quivering in my limbs was not entirely due to the cold, and I had to clench my teeth hard to prevent them from chattering. All my efforts to screw up my courage, all my fatalistic self-assurances that "what is to be, will be," became more and more useless, and hope seemed to ooze away with every second . . .

At last the order was passed along in a whisper to fix bayonets, and we knew that the time had come. It was almost a relief to do something. A few minutes later—glancing at the luminous dial of my watch, I saw that it was exactly 5.20—three big guns spoke out in regular sequence, from far in the rear : "One !——Two !—— Three !" The scream of their shells had hardly ceased to vibrate in our ears when, with a tremendous simultaneous crash, as though the vault of heaven had burst and was falling upon us, the Barrage opened.

Shells in hundreds, in thousands, of every size and calibre, shrieked down close over our heads and burst in front of the trench, at first close to the parapet, then gradually creeping towards the German lines, a flail of death-dealing eruptions which must surely sweep everything living from its path. Mere words can convey no idea of this great culminating barrage, surely the greatest and most intense in the history of war. Devilish force unchained, the power of Hell let loose, trampling the earth beneath fire-spurting feet, the mighty crash and clangour of ten thousand guns—imagination fails, and memory itself can retain only a tithe of the stupendous reality. Great gouts and fountains of flame, scarlet and green and gold— thousands of flashes stabbing the night incessantly—an indescribable hell of noise that numbed the senses and stupified the brain—that was the Barrage.

In the German lines, complete chaos seemed to reign for the first few minutes. Verey lights of every colour shot into the air as if fired in panic ; but very soon the enemy appeared to recover from their surprise, and their machine-guns swept the ground with a hail of bullets. The parapet just above our heads spurted with jets of earth as they traversed from side to side, and the high whine of ricochets was added to the din. The front line was evidently held in strength—indeed, it was afterwards reported, on the evidence of prisoners, that they themselves had planned an attack for about three hours later.

Then, all together, we were scrambling up the short ladders which had been placed against the side of the trench. Our chief thought was to get on our feet as quickly as possible, for the bullets were sweeping low and one stood in greater danger of a fatal wound while crawling over the parapet than when standing upright. Several men in the Platoon were hit during those first few seconds, and the Company Sergeant-Major, one of the most popular of our N.C.O.'s, was killed outright ; but I was untouched. We had, of course, strict orders not to stop to help casualties, but to leave them to the following stretcher-bearers. Once on top, we turned half-left, the trench being at an angle to the direction in which we had to advance, and moved in single-file at a sort of half-trot, picking our way by the flickering light of the explosions through the broken wire and shell-holes.

By this time the German guns were at work, laying down a counter-barrage, and shells were bursting all around and among us. Great fans and fountains of flame sprang up as if by magic from the ground, for the uproar was so great that one could no longer distinguish the sound of separate shell-bursts, even when close at hand ; they were all welded into a homogeneal solid-steel universe of thunder that seemed as material and all-pervading as the atmosphere, stabbed through by the zipp and whine of bullets. The acrid smell of lyddite fumes was everywhere. It seemed impossible that anyone could come alive through that cyclone of destruction.

The sensation of standing up and crossing open ground under heavy fire is one which I find difficult, almost impossible, to describe in any ordinary terms. On first scrambling to my feet, I had a feeling of being stark naked, without a vestige of protection ; and this was coupled with an extraordinary sensation—curiously like relief—that I was no longer personally responsible for my own safety. The issue was entirely out of my hands, I had nothing to do with it, and it mattered not at all whether I kept my head down or walked erect. As soon as we had started, my previous nervous qualms seemed to disappear, and my whole being became keyed up to a point where personal danger was meaningless ; it was as if I was in the grip of a power outside myself, whose bidding I had no choice but to obey. The terrific uproar around made conscious thought and feeling impossible, and I stumbled forward with the others over the churned-up ground, picking my way carefully and almost methodically through the unseen obstacles, heedless of the bullets which constantly cracked past, and watching, as if they did not concern me, the showers of sparks which shot up from the ground on all sides as shells exploded ; in the general din, they seemed to be almost noiseless. It was like walking in a nightmare of Hell, a whirlwind of thunder and flame.

But then comes a gap in my memory. For a space of what must have been about half-an-hour my memory is a complete blank; many times since I have tried to remember what happened during that time, but always without result—it is an impenetrable fog. We must have reached and passed the German front line, which ran between our starting point and the Canal, but whether it had been evacuated before we got there, or whether there was fighting, I do not know. My first distinct impression is of dropping into cover behind a low bank not far from the edge of the Canal with a number of men from my platoon, and remaining there for some time, while the advance seemed to be temporarily held up. It was still dark, though there was a greyness which enabled us to see nearby objects vaguely, and we were still being shelled heavily, but our own barrage had gone on over the Canal. Something had evidently gone wrong.

It was not until some time afterwards that I learned the reason for the delay, and how it was ended. It appears that on reaching the Canal bank the leading platoons found themselves under very heavy fire from " Mouse Post," a machine-gun emplacement at the far end of the broken bridge, which had been thought to have been destroyed earlier. It was sweeping the place where we should have to climb down into the Canal bed, and our fellows found it was impossible to go forward. As this was the key-point of the whole scheme, Captain Frisby realised the seriousness of failing to capture the Canal crossing, and, calling for volunteers, he, Corporal Jackson, and four other men rushed forward, clambered down into the Canal and, in the face of intense point-blank fire, succeeded in rushing and bombing the post, which was strongly fortified with steel girders and concrete blocks. For this gallant deed of almost super-human bravery, both the Captain and Cpl. Jackson were afterwards awarded the Victoria Cross, though in Jackson's case it was a posthumous decoration, for he was killed a few hours later. Captain Frisby received a bayonet wound in the leg, but carried on throughout the day.

Presently we had the signal to advance, and moved forward to the verge of the Canal, which was like a gigantic trench across our path. The steeply-sloping sides, originally faced with brickwork, were badly broken by shell-fire in many places, so that descent was comparatively easy ; we climbed and slithered to the bottom, crossed piles of rubble and pools of mud and water, and scrambled up the farther bank. Here, Captain Frisby was waiting, just below the summit, and despite the hail of bullets which was still sweeping the ground, he gave a helping hand to each of us who needed it and had a cheerful word for everyone as we passed him.

I have no idea how long these events were in happening, but by the time we were across the Canal it was getting quite light and

I could see my immediate surroundings plainly, so that it must have been nearly half-past six. The German counter-barrage was by now much less vigorous, though their machine-guns were still very active from the summit of the ridge. The various attacking units were becoming somewhat mixed up, and in the confusion and the half-light I had not gone far from the Canal bank before I realised that the men I was with were not my own section, but a Lewis-gun team of No. 8 Platoon. However, I decided to stay with them for the time, and we went for some distance along a trench leading away to the left, stepping over many corpses and throwing hand-grenades into the entrances of the dugouts we passed. We saw no living Germans. Presently the Corporal in charge found a position which he considered offered a suitable field of fire for his gun, and stopped there. He was afterwards awarded the D.C.M., though he always declared that he didn't know what for, since he stayed in the same spot all day and went to sleep !

I stayed with the team for a time, until it was fully daylight, and then thought that I ought to try to find my own platoon. I made my way back along the trench alone, without seeing anyone except dead bodies, and presently came to a point at the intersection of two roads which I took to be " Steve Post," at which, according to our " battle orders," we were to have re-assembled for the attack on the main Line. But there was no one to be seen and things were very much quieter, though there was still a little sporadic shelling and the sound of machine-guns at the top of the rise. I dropped into another trench, which appeared to lead roughly in an easterly direction, thinking that that was probably the way the others had gone. Moving warily and with my rifle at the " ready," for at any corner in the trench I might encounter one of the enemy, I had gone for perhaps a quarter of a mile when, to my great relief, I came upon Sergt. Reed and most of No. 6 Platoon.

We were there, I think, in the first of the double line of trenches which formed the main Hindenburg Line, and the Sergeant had received orders to stay there and consolidate the position. Away in front there was a good deal of noise of bombing, and apparently several small attempts to counter-attack were made, but none succeeded in getting through the troops ahead of us. A German aeroplane (the only one I remember seeing that day) came over, just skimming the ground, and sprayed us with bullets, but a few seconds later it crashed, probably brought down by a lucky shot.

Several other stragglers rejoined the Platoon during the morning, and presently the second main wave of the attack went through on our right, advancing in open order through fairly heavy shell-fire ; they seemed to be successful, for the battle receded out of our sight beyond the skyline. On all sides, we could see prisoners being marched in twos and threes to the rear. Sometimes, after being disarmed, they were sent back without escort, and then often made a somewhat grotesque sight as they ran for safety, stumbling over the rough ground but not daring to lower their arms.

Towards eleven o'clock orders were given that we were to go back a short distance to a part of the trench where there was a small dugout, and were then given permission to get out our rations. Evidently, our part in the attack was finished, and the enemy was in retreat. From where we now were I could see down the slope to the Canal, where already the Engineers were busy constructing a bridge or ramp at the place where we had crossed, despite the big long-range shells which occasionally dropped near them. Reports got about that Graincourt had fallen, but these proved to be premature ; actually, Flesquieres was captured in the early afternoon and Graincourt was not finally cleared until 4.30. By evening the British line ran approximately from Fontaine Notre Dame to the outskirts of Marcoing, and the Hindenburg Line was everywhere in our hands. Bourlon Hill had been stormed by the Canadians fairly early after an intense gas bombardment, and they (the Canadians) had joined up with our troops near Graincourt.

Once again, " for military reasons," the Germans had been obliged to " allow the English to occupy some devastated territory," but this time they could hardly claim that it was " according to plan ! "

Our meal of Bully, dry bread and biscuit was very welcome; for the first time since we went over the top I realised that I had had no breakfast, and that I was hungry ! The dugout to which we retired was of a kind apparently favoured by the Germans, but which I never saw in our own lines—little more than a deep " funk-hole," just a shaft of about a dozen steps, leading nowhere and very dangerous in a strafe because of its single entrance. It faced, too, the wrong way—from our point of view—but it was comforting to get below ground, and all who could crowded in.

The rest of the day was for us only a case of waiting for our relief. We had been told previous to the attack that if all went well we should start back to rest-billets about eleven in the morning; actually, the relieving troops did not turn up until eight o'clock at night. In the meantime, during the afternoon we were moved to a German trench running parallel with the Canal, and in consequence of a rumour that we were to remain there for the night, we started to make ourselves as comfortable as possible in the numerous dugouts with which it abounded. These were all of the kind just mentioned, and the one allotted to my platoon had received a direct hit which had brought down the roof-supports half-way down the shaft, leaving a hole only about two feet high to be crawled through. In the ordinary way, no doubt, we should have hesitated before trusting ourselves in such a potential death-trap, but such is the instinct to get below ground-level, although there was then very little shell-fire, that we hardly considered the possibility of a collapse.

The trench was littered with the belongings of its late occupants, and there were many souvenirs to be had for the trouble of carrying them away. I possessed myself of a leather belt with a " Gott Mit Uns " buckle, a clip of five unused bullets (two of which were plainly illegal dum-dums), some German equivalents of our " field-service postcards " and one or two other small objects, but I had no wish to add unduly to the weight of my already heavy kit. The parapet, along the whole length of the trench, fairly bristled with abandoned machine-guns and trench-mortars, and it was not difficult to account for the murderous fire which had greeted our attack. The wonder was that anyone at all could have got through in the face of such an imposing battery.

Later on, we pooled what water remained in our flasks, made small fires in the trench and had tea—if a meagre repast consisting of the scanty remains of our day's rations could be dignified by that name—and not long afterwards received word that our relief was on the way. About half-past seven we lined up on the Graincourt Road (surreptitiously jettisoning any remaining Mills-bombs and much surplus ammunition!) and half an hour later started off to the rear.

It was a noticeably smaller column which re-crossed the Canal by way of the new ramp, than the Battalion which had entered the trenches less than twenty-four hours earlier, for we had suffered rather heavy casualties, in killed, wounded and missing. It might be supposed—by those who only know the British soldier in France as " Tommy Atkins," of the propagandist, the cartoons of Bruce Bairnsfather, and the sentimental novelist—that we were " tired but happy, enlivening the road with cheerful songs and jokes." For had we not just helped to win a notable victory, broken the redoubtable Hindenburg Line and inflicted on the enemy what Sir Douglas Haig later described as " the decisive defeat of the war? "

But the reality was quite otherwise. We were all tired to the point of exhaustion, and limp from lack of food; our mouths and throats were dry as lime-kilns. Nerves were on edge and tempers frayed, as always after the intense strain of " going over the top," and any small disagreement was liable to flare into a quarrel. We trudged wearily along in the darkness, with little of the Guards' traditional smartness, although we instinctively tried to pull ourselves together when another body of anonymous troops passed us on their way to the line. True, one or two incurable optimists tried to start a song, but we lacked the energy or inclination to keep it going, and it died a natural death after a few bars. Many had other causes of discomfort besides weariness—slight wounds, sprains, blisters, or the like; for myself, the soles of my feet had become extremely tender and raw, from some unknown cause, so that it was painful to stand on them, to say nothing of marching over bad roads and shell-torn ground.

The march seemed to last for hours, and it must have been after midnight when we reached our destination, though the actual distance was little more than two miles " as the crow flies." Of course, we travelled slowly, and judging by the number of times the officer in charge of the platoon enquired the way it is probable that we went a good deal farther than was necessary, but it is still a mystery to me, after studying the map, how we took so long over the journey. Even when we reached Boursies, which should have been our halting-place, we lost our way again in the darkness and went right past the village, then came back and wandered about over open fields before we at last found the trench by the main road which was our designated billet. There should have been a hot meal ready for us on arrival, but for some reason the arrangements had miscarried and no food was forthcoming. However, our weariness was greater than our hunger, and we were only too thankful to be able to lie down and go to sleep. My last recollection that night is of Captain Frisby, exhausted as he must have been and wounded into the bargain, limping along the lines, asking if everyone was reasonably comfortable and apologising for the absence of supper.

Next morning we were not disturbed until late, and it was ten o'clock before we fell-in outside the trench. It was not exactly a cheerful parade, for self-congratulation was mingled with apprehension as we furtively searched the surrounding faces to see who was absent. As the Sergeant called the roll, and name after name brought no answering " Here ! " we began to realise how many of our number had " gone west " since yesterday morning. At each unanswered name, the Sergeant asked, " Does anyone know anything about him ? " and those who could give any information were cross-questioned by an officer; gradually, from confused and sometimes contradictory evidence, most of the casualties were definitely accounted for as killed or wounded, and those about whom nothing was known were listed as " missing." Among the men with whom I had been in closest contact (though I had made no intimate friends during the bare four weeks I had served in the Company) Bristow, Whitlock and Carson were dead, Farley and Cpl. Macready were wounded, and Dobson was listed as missing—though the last-named afterwards proved to have been slightly wounded also, and re-joined the Company about three months later.

We spent nine days at Boursies, where we converted the old trench into a quite comfortable abode (by current standards) by widening sections of it and roofing them with sheets of corrugated-iron and tarpaulins scrounged from some ruined huts a few hundred yards away. The trench lay alongside the main road, just outside the village, and in front of us a broad slope of open ground led down towards the heap of rubble that had been Demicourt, in which the Divisional Canteen was established (though it seldom had anything to sell). Every yard of the ground was scarred and pitted with shell-holes, many of them old and overgrown, but most of recent origin. (The way in which they overlapped each other was sufficient evidence to disprove the popular belief that " two shells never fall on the same spot " !) Away to our left-front was the dark hump of Bourlon Hill, now no longer a menace, and the Canal was hidden from our view by slightly-rising ground. The fighting-line was already so far ahead that we were out of artillery range and well behind our own guns.

Boursies seemed to have been a fair-sized village once, extending for about half a mile on both sides of the Bapaume-Cambrai " route nationale," but it was now literally razed to the ground. A few tottering walls still stood up crazily among the heaps of shattered brickwork, and the barely traceable cottage gardens, the splintered remnants of orchards, a wayside shrine and a broken pump were all that was left of a once-flourishing community. I often wondered what would be the feelings of the villagers when they returned to their homes.

Rations were quite plentiful for the first few days—for obvious reasons. There was as much bread as we wanted (and more of biscuit), " beaucoup " tea and " pozzy," cheese and margarine, while tins of " Frey Bentos " and " Maconochie " were at a discount. We had all we could eat, and more. This state of affairs, however, only lasted until—on the fifth day, I think it was—a new draft of reinforcements joined us. A welcome variety was provided by the food parcels arriving from home, some of which were addressed to men who had become casualties. These were opened and their contents shared among the survivors; it was not pleasant to think that we might be enjoying dainties which had been prepared with loving care for someone we had known and who might now be dead—but we did not refuse them on that account. In any case, even if he was in hospital or in Blighty, they were of no use to him, and had he been with us he would probably have shared with us, as we with him.

German planes came over regularly every night, and often dropped bombs in our neighbourhood, though without—so far as I know—doing much damage. Wet or fine, as soon as it was dark the shrill whistles of the look-out men gave warning of their approach, and every light had to be extinguished. In daylight, however, they left us severely alone. One evening, I recall, two of the fellows—" Mary," so-called because of his clever impersonations of a cockney " char " in the Battalion Concert Party, and " Bermo," who hailed from Bermondsey—and I were trying to heat up a tinned meat-pie which I had just received from home, over a fire which had taken a lot of coaxing before it would burn, and in a mess-tin which was almost too small for the purpose. Just as success was in sight and we had begun to anticipate an appetising supper, the air-raid warning was given, and we had to throw our nearly-boiling water on the fire. " Sich wyste, Mrs. May ! " screamed " Mary," in his falsetto stage-voice; " I never seed anything so disgriceful in all me born dyes ! " But the pie was not entirely wasted: we ate most of it in the dark, lukewarm and half-congealed.

At the first opportunity after we came to Boursies, I went in search of the dugout in the sunken road in which we had lived before the attack—only four days ago, but it seemed now more like a month ! I wanted to recover a book which I had not finished reading, and which I remembered thrusting behind one of the roof-timbers just before we started for the trenches; it was still there. Coming up out of the musty darkness of the dugout, it seemed almost unnatural not to hear the roar of near-by batteries or the scream of an approaching shell. All those battered fields were quiet at last.

Next day the whole Battalion went on a road-making fatigue between Flesquires and Ribécourt. In order to get there, we marched—in column-of-route—across the same ground over which we had stumbled in the dark behind the barrage on that eventful morning, and crossed the Canal by way of the temporary ramp close to where we had scrambled up the bank under machine-gun fire. It was extremely interesting to see it again by daylight and in less strenuous circumstances, but the scene on the other side of the Canal was already almost unrecognisable. Roads and bridges were being made and repaired, huts and tents had sprung up everywhere, and at Ribécourt the railway was being energetically re-layed and a huge naval gun on railway mountings had been brought up. At Flesquieres a large Field Ambulance Station was in course of construction. The " front " was by now beyond the river " Scheldt," a good three miles farther east, and it was evident that every effort was being made to keep the enemy on the run.

I mentioned above that after the action on the 27th my feet had become extremely sore; for several days afterwards I could only hobble about with considerable difficulty, but would not go sick for fear of seeming to " dodge the column." However, after the road-making fatigue I could stick it no longer, and decided to see the M.O. The soles of my feet felt as if they had been flayed, and were extremely tender and inflamed; I never discovered the cause—it was not a case of " trench feet," for there was no swelling —and the doctor suggested no explanation, but he excused me from all duties for several days and prescribed a liniment with which to rub the affected parts. They were quite recovered by the time we left Boursies.

After three or four days the Regimental Band came up to the neighbourhood—" a sure sign," said someone, " that it is now a safe area and the Germans are on the run!"—and every fine evening " did their stuff " on what might be called " the village green "—though there was not much green about it. Troops gathered from miles around to hear the concerts.

About this time I had some hopes of a re-union with Arthur Brookes, my Windsor pal of a year ago. Since I left England we had corresponded more or less regularly, and during September he wrote to say that he expected to " come out " almost at once; now, two or three days before we left Boursies, I had a short note saying that he was in France, had taken part in the " stunt " on the 27th, and was trying to find me. After the disbandment of the Household Battalion he had gone into the Welsh Guards and, while he was fortunate to have remained in England for so long, it was very hard luck to have been rushed into action as soon as he reached the front for the first time. But although we were both in the same Division, and probably within a mile or two of each other, the censorship did not allow us to give any indication of our whereabouts and, despite many enquiries on both sides, we did not succeed in meeting then or until four months later, when the war was over and we were both in Cologne. No doubt we should have run across each other sooner, had I not had the misfortune (?) to be wounded again and sent down the line.

On the evening of Monday, October 7th, our spell of rest and refitment came to an end, and we left Boursies at dusk on the way to a new attack. The weather, which during the greater part of our stay there had been excellent, now broke and the march was performed in a persistent drizzle, over ground heavy with mud. Our route ran through Demicourt and across the Canal to Flesquieres, and thence to some trenches on the near side of Ribécourt. The march was without incident, except that a few long-range shells fell on Flesquieres as we passed through, one of which exploded close enough to us to shower us with brickdust and rubble, though without causing any casualties. We spent the night under tarpaulin shelters in the trench at Ribécourt.

The next day showed some improvement in the weather, and the sun broke through the clouds with increasing frequency as time went on. We did not resume the march until afternoon; at dawn an attack was launched some four or five miles ahead, and we could see the enemy's shells bursting thickly on the crest of the ridge facing us. The truck-mounted gun was firing with a great noise from the railway near Ribécourt. It appears that it was because this attack was not as successful as was expected, that our departure was delayed; otherwise, we were to have gone into action that day. So we hung about in the neighbourhood of the trench during the morning, awaiting fresh orders. In accordance with a recent Army Order, we now had to go into action in full marching kit, wearing our packs—a considerable increase in weight, no doubt made necessary by the new conditions of " open warfare " and the consequent difficulty of keeping in touch with Battalion H.Q.

H

No. 2 Company was not under the direct leadership of Capt. Frisby on this occasion. The Colonel had been slightly wounded on September 27th and the Major was on leave, so the command of the Battalion had temporarily devolved upon the Captain. One of the other officers was in charge of No. 2—not a change for the better, in our opinion.

We moved off in the early afternoon. The march was for the most part over open fields and we saw no decent roads, so that it is difficult for me to trace our route with any accuracy. Mounting the rise to the right of Flesquieres, we bore north-east to the edge of the Bois de Neuf, and then eastwards until we reached the canalised River Scheldt between Marcoing and Noyelles. Crossing by way of a temporary wooden bridge, we passed through a line of heavy guns and then over a high railway embankment; half a mile farther on we came to a halt alongside a shallow and much-battered trench near the summit of the rise. In front of us, across the ridge, could be seen the tops of the houses in the village of Rumilly, now haloed in a cloud of red, sun-illumined dust as shells burst among the ruins. On the left, seemingly only a short distance away, was a church steeple which marked the outskirts of the immediate goal of the advance—Cambrai itself !

We remained here, in that shallow trench which was little more than a ditch, but which we knew was not worth the trouble of improving—for there seemed no danger of an attack from the enemy—from about six in the evening until midnight. During the halt a small incident took place which deeply impressed me at the time by its significance. Near that part of the trench occupied by No. 2 Coy. we found the dead body of a German soldier, apparently killed only a few hours earlier; he was little more than a boy, perhaps eighteen or nineteen years old. At the suggestion of our officer, a volunteer party was formed and a grave dug, and the German was buried with all the honours we might have shown to one of our own men. The Company stood round with bared heads while the Padre read the Burial Service, and the body was lowered reverently into the grave. Some of the men showed openly the emotion which I think we all felt, at the spectacle of this interment of an unknown boy by his " enemies " in an alien land.

I mention this incident, not because it was unique—it was not —but because it seemed to me to demonstrate how little personal hostility there was, in cold blood, between the combatants in the war. Civilian " patriots " at home, to whom all Germans were " unspeakable Huns," were far more pugnacious in their talk towards the enemy than we were, and I think few men at the front bore much personal malice towards the individual " Jerries " who fought because they had to and carried out orders they were compelled to obey. On the contrary, the history of the war is full of unofficial instances where men on either side have risked their

lives to get a wounded " enemy " to safety, or have shared their
rations with him when lying out under fire in No-man's-land.   I
have myself seen men give a priceless cigarette to a wounded
" Fritz " and treat him with all the care and consideration they
would show to one of their own comrades.   There was, I think,
an underlying feeling that we were all, friend and foe alike, helpless victims caught in the same net of inexorable circumstances,
and that, as the Prime Minister said—though in a much wider and
more catholic sense than he intended—that our real enemies were
not the people, but those in high places who misled them.

One evening at Boursies, an argument had started in my
platoon, about the German rear-guards who sometimes held out
against us in isolated posts long after all hope of rescue had gone.
Should the survivors be allowed to surrender at the last, or should
they all be killed ?   One or two men said they ought to be wiped
out, even if they put up their hands; they had killed many of our
men to no purpose, and should pay the price, the dirty bastards !
But the great majority disagreed.   They were brave men, they
asserted, who had sacrificed themselves so that their comrades
might get away.   Many British troops had done the same thing
in similar circumstances, and were accounted heroes; if they were
forced to surrender, they were entitled to be taken prisoner.   (Of
course, this was a theoretical discussion—what happens in hot
blood, in the midst of battle, is seldom determined by logic.)

But, unfortunately for the peace of the world, the rank-and-
file had no voice in the Peace Conference, and the spirit of
reasonable reconciliation for which I am sure the majority of front-
line soldiers would have voted found no place in the treaties.   The
final tragedy of the war was that, by our very victory, we placed
unlimited power in the hands of the " hard-faced men," who
promptly and cynically betrayed every ideal for which we had
fought.

.   .   .   .

Shortly after midnight the cooks took leave of us with a final
dixie of tea, and we moved off by platoons to take up our final
positions for the attack at dawn.   Our way led through Rumilly,
shattered and fantastic in the darkness, and as we emerged on the
farther side of the village we were greeted by a number of
gas-shells, which burst on both sides of the road with their
distinctive subdued "plop" like a "dud," and filled the air with
deadly fumes.   At once we put on our respirators, but in the dark
it was even more impossible to see our way along the broken road
through the mica goggles.   After stumbling helplessly about for
some minutes, most of us pulled off the face-covering, leaving only
the nose-clip in position and the mouth-piece between our teeth
to breathe through.   It was a risky thing to do, for there might
be mustard-gas among the fumes, which would have a corrosive
effect on the skin, but we had little choice and the gas was apparently

not strong, for we felt no ill-effects at the time. After about ten minutes we took the masks off altogether.

We finally came to a halt about half-past one, in the middle of what seemed to be a wide stretch of open fields. Profound silence reigned around, and we might have been miles from the war. There was no gun-fire and scarcely even the crack of a rifle audible at long intervals over that empty black void ; the darkness ahead was only broken now-and-again by a rare star-shell, and once or twice a distant searchlight followed an aeroplane across the sky. I saw no signs of the troops we were relieving—if, indeed, we were relieving anyone—for by now the whole front was in a state of flux, there were no trenches and scarcely any definite continuous line such as we had known in the past.

As soon as we halted, we lay down under cover of a low bank, and our officer gave us our instructions for the morning in a subdued voice—for, although the Germans were probably some distance away, we couldn't be sure. We were to move forward again for a short distance at 4.30 a.m., in readiness to follow the barrage which was timed to begin at 5.20 ; once on the move we were to go on as far as possible in a straight line, until definitely held up by enemy resistance, when we should take cover and dig in ; the supports would then go through our line and continue the advance. A railway line running south-east from Cambrai was to be our first objective. After synchronising our watches with the officer's, he told us to get as much sleep as we could during the three hours that remained.

Away to our left, Cambrai seemed to be burning furiously behind the rising ground, for clouds of lurid smoke rolled along the northern horizon.

.   .   .   .   .   .

At the appointed time we moved silently forwards in the dusk of the dawn, to within a short distance of the road from Cambrai which led to Esnes, along which the barrage was to open. " Summer Time " had ended a few days before, so that dawn was an hour " earlier " than on the morning of the Canal du Nord attack and this time, though we " went over " at the same time by the clock, we had daylight from the start. We took cover in some big craters about thirty yards short of the road—they were huge excavations, almost big enough to " bury a house," and I think they were probably made by large bombs, rather than shells—and waited for the " show " to begin.

Punctual to the minute, the artillery opened up at 5.20, but the performance was not so awe-inspiring nor so accurate as on the 27th —perhaps inevitably so, for the former occasion had been prepared for and the guns ranged for weeks ahead, whereas now the artillery was extremely mobile and constantly moving into unfamiliar country. The fire, though heavy, was somewhat ragged, and from the first a number of shells fell short, causing casualties in our ranks as soon as we left the shelter of the craters.

Five minutes or so after the barrage started, we scrambled out into the open, and formed line. There was no hostile reply, either from guns or bullets, this time, and we moved forward at walking pace without opposition. It was quite the most spectacular advance I had seen. Apart from the noise of the barrage, we might have been performing an exercise in field-training. The country was open, nearly level fields with a few trees here and there, and there were no trenches—it was a real "war of movement" at last. The wall of bursting shells in front, with the smoke of the explosions drifting away on a light breeze, and following the barrage an unbroken line of men at intervals of about ten feet from each other, moving forward with fixed bayonets and rifles at the trail; then splitting into sections in single file regularly spaced, each platoon led by an officer a few feet in advance, who signalled us on with his revolver—it was the sort of picture one might see in a romantic Hollywood war-film!

We moved slowly forward for some time, keeping as close as was prudent to the barrage, without seeing any sign of the enemy, except for a short burst of machine-gun fire from a rear-guard post in the ruins of Forenville, some distance away to our right. We did not go unscathed, however, for shells continued to fall short at intervals and several of our men were hit. There seemed to be one particular gun on our sector whose elevation was insufficient, for at regular intervals a shell pitched some fifty yards short of the barrage, right on the line of advancing men. I saw one of our Corporals struck in the thigh by a splinter and stagger a few paces with the blood spouting like a fountain; someone ran to his help, but a main artery had been severed and he died in less than a minute.

We continued to walk forward over the churned grass, and had gone perhaps a mile from the starting-point when we were signalled to halt for a few moments. We were getting too close to the barrage, and had dropped on one knee while waiting for it to go forward again, when another of those badly-ranged shells screamed close over my head (or seemed to) and burst with an immense impact a few yards directly in front of me.

I felt a sharp blow on my left leg as the concussion knocked me over, and on picking myself up I saw a piece of metal sticking in my puttee below the knee. I pulled it out and dropped it quickly it was hot!—and, as I could feel no pain, apart from a general numbness in the leg which I attributed to the blow, I thought it had done no damage. When we had gone on for about another hundred yards, however, glancing down I noticed blood oozing through the hole in my puttee, and told my nearest neighbour that I had "stopped one." He looked at the place and strongly advised me to go back, toute suite, and find the Aid Post, adding a heartfelt "You lucky devil!"

But I was doubtful whether I was morally justified in "packing up" for a wound which, although certainly genuine, might be—probably was—little more than a scratch, so I continued to go forward. I didn't want it to look as if I was deserting ! I had not gone far, though, before the temptation to take advantage of a perfectly legitimate excuse to retire from the action overcame whatever scruples I had. I remembered, most opportunely, that we had recently received orders to the effect that any man who was wounded, however slightly, should have his injuries dressed and be injected against tetanus as soon as possible, and I soon persuaded myself that it was my duty to go back and get this done.

So I turned round and went in search of a stretcher-bearer. I soon found one, who cut away my puttee and disclosed a hole about the size of a shilling in my calf. It seemed to be fairly deep, but to have missed any important veins and was not bleeding very much, so he bound it up with a field-dressing and told me to wait there until the M.O. arrived. I lay down on the ground and waited for a long time—an hour, at least—but there was no sign of the Doctor, or of anyone else, so at last I determined to go myself in search of the Dressing Station, especially as my leg was beginning to throb quite a bit. Therefore, dumping my rifle and equipment, very glad that as a casualty I was entitled to get rid of their weight, I started off.

Re-crossing the road from which we had started the advance, I pushed off as nearly as possible in the direction from which we had come during the night—that is to say, more or less due west. As the numbness wore off, my leg got very sore, and I made slow progress in consequence. My way lay across fields of dry stubble from which the grain had been harvested fairly recently, which made rather rough ground over which to limp, and I was obliged to stop and rest several times. There seemed to be no sign of life anywhere in sight, and the gunfire gradually died down. The morning sun shone brilliantly, with a touch of freshness in the air, and despite the pain of my leg I felt exhilarated at the prospect of a respite from soldiering. I suppose that, rightly, I ought to have been disappointed at not being able to stay with the Regiment in their triumphant march to victory ; but, bad soldier and worse Guardsman that I was, I felt no such regrets at the time—only relief and self-congratulation at the chance to "get away from it all," even if it was only for a short while !

After rather more than an hour, I saw troops in the distance, near the summit of a slight rise, and on reaching them found they were the 2nd Scots Guards, in Brigade support, waiting to go forward. Enquiring the way to the Dressing Station, I was told that it was about two kilos farther on, in Masnieres ; but before being allowed to proceed, a Sergeant told me that all walking-casualties were to report to the Brigadier-General. He was close at hand and asked me a number of questions about the progress of the advance. I told him what little I knew, and then spoke of the trouble our fellows were having from badly-ranged gun-fire. The General expressed great concern that we should be losing men by our own shells, and gave orders immediately that the offending gun should be located.

After being dismissed, I started for Masnieres, but had not got far along the road when I came upon a wounded man, lying unconscious by the roadside. When I had satisfied myself that he was not dead, I was wondering whether I had better go back for assistance, when an ambulance car appeared from the direction in which I was heading. It pulled up beside me, and the officer-in-charge, on making enquiries, told me to wait there until he returned. In a short while the car came back, and the unconscious man and myself were taken on board. A quick run brought us to Masnieres and the Guards' Main Dressing Station, where my wound was properly dressed and I received an A.T. injection, after which I was given a very welcome drink of tea, a meat sandwich, some chocolate and a packet of cigarettes. There were a large number of wounded men at the Dressing Station, both from our own and neighbouring Divisions, and while I was there some German casualties were brought in, who I noticed were treated exactly the same as our own men. My stay there was brief, and about an hour later I was en route for the C.C.S., sitting on the floor of a Red Cross car between four stretcher-cases. Almost the last thing I heard before leaving Masnieres was that Cambrai had fallen to our troops that morning.

The two-hours' run in the little ambulance must have been a gruelling ordeal for the stretcher-cases, who were all badly hurt. One of them was, I think, unconscious or doped, but the others were groaning or crying out every now and again. The road was very bad, and although the driver went as carefully as possible, there were continual jolts and shakings which were very painful to the helpless men. I was busy all the time doing what I could (without much success) to steady them against the worst bumpings and lurchings of the car.

At last, thankfully, we reached Grevillers, near Bapaume, and disembarked at the 49th C.C.S. After my leg had been examined again and re-dressed, I was given dinner, for which I was very ready, and then rested for an hour or so in one of the marquees. My luck still held, for about three o'clock in the afternoon I was detailed for the first hospital-train to leave Grevillers after my arrival there, and very soon afterwards was on my way to the Base.

The journey was uneventful and comparatively rapid, though it was somewhat uncomfortable, for the carriage in which I travelled was an ordinary third-class compartment rather the worse for wear, and we—the "walking" cases—were rather crowded ; there was nowhere to stretch out my "bad leg" except under the opposite seat. But minor discomforts like that were as nothing compared with the fact that we were going down the line, some of us to

Blighty, and might even have seen the last of the war. No one in my carriage was in low spirits!

Etaples was reached about ten o'clock, and after a snack of cocoa, buns and cigarettes, provided free by the Y.M.C.A., at the station, a convoy of ambulances conveyed us to the 4th General Hospital at Camiers. The usual formalities of reception were soon completed and we were conducted to our respective wards. It was with a feeling of most profound relief that I took my clothes off and fell asleep almost immediately, between white sheets in a real bed. I had not been able to undress properly or sleep other than on the floor for several weeks. I could hardly believe my luck, or realise that only that morning I had " gone over the top " behind the barrage!

. . . . . .

That was the end of the war, so far as my insignificant personal part in it went, and I was no more than a spectator, at second-hand, of the final scenes in the long drama. The wound which had taken me out of the firing-line turned out to be, as I had suspected, not at all serious and caused me little discomfort. The leg was sore and partially numbed for a week or two, and the M.O. at Camiers thought there might still be a small splinter or two of metal embedded in it ; but if this was so, they did not prevent it from healing up completely in about three weeks.

I sometimes wondered uneasily whether I had not been too ready to " pack up " after receiving so slight an injury, or whether I ought, for the sake of my comrades and the Company, to have tried to ignore it and carry on. But there were not many men at the front who would not have jumped at the chance of a " cushy one." On Active Service most soldiers are, whether they acknowledge it or not, superstitious ; there was a widespread belief, particularly towards the end, that if one deliberately interfered with the course of events by refusing such a chance—if it came honourably and unsought—disaster was bound to follow. " Obey orders if you're detailed, but don't volunteer for anything," was the general attitude.

In any case, apart from the " G.S.W.," I should almost certainly have been sent to hospital by reason of the gas-burns which began to show themselves within twenty-four hours of the shelling in Rumilly to which I have referred.

I did not stay long at Camiers, which was at that time being used as a clearing depôt, some cases being sent to England and others—mostly the lightly-wounded casualties—being distributed among Convalescent Camps along the coast. I had some slight hopes of getting across to Blighty on the strength of my wound, thinking that the fact that I had now been " out " for almost twelve months and therefore due for leave in any case, might carry some weight (as it did in some cases). But my luck did not hold to such extreme lengths! However, I was not unduly disappointed, and on the 12th found myself in No. 6 Con. Depôt at Etaples. Here we were housed in bell-tents, which, although not uncomfortably crowded and supplied with bed-boards and mattresses, were not very warm at this time of the year. However, this camp again was only a distributing centre, and I was only there for three days. Rumours of the end of the war were now becoming common, and when one evening some guns near the harbour fired a salute, for some unknown reason, everyone took it for the signal for the cessation of hostilities, and great excitement prevailed for the time.

While there, I had an opportunity of seeing the hospital in Etaples, the bombing of which last May had roused such a storm of indignation in the English Press. From what I saw, I felt that there was something to be said for the enemy's contention that the attack on the hospital, as such, had been accidental. It was entirely and closely surrounded by training camps, munition dumps, store depôts, and other "military objectives," and would have been almost impossible to distinguish by night. To accuse the Germans of deliberately "bombing the wounded" was, in my opinion, under the circumstances, a piece of unscrupulous propaganda, and others beside myself have felt that the real criminals were those members of the "Gilded Staff" who had needlessly exposed helpless patients and nurses to danger by placing the hospital there. Hospitals did not *have* to be in crowded Base towns, which were bound to be attacked; there were always plenty of country chateaux available when Generals and their retinue required accommodation. The Germans committed many "atrocities," no doubt—as who in war does not?—but intentional desecration of the Red Cross was not one of them, and it did our cause no good in the long run to accuse our enemies of unsubstantiated crimes.

. . . . . .

My next move was a slow and uncomfortable train journey, in incessant rain, to No. 5 Convalescent Camp at Cayeux. There were some two score of us in the party from Etaples, and we arrived at about three in the afternoon, in a rather disgruntled frame of mind, for we had been despatched in the early hours of the morning without breakfast, and had had no food since. A good meal awaited us at the Camp, however, and, as can be imagined, we did ample justice to it.

Cayeux was a small town near the mouth of the river Somme, and the Camp was situated about two miles to the north, close to the sea-shore. The nearest civilian habitations were a few fishermen's cottages clustering round a lighthouse — a hamlet which, though it was called "Nouveau Brighton," bore little resemblance to its English namesake! The Camp, which was a great improvement on Etaples, was composed of a large number of wooden huts arranged symetrically around a central parade-ground, and could accommodate about ten thousand men. It was well provided with recreation-huts under the auspices of the various war-charity institutions, and the Y.M.C.A. ran a large cinema, at which there were showings every evening.

I found a bed assigned to me in the only hut which was built of stone, known as the "Markham Hut," in which were housed about thirty of us, belonging to many different regiments. It was adequately furnished with bed-boards and mattresses, and we were not overcrowded. Life at the Camp was very easy; there was a roll-call each morning and again at night, and a short, very light parade for those fit to attend at nine o'clock—though one usually dodged it, if possible, on principle! We attended at the "surgery" every morning to have our injuries dressed or receive the prescribed dose of medicine, and there was an inspection by the M.O. once a week. Apart from these, the day was usually at our own disposal.

The town of Cayeux was "out of bounds" to the inmates of the Camp, and the main road leading thither was patrolled by Military Police, but that didn't worry us. It was quite easy to go there, if we wished, by walking along the sands at low tide, and as we wore ordinary service uniforms, not hospital "blues," there was not much risk of being caught. But it was an uninteresting place, with little beyond the charm of "forbidden fruit" to recommend it; personally, I preferred strolling on the sands or through the inland woods, and there were plenty of amusements in the Camp itself during the evenings. Besides the Cinema, there was a theatre, and in most of the recreation huts one could play billiards, draughts, bagatelle, chess, etc., listen to lectures or join in community-singing. I soon discovered several well-stocked libraries, and made good use of them during my stay.

One rather odd result of living among men from so many different regiments was that, although there was no compulsion to do so, while at the Camp I "poshed-up" more thoroughly than ever. When with the Battalion, I used to grouse as loudly as anyone about the absurdity of "spit-and-polish" in war-time and the insistence on standards of appearance which did not, so far as I could see, affect our military efficiency. But now, surrounded by members of what we somewhat contemptuously called "grabby mobs," I felt impelled to maintain, to the best of my ability, the reputation of the Guards for smartness in dress and bearing. Voluntarily, I polished my cap-star and buttons, brushed my clothes, creased my slacks and shaved meticulously, as if for a General Inspection. In that environment, I saw—or thought I saw—how much superior in every military sense were the Guards to any other branch of the Service, and though I had little claim, personally, to consider myself a typical representative, I was very proud to know that I was a Guardsman. In this, I think, I was not alone. Most Guardsmen had an instinctive conviction, whether they acknowledged it or not, that they were the *élite* of the British

Army, and when separated from their unit had a sense of responsibility for the honour of their Regiment.

Of course, it was mainly "swank," on our part. In essential military or personal qualities the Guards probably excelled few of the "first-line" regiments; only, perhaps, in discipline, "esprit-de-corps" and parade-ground smartness were they pre-eminent—but we had a renowned history, an unrivalled tradition and a reputation which was the envy of other troops, and to be a Guardsman—a member of the Brigade of Guards, the personal bodyguard of the Sovereign—was a source of real, if unexpressed, pride to each one of us.

There were several Guardsmen in the Camp at that time, though none besides myself from the 1st Coldstream, and I fell in with one or two who had formerly been in the Household Battalion, notably a Welsh Guards Sergeant who had been a Corporal-of-Horse at Windsor when I was there. Another man I was surprised to find was still wearing the H.B. badge; it seems that he had been sent to the Camp as a convalescent shortly before the disbandment of the Battalion, and having "dug himself in," in a permanent appointment on the Camp staff, had never been transferred to another regiment like the rest of us, and so was still officially a member of a unit which had long since ceased to exist!

.   .   .   .   .   .

The mustard-gas burns I mentioned first began to show themselves on the day after I was wounded, and the M.O. at Etaples diagnosed them as the result of the gas shells which fell near us the previous night, when we had partially removed our masks in order to see our way in the dark. They manifested themselves as open, running sores, not painful but very unsightly, and refused obstinately to heal up, despite the variety of lotions which were tried. In two or three days they covered my face and neck, and after a week at Cayeux the M.O. there sent me to a small hospital camp in a pine wood on the outskirts of the huts. Here a dozen or so of similar cases slept in bell-tents, which were not so comfortable as the huts at that season, but the food was very good and there was plenty of it; in the day-time we had a well-warmed "common room" in which to amuse ourselves. We were not supposed to leave the enclosure, but some of us used to get out after dark through a break in the barbed-wire fence, and visit the canteens in the Camp. As my face and head were well camouflaged in bandages, I had to be particularly circumspect in avoiding officers, and often thought what a "wounded hero" I should look if I could walk about the streets at home in my present disguise!

The burns still refused to respond to the treatment, however, so after a few days the doctor sent me before the Camp Commandant as a "special case," and the latter decided that treatment in a regular hospital was needed. Consequently, on the following Monday evening I left the Camp, in company with a number of other "specials," for Abbeville. We travelled by road in a couple of ambulances, and—after a breakdown on the way which delayed us for about half-an-hour — reached the 3rd Australian General Hospital. I thought myself to be in luck's way to be sent to a Colonial hospital again, for I had always considered them to be the cushiest, and in this case also I was not disappointed. The ward in which I found myself was very comfortable, and the Sisters most pleasant, cheerful and considerate. They were all Australian, and talked a lot about "down under," comparing their native land with England, not always, naturally, to the advantage of the Mother Country. The people, the climate, the scenery, they maintained were far superior in Australia ; the only thing in which they "gave us best" was "your lovely long Summer twilights—we have nothing like them at home."

Throughout the week I spent in the hospital I was kept in bed, for no particular reason that I could see, but I thoroughly enjoyed the long rest, and the time was by no means monotonous. I had books in plenty, newspapers were delivered in the ward every day, and I made some pleasant acquaintances among the other patients. Several fellow-Guardsmen who happened to be in the hospital at the time paid me visits, one of whom was a Coldstreamer of No. 2 Company. He had been in the advance on the morning when I was hit, and told how they had eventually caught up with the enemy, but said that there had been no more than a "token" resistance. He himself had been sent down with a slight wound a few days later.

The general war-news in the papers was becoming more and more exciting day by day. Turkey and Bulgaria were already out of the war, and Austria surrendered on November 4th, leaving Germany alone to continue the hopeless struggle. No one doubted that the end was at hand, and when one morning long before dawn several men from the ward were sent to Blighty great excitement prevailed, both among those who were going and those who remained ; we all felt that it would not be long before we, too, were homeward-bound.

I cannot recall anything about the kind of treatment which was applied to my burns, but it was entirely successful and the sores healed up completely in a few days. I returned to the Camp at Cayeux on November 5th, and found everyone in a state of tension, expecting the news of Germany's surrender at any moment. No one knew how or when the tidings would come, and the slightest rumour was sufficient to produce an uproar. The premature outbreak of excitement on the evening of November 7th demonstrates the almost hysterical state we were in.

It was half-past nine ; "Last Post" was just about to sound, and nearly everyone in my hut was in bed. I was reading, I remember, "The First Hundred Thousand." Suddenly, through the pandemonium which always preceded "Lights Out," could be heard the sound of distant cheering, apparently from the far side of the Camp. At first it was greeted with sarcastic laughter and a few ironical counter-cheers, but the sound increased, and presently the throbbing of a drum mingled with the shouting.

At that, the noise in the hut was suddenly silenced. Men gazed at each other with eager, questioning eyes. "Can it be?" was the unspoken query—"It is!" and with a simultaneous movement, everybody huddled on their clothes and poured out on to the parade-ground. On all sides, the other huts were disgorging their occupants and in a few minutes the huge open space was black with excited men. The rumour and the cheering spread like a conflagration: "Germany has surrendered!" and the whole eight or ten thousand of us yelled ourselves hoarse. With one accord, the whole throng burst into unanimous song :—

> "Take me back to dear old Blighty,
>   Put me on the train for London town ;
> Drop me over there, any-blooming-where :
>   Birmingham, Leeds or Manchester——
> Well, I don't care . . ."

Backwards and forwards we swayed, arms linked, shouting, cheering and singing. The uproar was indescribable, and it never occurred to us to doubt the truth of the rumour. I remember thinking : "This is the happiest moment of my life. I must fix it in my memory for ever!"

Someone found a box of Verey lights and there was an impromptu firework display. "Lights Out" sounded on the bugle, but the power-house was seized and the dynamo attendants forcibly prevented from turning off the current. Presently, some of the wilder spirits began to get out of hand ; a number of men raided the Guard-room and tried to release the defaulters in detention (who wisely refused to be released), and drenched the R.S.M. in the contents of a fire-bucket. Then a small crowd broke camp and marched into Cayeux in a body ; they returned during the small hours of the morning, still singing.

But, after the first excitement, the great majority of us began to wonder whether the celebrations were not after all a little premature, since no official confirmation of the news was forthcoming, and gradually we dispersed to our huts again. Next day, at dinner-time, the Camp Commandant visited the large mess-hut in which we took our meals, and addressed us. Without recriminations, he said that he sympathised with our feelings, but asked us not to repeat the performance. He pledged his word that as soon as he received official news of the Armistice, the "Fall in" would be sounded and he would announce the fact on parade ; then we should have all the opportunity for celebration we desired.

That was all, and we felt that it was quite reasonable, so we settled down to wait as patiently as we might.

.   .   .   .   .

Another extract from one of my letters written at this time, shows that despite the almost delirious excitement which everybody felt at the end to four years of suffering and horror, and the universal relief, there was room for grave doubts as to what use would be made of our victory now we had got it.

"Do you think Germany is really in earnest over the Armistice ? The Allies certainly don't seem inclined to let her down gently—nor do I think they should. But at the same time, they must be careful not to allow the elation of victory to run away with them. In my opinion, this is a most critical and dangerous time for us—the greatest danger we have yet faced. For it is not now the danger of defeat, it is the peril of victory. In the enthusiasm of success, will England remember the ideals for which we went to war ? Will she be true to the principles she professes ? It is so very possible that in the first glow of unlimited power for good or evil, she may yield to the "Junker" element in the nation, and cast aside the unselfish aims of justice and freedom for which so many thousands have laid down their lives . . . A lasting peace it must be, but it must also be an absolutely *clean* peace. Otherwise, the war has been in vain."

Many people, far more gifted and articulate than I, were feeling the same anxious doubts about the future which I expressed so crudely. But unfortunately their voices were drowned in the primitive orgy of hatred towards a defeated foe which swept the country and the "civilised" world. "Hang the Kaiser" and "Squeeze Germany until the pips squeak!" became the order of the day — with the results we all know now only too well.

The three days following the "dress-rehearsal" just described dragged by on leaden feet. The first notes of every bugle-call were listened to with bated breath, as we waited for the promised "Fall In," and no one dared go far from the hut, by day or night. The wildest rumours were received with enthusiasm and evoked cheers at the slightest excuse, though indeed the authentic news posted daily at the Camp Guard-room door almost outran our most optimistic imagination. Events crowded upon each other with bewildering rapidity : the Kaiser in flight to Holland—the British at Bruges and Ghent and Mons—the Americans at Sedan—the Guards in Maubeuge and over the Belgian frontier—we felt positively dizzy with the thrill of it !

The culminating point of suspense was reached on Sunday, at tea-time, when the C.O. again addressed us in the dining-hall. He had not yet received official news of the signing of an Armistice, he said, but it might come at any moment. As soon as he heard, the troops would be called on parade, and he would then detail the plans for celebrating the occasion.

Next day, the memorable Eleventh of November, there was no morning parade, and we passed the time hanging around the huts, tensely awaiting the signal. The Commandant did not keep his promise to the strict letter, for no word reached us until after dinner, though apparently the news was known in Cayeux three hours earlier. But at two o'clock the Camp was electrified by the sound of a bugle. Out we poured, pell-mell—the sick, the lame, the disabled and the whole—and formed up in our Companies in double-quick time. There was no dodging *that* parade! I am very sure that there was not a man missing who could by any means crawl there.

As soon as all the Companies had marched into position on the great central parade-ground, the Commandant took his stand facing us, attended by all the officers in camp, and called us to attention. Amid a silence in which the proverbial dropped-pin would have made a clatter, he made the momentous announcement. "Boys, Germany has surrendered. The Armistice was signed this morning!"

He got no further, for—crash upon crash—the pent-up cheers broke loose. Caps were flung in the air, hands were shaken on all sides, and everyone yelled to the utmost extent of their lungs, many with tears of joy running unheeded down their faces. It was the moment all had been waiting for, a moment of such undiluted happiness and emotion as I had never known and probably shall never know again—no longer an imagined hope for the future, but actually here!

When he could make himself heard, about five minutes later, the C.O. proceeded to outline the plans for celebration. For forty-eight hours there was to be complete freedom for everyone — no parades or roll-calls, all rules suspended and all bounds raised; we were free to go where we would and to do what we liked, provided that we returned to the Camp at night and answered our names at the roll-call on Wednesday afternoon. He placed us all "on our honour" to "play the game," and to report present at the end of the holiday—and as far as I am aware there was no case in which his confidence was misplaced. Only the permanent staff of the Camp were asked to remain on duty, to provide our meals and other indispensable needs, and to them would be given special privileges later. The festivities would be preceded by immediate services of Thanksgiving for all denominations, and then there was to be a round of concerts, dances and cinema-shows during the evening, after which an immense bonfire would consume an effigy of the Kaiser. Next day, there were to be football, hockey and baseball matches, and a smoking-concert in the evening.

Then, almost apologetically, he asked us to sing "God, Save the King," and such was the spirit of goodwill abroad at the moment that it was almost unanimously responded to. (For some months past, the National Anthem had been silently boycotted by the troops in France. Even in the Guards, when it was played during Church

Parade or on other ceremonial occasions, the only people who sang were the officers and a few senior warrant-officers ; the rest of us stood rigidly to attention, silent. I do not think that this was due to any disloyalty or republican sentiment, but was a spontaneous unspoken expression of disgust with things in general.)

After that, the C.O. took off his cap and, waving it over his head, shouted : "Now, boys, three ringing cheers for the end of the war!"

Pandemonium broke loose again—the cheers might almost have been heard across the Channel! The band played "Tipperary" and "Good-bye-ee," and the parade broke up into cheering groups.

After the Thanksgiving Service in the Church Army hut, a simple but very sincere and affecting ceremony, I assisted in the work of carrying logs of wood from the dump where they had been stacked in readiness to the centre of the parade-ground, and building them in a huge pile ready for the bonfire. This was a "fatigue" for which there were so many volunteers that it was all done in a few minutes. Then—after dashing off an ecstatic and almost incoherent note to my parents—I followed the crowd to the cinema. The performance was not due to commence until six o'clock, but before five the house was crowded, so they began at once ; the programme was interrupted several times by failure of the current, but nobody cared, for we nearly lifted the roof off with popular songs each time.

I was determined to take part in everything that was doing on this day of all days, so made a round of all the recreation huts and canteens in turn, in each of which there was a "sing-song" and dancing. The Depot Concert Party visited each hut during the evening, with an appropriate programme of songs and sketches, every item of which was applauded to the echo.

At nine o'clock the C.O. applied a torch to the giant bonfire, which stood twenty feet high in the midst of the Camp, surmounted by a rough effigy of the Kaiser, complete with bristling moustache and clad in a German uniform. As the flames soared upwards and the petrol-soaked wood crackled furiously, all restraint was flung aside, and the troops danced and whirled round the blazing pyre in an orgy of primitive self-abandonment. When at last the "Kaiser" tottered to his fiery doom, there was a great outburst of cheering, and the band struck up popular tunes. We went through the whole repertoire, from "Rule Britannia" to "Dixieland," everybody singing whether they knew the words or not, for three hours, until we could sing or dance no longer. At last, there was a unanimous demand for "Home, Sweet Home," and on that note, tired out, we gradually dispersed to bed.

．　　．　　．　　．　　．　　．

That, then, was how one camp in France celebrated the Armistice. It was a wild outburst of "mafeking," a release of long-pent-up spirits more suited to the civilan crowds of a great city, and perhaps hardly worthy of so momentous an occasion. In the line, I heard later, the troops had re-acted somewhat differently. Our Battalion was at Maubeuge, and the cessation of hostilities was announced on parade quietly, almost as if it was a routine order. Most of the men were bewildered and half-incredulous at first, and hardly knew whether to believe the news, after the spate of unconfirmed rumours which had long been going round. It took time for the truth to sink in, and full realisation came slowly. They were dazed by the thought that, after months of fighting and danger, they had really "come through" the war safely and would see their homes and families again. For the first day or two there was an unspoken fear lest, after all, there might be "a catch in it," and the distant sound of demolition explosions gave rise to momentary alarming surmises. "At first," one of the fellows told me afterwards, "the silence of the guns was almost frightening." Of course, there was cheering and singing, too, especially among the newest-comers, the "Maubeuge Draft," who had joined the Battalion just before the Armistice; but generally speaking the rejoicings were sober and restrained, the expression of a relief too great for shouting. I cannot help thinking that they must have been more in keeping with the magnitude of the "Great Deliverance" than was our orgy of noisy excitement at No. 5 Convalescent Depot.

AFTER THE ARMISTICE

WHEN I first roused next morning, it seemed as though I had been dreaming of some impossible happiness, but the full waking realisation was more wonderful than any dream. The war was over! There could be no doubt about it, incredible though it seemed; ten thousand witnesses on all sides of me confirmed the news, so it must be true!

After breakfast, I slipped away from the crowd by myself and rambled along the sea-shore, trying to grasp in solitude the full significance of yesterday's event. The weather had cleared after the slight drizzle of the previous evening, and the sun shone brightly, with considerable warmth for November. As I walked along the edge of the waves, with a light breeze just ruffling the calm surface of the sea and the pale gold sunlight gleaming back from the wet sands, the Sabbath stillness seemed to be a concrete expression of the new Peace which had come to the world, as if even Nature was resting after labour.

Away from the noisy excitement of the Camp, alone under the great arch of the clean sky, I began to comprehend something of the magnitude of our deliverance. All over the world, I thought, the shadow has lifted, and the dead weight of tragedy which had pressed on every living soul is taken away. The night has ended, and civilisation, re-born from the flames of its own conflagration, is given a new chance to realise its great possibilities.

For the first time for more than four years, the guns were silent, the scream of shells ceased to torture the air, and the ground was no longer rent by explosions. The last torpedo had been fired, the last bomb dropped, and the last humble village levelled with the ground. More wonderful than all, was the knowledge that men were no longer being killed by their fellow-men, dying in horrible ways or being maimed for life by means of devilish machines which were at once the most ingenious triumphs and the deepest degradation of the human mind. No more must we grub out precarious shelters in the mud against the hail of death; no longer need we live like animals in underground burrows, in rain and filth, infested with vermin, suffering hunger and thirst and interminable weariness of body and mind, enduring our lives from day to day without daring to look ahead to the future. Never again should we cower in secret terror while the universe crashed and roared around us; never again should we walk deliberately into Hell in the grey dawn of day. All that was over — marvellously, unbelievably over! — and henceforward disaster and death, danger and discomfort, instead of being the daily pattern of our lives, were once more relegated to their normal proportions in an ordered existence. Life was before us—happiness —Home . . . .

.　　.　　.　　.　　.

I went on along the sands to Cayeux, where the little town was "en fete." A band was playing in the Place (although its repertoire appeared to consist almost solely of "Tipperary," "Colonel Bogey" and the "Marseillaise," it rendered them repeatedly with the utmost verve), the houses were decked with flags, and soldiers and girls were dancing in the street. In the afternoon, I watched some of the sporting events which had been arranged in the Camp, and later went to the smoking-concert which packed to suffocation the large dining-hall.

I remained at the Camp for little more than a week after the Armistice, and was "marked out" as fit on the 19th. Despite the very easy and pleasant life of the Camp, I was, indeed, eager to go, for I had now been in France for nearly thirteen months and was "bobbing on the top line" (as the phrase was) for Leave, which I thought I should in all probability get when I reached the Base at Harfleur. The prospect was even more attractive now that the war was over; although hitherto I had longed for the chance to see my home, as a saint longs for heaven, I am sure that the thought of having to return to the front afterwards would have taken away half the pleasure. Now, there was no question of that; at most I should return for a few months' garrison service in Germany. More than this, there was quite a good chance, according to rumours going about, that I might even get demobilised while on leave, without having to come overseas again. But in both of these hopes I was destined to be disappointed.

I left Cayeux on November 21st, and after breaking the train journey at Noyelles for a few hours, reached Harfleur the following afternoon. I reported at the Guards Base Depôt and took up my quarters in the tent-lines. Nothing of note occurred during the next two days. I drew a new outfit in replacement of my kit "lost in action," and learned that we—the casualties returned from hospital—were to rejoin our respective Battalions very shortly.

On the 25th, however, I had the surprise of my life. I was sent for by the Regimental Sergeant-Major and placed under arrest!

The reason was that—being in a rather "fed-up" frame of mind, due to having learned that Leave was being granted from the Base only after fifteen months' service abroad and that I was consequently out of the running—I had written a very disgruntled letter home, in which I had imprudently alluded to reports that no celebration of the Armistice had been allowed in the Guards Base Depôt (on the contrary, it was said that the troops had been confined to camp on that day) and I had also referred very scathingly to the militaristic regulations of " this Grenadier-ridden hole."

No doubt I was to blame for giving way to my bad temper, and especially foolish to have expressed my grouses in a letter which was bound to be censored ; after all, my Leave was probably only delayed until I re-joined the Battalion. That the Base Depôt was a " militaristic . . . . hole " was, in my opinion, only too true. The worst types, both of officers and non-coms. seemed to gravitate to permanent employment there: the atmosphere in the service units was entirely different—but it was silly to say so openly. My letter had been passed to the R.S.M., himself a Grenadier, who was one of those fat, uneducated bullies who in such places often achieved promotion by no other apparent merit beyond a raucous voice and a blustering manner. It was well known that he " had it in for " all Coldstreamers, and was cordially hated by everyone who came to the Depôt. When I reported to him, he was livid with fury and raged at me in terms impossible to reproduce, while I stood rigidly at attention. In the end I was informed that I was under open arrest and was ordered to appear at " C.O.'s Orders " next morning.

When I was marched into the Orderly Room under escort, at the usual breakneck speed and to the accompaniment of shouting N.C.O.'s, the charge was read and the C.O. asked if I had anything to say in my own defence ; but I had scarcely opened my mouth before the Sergeant-Major shouted " Silence ! " The C.O. then said, " Will you accept my sentence, or do you wish to appeal to a Court-Martial? " I did not believe that a Court-Martial, in which I was allowed to state my case, would have convicted me ; for what, after all, had I done?—repeated, in a private letter, what was the common talk of the Depôt, and made some ill-tempered and possibly unjustified remarks about the Camp. I had revealed no military secrets, which was the ostensible reason for the censorship. My real offence, I think, was that I had been disrespectful to a great brother-regiment, and in this I freely admit I was wrong ; R.S.M.—and Colonel—were not typical representatives of the Grenadier Guards.

But to carry the matter further would have meant a delay, probably, of several weeks, and I was confident of getting my Leave as soon as I re-joined the Battalion ; so I thought the quickest and simplest way was to accept the C.O.'s sentence, and said so. I was hardly prepared, however, for the severity of the penalty imposed (in relation to my " crime ")—seven days' No. 1 Field Punishment, the most rigorous sentence for a minor offence in the Army Code, and which in the ordinary way included the notorious " crucifixion " (being tied to the wheel of a gun-carriage in public for several hours each day). However, I had accepted the sentence in advance, so there was nothing to be said.

I was then locked up in the Guard Room, where there were several other defaulters, one of whom I recognised as a man from my old platoon in the 3rd Battalion, whom I had not seen since those days. We were both pleased at the unexpected meeting, and spent much of the day in talking and exchanging reminiscences. Among other things, I learned something of the Armistice Day excitements in London, for my friend had been on Leave at the time. Indeed, his Leave had expired on November 11th, and it was because he had not started back for France almost at the very minute when the Armistice had been announced that he had been arrested on a charge of being twenty-four hours " A.W.O.L." None the less, he considered that it had been worth it!

As things turned out, I did not have to undergo the full rigours of my sentence, after all, for next day all Coldstream " details " in the Depôt were sent to join their respective units at the " front," defaulters included. Although nominally under close arrest, I travelled with the rest of the detachment exactly the same as any of the others; the Corporal in charge of the cattle-truck was responsible for my safe custody, but he was a decent sort and allowed me just as much liberty as anyone, so long as he was satisfied from time to time that I was still there. We marched into Havre, entrained at five o'clock and finally got under way at eight-thirty in the evening. I don't know why it was, but every time I had left the Base we boarded the train several hours before it was due to start, and hung about in the meantime with nothing to do. It was apparently the normal procedure.

Chaulnes was reached at six o'clock next morning, and there was then one of those mysterious halts on sidings which were an almost inevitable feature of troop-train journeys in France. We were there on this occasion for more than fourteen hours, and were not allowed to leave the train, other than to walk about on the permanent-way alongside. After a short halt at Cambrai early in the morning of the 29th, we arrived at our destination, Solesmes, about 8.30—a total distance of about one hundred and fifty miles in thirty-six hours!

.   .   .   .   .

Solesmes, a small town on the river Selle, five or six miles north of Le Cateau, was the temporary location of the " Guards' Reinforcement Camp," whither all Guards " details " were at that time being sent before going on to their respective units in Germany. The town was less damaged than most in the war-area, having been well behind the German lines until the last two or three weeks, and there were still a good many civilians there. But it was quite uninteresting, and seemed to be cut off from the outside world, for while I was there we had no newspapers at all, and very few letters. There was only one shop in the place open for business, and that was a small haberdasher's which had little in stock of use to us, except an occasional candle at 7½d. each. Our own Canteen was almost always closed for lack of supplies ; one afternoon I stood in a queue for two-and-a-half hours to obtain one franc's worth of biscuits and a tin of herrings—all the variety there was to buy.

When we arrived, I and the rest of the defaulters were taken to the Headquarters Guardroom, a vault beneath a brewery, where we slept on loose straw, surrounded by barrels (empty, of course!) The Sergeants of the Guard, who had charge of us, were quite decent, and, although we were nominally in close confinement, they allowed us to go into the town after dark, "sub rosa." During the daytime we had some fatigues to perform, none of which were very strenuous, and considered that we were serving our sentences in a very cushy manner. On December 1st, however, I was transferred to the 2nd Brigade Guard-room, where, although living conditions were no worse, we had "pack-drill" each afternoon. But by that time there were only two days left of my "Seven Days," and on the 3rd I was released and joined the 1st Coldstream section in another part of the same building.

The next fortnight was passed in a state of growing depression. We were marooned in this taudry oasis, forgotten, it seemed, by the world ; for we had practically no news from outside, where we knew that great events must be taking place and the Peace we had helped to win was being shaped. A General Election campaign was in full swing in England and, under the new Parliament Act, we all had votes, but no word of the issues before the electors reached us. It almost seemed to us that we were being deliberately kept in the dark, and when at last postal ballot-papers were distributed most of us tore them up in disgust. To have voted for candidates about whose views we knew nothing would have been farcical.

Solesmes was destitute of any kind of amusement or interest. The civilian inhabitants were poor and seemed half-starved, and there were no public services, gas or electricity ; candles were almost unobtainable, and the long winter evenings seemed longer than ever, with only desultory conversation or games of cards by fire-light to pass the time. Fortunately, we were not short of fuel, though the source of supply was somewhat unorthodox. The top of the large building in which we were billeted (originally a convent of some kind) had been wrecked by a shell, and when we wanted fire-wood we just went upstairs and stripped the woodwork from the upper rooms !

The daylight hours were mainly occupied by parades and fatigues, but sometimes there was a route-march over the surrounding country, in the course of which we crossed ground which had been the scene of one of the fiercest of the German rear-guard actions in which our Battalion had taken part. On a hill near St. Python there was a shrine by the roadside, entirely shattered by gunfire except the Figure, which stood in the midst of the ruin untouched. There was a superstition among the troops that such wayside crucifixes could not be destroyed by artillery or bombs, and it was remarkable how many one saw which had remained intact—but, in truth, there were at least as many more which had been smashed.

It was at this time that the title of the rank-and-file of the Guards regiments was changed—presumably in recognition of "The Brigade's" services during the war. Henceforth, we were no longer "Privates," but "Guardsmen."

And while I was at Solesmes I learned of the award of the Victoria Cross to Captain Frisby and Corporal Jackson. I had not known Cpl. Jackson personally; he had been in another platoon and I had not come into close contact with him during the three weeks or so I had been in the Company before his death. But there was no one for whom I could have been better pleased, because he had won his Country's highest military honour, than Captain Frisby. He was universally admired and respected in the Battalion, and was a Leader we were proud to follow.

All this time at the Guards' Reception Camp we were fretting to get back to our Battalions, who we pictured as living in clover in Germany. Solesmes became to us a prison from which there seemed to be no hope of escape, and some said that we were to be kept there until the next war! But actually, while we were kicking our heels in idleness—or comparative idleness—we were being saved a very strenuous ordeal. The Guards Division marched all the way from Maubeuge to Cologne, in full fighting order, with brasses shining, trousers creased and boots polished—one of the most prolonged and exacting route-marches in their history, nearly a month of daily foot-slogging! I would like to have been on that march. Most of those who were there probably wished themselves anywhere else at the time, and so, I expect, should I have done; but—mark my phrase, "to have been"—it must have been an experience to remember, to look back upon with pride, however great a test of endurance it was in the doing. And, as I have been told, it was a Triumphal March of Liberation, for in each town or village of France or Belgium through which they passed the inhabitants went wild with joy, and some unforgettable scenes occurred.

However, at long last the order came through for us to re-join our respective regiments—by train—and we left Solesmes on the morning of December 16th. We passed through Le Quesnoy and Valenciennes, and halted for a time at Mons. I was glad to have the opportunity of seeing the famous battlefield where the British first met the German army in 1914. Then we proceeded towards La Louviere; but just as we reached the outskirts of the town the couplings broke between two of the cattle-trucks, and about half of the train, my car included, ran backwards down the incline. At first we noticed nothing wrong. The train seemed to come to a standstill, and then to move slowly back—we thought we were merely shunting into yet another siding. But soon we began to remark on the unusual speed at which we were travelling, and when we saw men by the railside leave their work and run after us, shouting and gesticulating, we realised what had happened. Every alternate truck was fitted with hand-brakes, and these were immediately applied. We must have reached a speed of forty or fifty miles an hour before we began to slow down, and had we come to a sharp curve or points we must certainly have smashed up. Fortunately, the line was almost dead straight for about twenty miles, and we came safely to a standstill after running back nearly to Mons. A half-hour later the rest of the train, which had not, apparently, at first noticed our "desertion," came back in search of us, we were hitched on and continued the journey.

We passed through Luttre after nightfall, where there were many acres of smashed and twisted trains and railway lines—the result either of raids or demolitions—and stopped at Charleroi. Here we were definitely right out of the war-area at last, and back in untouched civilisation, and it gave us a real thrill to see the great covered station blazing with lights and to walk on the smooth platform. We got out and tramped up and down for the sheer joy of the feel of a real pavement under our feet. Namur and Liege were passed while I was asleep, but I awoke in time to realise that we were crossing the German frontier.

There was a brief halt at a small station just across the border, where the inhabitants seemed very much alive to our arrival, and even raised a feeble cheer. This indication of goodwill surprised me very much, for I had expected nothing but sullen looks and impotent hostility from the inhabitants of the Occupied Area ; but it appeared that the allocation of that part of the Rhineland to the British was a great relief to the population, who had been terrified at the prospect of being under French rule—and well they might be ! After stopping again at Aachen (Aix-la-Chapelle) and also at Duren, we reached Cologne at ten o'clock in the evening of December 17th.

.   .   .   .   .   .

The station at which we left the train was in one of the northern suburbs of the city, but it was too dark to see much of our surroundings and I never learned its name. We remained in the station yard for some three hours, while baggage and stores were unloaded from the train, during which time we collected firewood, made fires between the lines and fried our ration of bacon for supper. Some time after midnight we fell in and marched off, all of us in high spirits. It was a great moment, to know that we were marching, as conquerors, through one of the enemy's principal cities, and we waked the echoes of the sleeping streets with all the popular songs of the time, among which "Good-bye-ee" was, rather inappropriately, the first favourite just then. We were billeted for the night in some school buildings, and next day, having "poshed-up" thoroughly after the journey, we re-joined the Battalion in the Barracks at Riehl, one of the northern suburbs, where the 2nd

Guards Brigade was stationed. They had apparently arrived by road only a day or two before we did.

Of the many and varied interests of Cologne it is not necessary to say much here, and indeed I did not have much opportunity of seeing the city on this occasion. It was the first large town I had been in for more than a year, apart from poor shattered Arras, and the first thing about it that impressed me very strongly was the clean neatness of the streets and the spacious planning of the more modern districts. A series of magnificent boulevards, tree-shaded and lined with imposing buildings, formed a semi-circle whose ends opened upon the river and which enclosed the " Old City," where although more crowded, many of the streets preserved a fascinating air of medieval quaintness, with the sculptured wonder of the Cathedral rising in their midst.

The Riehl Barracks, in which we were quartered, were extremely comfortable by English standards and much more modern in construction than any of the Windsor or London barracks with which I had any acquaintance. We lived in spacious and well-ventilated rooms, slept in excellent beds and had every convenience for storing our kit and other belongings. The whole place was spotlessly clean, and so designed that a minimum of labour was required to keep it so. There was a theatre in the Barracks, and an excellently furnished Canteen, though the effects of the blockade were to be seen in the extraordinary synthetic articles sold in the latter. The native cigarettes, for instance, consisted of about an inch-and-a-half of some kind of dried herb (certainly not tobacco) at the end of a cardboard tube, and cost the equivalent of fourpence each. However, the troops were not dependent on these, but could obtain a good supply of English brands at tax-free prices. On the walls of this Canteen, which was run by Germans, I was surprised to see a framed photograph of Bexhill-on-Sea !

We were allowed unlimited use of the municipal tramway system and might travel to any part of the city without payment, even being entitled, I believe, to demand that civilians should give up their seats to us in a crowded car, though this right was seldom exercised. On the contrary, I often observed the expressions of pleased surprise with which ladies greeted the offer of his seat by a soldier. It was apparently a courtesy much less usual in Germany than in England, particularly by the military. The tramway route into Cologne from Riehl passed the Barrack gates, and was a great convenience to us when off duty. In the early days of the Occupation we were only allowed out in couples wearing bayonets, but there was little or no indication of hostility on the part of the people, and the rule was soon abandoned.

In fact, for the most part the civilian population was remarkably well-disposed towards the troops ; one might have thought that we were allies rather than enemies. All classes showed a friendliness and willingness to please which was surprising and, at first, somewhat disconcerting. We had come prepared for hostility, but were met with smiles! Many men who had been loudest in their threats of what they would do to " the dirty Hun " when they got the chance, speedily reversed their attitude. Later, when on sentry in the city, most passers-by would give me a pleasant " Morgen ! " or " Guten nacht ! " and I heard that men who had the luck to be billeted on private families were made extremely comfortable. In the shops, too, there was little disposition to raise prices against us, or to take advantage of the troops' ignorance of the rate of exchange. (While in Germany, we were paid in marks and pfennigs, though English and French notes were also current.) In fact, it was often the other way about, and I was several times ashamed to see whole-sale " shoplifting " going on openly, while the perspiring shopkeeper was endeavouring to attend to the wants of a crowd of souvenir-hunters. That was, however, only the case during the early days ; some types of men apparently considered themselves entitled to " spoil the Egyptians," but soon, in the absence of provocation and the return to more normal conditions of civilised life, their civilian respect for the conventions of property reasserted itself. German ex-soldiers, too, were often eager to fraternise with our men and to exchange war-reminiscences, so far as the language difficulty would permit. I came across one man, now serving behind the counter of a shop where I was buying a bottle of " Eau-de-Cologne " to take home, who, it seemed, had been in the German trenches opposite Monchy last winter, on the same part of the front as I had been at the time.

Was all this conciliation no more than a cunning conspiracy to secure better treatment for themselves ? Perhaps ; it's hard to be sure. But if it was deliberate, it was remarkably unanimous and widespread, not only in Cologne but, as I heard, in the smallest country villages of the Occupied Zone. The people welcomed us, not as conquerors, but as deliverers from war. That was the universal feeling: relief that the war was over, at any price. Also, our presence was a safeguard against the turmoil of revolution, which was rampant in the rest of Germany. And our men, by their correct behaviour and lack of " Prussian " swagger, soon became genuinely popular.

During that Christmas-tide of 1918, I think that, could matters have been left to the soldiers and common people, such a Peace of reconciliation and mutual good-will could have been made which would not only have fulfilled the ideals for which millions had died, but would have secured a lasting friendship between the erst-while enemies. The men who had fought and suffered, on both sides, had had their fill of war, and were ready for a peace based on Christian concord without malice. But the soldiers were virtually disfranchised, the politicians took control and imposed a vindictive treaty the like of which had never been seen in the modern world before. All our subsequent troubles and frustrations date from that; the supreme opportunity was thrown away.

My stay in Cologne on this occasion, however, was very brief, and I did not have much opportunity for exploration of the city until later. As soon as I re-joined the Battalion I put in my name for Leave, which was now much over-due, and to my great satisfaction it was granted almost at once. We were not allowed out of barracks until after five in the afternoon, so that I only had time to scurry round and secure a few souvenirs before I left. The shops seemed to be quite well stocked with most things—except food— and the brightly-lit windows were gay with Christmas displays. It was " touch and go " whether I should manage to get home before Christmas Day, but the Company Office was exceptionally co-operative, my pass was signed without delay, I was issued with a ration-card and packed my kit, and was away by the leave-train which left the central Bahnhof in Cologne at 3.53 on the afternoon of Sunday, the 22nd.

The first part of the journey was accomplished in luxury. To my pleased surprise, the train was not composed of the cattle-trucks ("40 hommes, 8 chevaux") in which the troops were usually conveyed, but was a line of magnificent corridor-coaches commandeered from the Germans. I managed to secure a comfortable seat by the window, and disposing my kit on the rack overhead settled down to enjoy a luxurious journey. The compartment had a door only on the corridor side and the window against which I sat was a single large sheet of glass, affording an uninterrupted view of the passing scenery, and below which was a hinged table, very convenient for meals or for playing cards. It seemed that we were to travel in style.

At first, all went well. The train travelled at a fair speed, and the well-sprung coaches were a welcome change from the banging and jolting trucks in which most of my train-journeys had been performed during the last fifteen months. It was pleasant to lean back in my well-cushioned corner and to think that this was only a foretaste of the civilised comforts to come. My fellow-travellers —the train was crowded with men all bound on the same errand as myself—were a pleasant lot and needless to say all in very good spirits.

Despite my window-seat, the early fall of darkness prevented my seeing much of the country after we had passed Duren; constellations of lights in a formless mass of dark buildings was all I saw of Aachen, Liege and Namur. As the night wore on, conversation in the carriage slackened and, one after another, we dropped into an uneasy sleep, feet stretched under the opposite seat and heads lolling at uncomfortable angles. Our repose was by no means uninterrupted, however, for—as seemed inseparable from any journey in which troops were involved—there were frequent stops, shuntings and inexplicable delays on obscure sidings, each of which brought sleepy groans, curses and sarcastic remarks from the long-suffering travellers.

When dawn broke we were approaching Charleroi, where we stopped for some time in the station and were able to buy newspapers. Then the journey was continued without incident, until Mons was reached. Here we had a most unpleasant surprise, when we were unexpectedly told to leave the train. Bewildered, we collected our kit and bundled out on to the platform. No sooner had everyone alighted than the train moved away empty and we were left stranded under the station roof, completely at a loss as to the reason for this unforeseen break in our journey. Presently an R.T. officer came along, and explained that the train in which we had arrived did not go beyond this point, but that we should be off again very shortly. In the meantime, rations would be distributed.

Well, the rations duly arrived, but the train did not, and after a couple of hours on the draughty platform we began to get impatient. There was a cold wind blowing, and a leaden sky from which a persistent drizzle fell steadily. One humourist was heard to remark that he was not surprised that the British Army had retreated from Mons if it was like this—he was only too ready to do likewise !

Then, about three o'clock, a Sergeant-Major loomed out of the mist, and ordered us to fall in. We did so wonderingly, but when he went on to say that we were to march to a rest-camp in the town and spend the night there, our dissatisfaction could no longer be concealed. Stop in this God-forsaken hole until tomorrow, and lose our last chance of Christmas in Blighty? Not bloody-well likely! Ominous mutterings and growls swelled rapidly into angry shouts, and the orderly ranks broke up into an indignant mob. The Sergeant-Major's voice was lost in the din, and we saw no more of him. Someone shouted, " See the R.T.O. about it! " and a concerted movement was made in the direction of the official hut at the far end of the platform.

But just at that moment a long train of cattle-trucks was seen approaching from the east ; it came to a stop opposite our platform, three sets of rails away. Somehow or other—I don't know quite how—the word went round that it was bound for Boulogne. A cry went up, " Come on, boys! " and with one accord we streamed across the permanent-way and stormed the trucks. They were all occupied, but we cared nothing for that. Without regard to the protests of those inside, we hurled our kit through the doors and squeezed ourselves after it, and no amount of official remonstrance could dislodge us. Railway officials and military police ran frenziedly up and down the length of the train, threatening all sorts of dire penalties and promising us another train if we would only wait, but we were determined not to trust them again. Time was too short to risk another disappointment.

At last they apparently realised that nothing short of force would eject us, and—possibly because those in authority were not without sympathy with our special reason for wanting to get away —the signal was given for the train to start, and we were once more on the move.

We were now in very different circumstances from the first part of the journey. Instead of a comfortably upholstered and well-sprung coach, lit with incandescent gas, fitted with racks for our kit and steam pipes to keep out the cold, we had now only the hard and grimy floor of the truck, which jolted and banged with disconcerting irregularity as we stood swaying and clutching at any support. For the trucks were so crowded that there was literally not room for all of us to sit down at one time. The one I was in, which had an official limit of capacity for forty men and could hardly have accommodated thirty with any degree of approximate comfort, now held fully sixty of us, and we were obliged to take turns in squatting on each other's kit, while the rest stood wedged in between holding on to the shoulders of the nearest man and overbalancing every time the train gave an unexpected lurch. There was no light except what came in through the open door, and of course no room for a brazier fire, such as we had always carried before on winter journeys.

Mons had marked the completion of about half our journey to the coast, and so far, although unbelievably slow by civilian standards, we had travelled at quite a fair speed for a troop train. The hundred and twenty miles had been covered in about sixteen hours. But now, whether because of the length and overloading of the train, or perhaps because the track crossing the old war-area had been hastily and insecurely laid, our rate was even slower. The distance from Mons to Boulogne, by the route we traversed, is something like a hundred and thirty miles, and the journey lasted nearly thirty hours ! Of course, considerable allowance must be made for stops and shuntings, but even so our best speed can hardly have exceeded ten miles an hour, and at times it would have been quite practicable to walk along side while the train was in motion. And all this time we travelled in the conditions I have described— surely the longest spell of " strap-hanging " on record ! But we were homeward-bound, and would willingly have put up with much greater hardships.

With the fall of darkness, the weather cleared and the stars sparkled in a cloudless sky. From my position well inside the truck I could see little of the country we passed, and it was not until we stopped just outside Arras in the small hours of the morning that I was able to extricate myself and stretch my cramped limbs. It was difficult to realise, standing there between the rails in the frosty light of the moon, that this was indeed Arras once more, the city in which, more than a year ago, I had made my first acquaintance with the war, and near which I had spent the previous Christmas.

How much had happened since then, and how different were my prospects now!

The silent town, its ruins bathed in the light of the moon, looked curiously unreal, like a dream of the past—the more so because the flash and rumble of the guns, so inseparable a part of my memory of it, were now absent; never once during my three months in the neighbourhood had their thunder ceased. What was it like in Arras now, I wondered—now that the war had gone but life could hardly have returned to the mangled streets? Were there troops still in Schramm Barracks and the Ecole Communale? "Wilderness" and "Bully-beef" Camps had no doubt been demolished, and the Fosse Farm Caves were empty. I wished I had an opportunity to re-visit the trenches around Monchy, now mouldering in silence under the moon. I could not—and I still cannot—picture all that countryside as cultivated and prosperous; to me, it will always be a barren waste of tumbled earth, rusty wire and shell craters.

The train had stopped just outside the main station, which still reared its gaunt skeleton of shattered ironwork against the sky; and across the Place de la Gare, through which we had so often marched on our way to and from the line, the row of smashed houses still stood, even more ruinous than when I had last seen them. We remained there for about an hour, during which time we managed to get a small fire going by the railside and brewed some tea. We dared not leave the vicinity of the trucks, however, for the train might start at any moment, and it was no easy matter to fit ourselves into the cramped space again at short notice. As it was, one man nearly got left behind and had to run alongside for some distance before he could be hauled into the truck.

I remember very little about the rest of the journey, which lasted throughout the next day. I was getting very weary and somewhat dazed from lack of sleep, and all my attention was needed to maintain my balance in the swaying train. The day, so far as I have any recollection of it, was a long purgatory of cold, of cramped and aching limbs, and of an almost uncontrollable desire to fall down anyhow and sleep. Thoughts of the home I was going to and of those I should see again after so long an absence gave place almost exclusively to a seductive vision of the comfortable bed which awaited me and the blessed prospect of undisturbed rest.

We got to Boulogne about half-past eight that night—Christmas Eve—and, after an interval of which my memory is little more than a blur of lights, shining rails and narrow streets, I found myself in a large, brightly-lit room fitted with bunks—evidently a rest-hostel for men going on leave. I was by that time so dazed with fatigue that I remember nothing more at all clearly, though I have a vague recollection of queueing-up for passes to be examined and of having a much-needed meal, the first fresh food we had received since the issue of the rations at Mons. Then I slept like the proverbial log until about six the next morning.

There were several hundreds of us going across the Channel that morning, and after breakfast had been disposed of we lost no time in getting our kit together—we travelled in full-pack order, with rifles, bayonets and sundry private parcels—ready to depart at the earliest possible moment. It was Christmas morning, and everyone was on a tip-toe of excitement ; the general atmosphere was like that of breaking-up for the school holidays—only more so ! At first there was some delay, and alarming rumours spread that the boats were not running, owing to the Christmas holiday. But all was well, and at last we lined up in a final queue to have our passes stamped. The boat was already at the quayside when we marched down to the harbour, and at about eleven o'clock we steamed out into the open Channel—really !—incredibly !—bound for Blighty.

The weather was perfect, the sky cloudless, and a million sun-sparkles flashed from the pale green surface of the sea. The frosty tang of the clear air set the blood tingling in our veins, and— if my own feelings were any criterion—it was difficult to refrain from a most " un-English " exhibition of exuberance. I stayed on deck throughout the crossing, continually straining my eyes towards the brown shores of Blighty, which momentarily came nearer— obscured once or twice, I must confess by a mistiness which did not come from the atmosphere. As we approached the entrance to Dover harbour we were surprised to hear strains of music, and, drawing alongside the quay, we beheld nothing less than a brass band and a small crowd of people, who cheered loudly as we filed down the gangway. Ours was the Christmas Leave-boat and was welcomed in appropriate style, which we, of course, thoroughly appreciated. When, too, our train drew out of the station, the windows of many of the houses overlooking the railway were filled with people, who must have left their Christmas dinners to wave and shout greetings—to which we naturally responded in kind.

The run to Victoria seemed almost inconceivably rapid, compared with our crawl through Belgium and France. Arriving at the famous terminus, beginning and end of so many war-time journeys, I handed in my pay-book at the appropriate office, so that the accumulated arrears of my pay could be assessed and forwarded to me, and from which a trusting Government allowed me to draw £2 on account. Then I made for the Underground and Charing Cross, only to find that there was no train to my destination before that evening. But, eager as I was to reach home, the delay mattered little, for nothing could now prevent my arrival, and in the meantime it was good to walk the streets of London again, and to breathe its delightfully soot-stained air !

At last I was actually on the train, and on the last stage of my long trek. The lights of London, still hardly restored from their war-time dimness, were left behind and succeeded by the dark countryside, with its scattered friendly gleams from cottage and homestead. One by one, the well-remembered station names flashed by, and the miles separating me from my goal diminished. Presently, the roar of the last tunnel slackened and ceased, and *the* name—of the whole gazetteer, the name I had most wished to see—came slowly to rest opposite the carriage door.

I surrendered my railway-warrant at the barrier, and climbed the hill from the station, as I had so often during the last months pictured myself doing. A few minutes more, and I stood at the gate through which, a year and a half ago, on a drenching summer morning, I had gone into the unknown world of Army life, expecting much but anticipating little of the varied experience that was before me. It seemed to me that I was considerably more than eighteen months older now !

Outside the door, I paused, with an almost nervous hesitation. My arrival would be entirely unexpected, for I had not been able to send word of my coming, and I had to prepare myself for the stir which it would cause.

Then I pressed the bell.

.   .   .   .   .   .

I shall say nothing about my leave, except that it was all I had looked forward to during the long months of anticipation. Successive applications to the War Office gained me extensions of time, until instead of fourteen days I had, in all, eight weeks at home. The authorities were being very generous at that time in the matter of granting extensions to men on Leave, but I was told, when I returned to Cologne, that mine constituted a "record" for the Battalion. A contemporary effort by my Father to secure my demobilisation on business grounds, however, was not successful, but brought a letter from Captain Frisby (who at that time was in command of the Battalion Demob. Office) saying, in effect, that the Battalion could not yet dispense with my services ! I left Tunbridge Wells on the return journey on February 15th, travelling direct to Folkestone, and boarded the Leave-boat at eleven o'clock.

.   .   .   .   .   .

We landed, to everyone's surprise, at Calais instead of Boulogne (though I heard afterwards that the latter town was now being used as a "demobilisation port" only) and were accommodated for the night in a Rest Camp. Next morning we entrained for Germany, and travelled in great comfort in a German corridor-coach, without this time having to change trains en route. There were seven other men in my compartment, who were excellent company—they were all Hussars, who had been "out" since the beginning of the war (or so they said)—and the journey passed very pleasantly. Our route passed through St. Omer, Hazebroucke, Bailleul, Nieppe, Armentieres, Lille (all famous names during the war) Tournai, Ath and Luttre ;

and then followed the same course as I had travelled on the first journey. The speed of the train, the stops and shuntings, were of course as usual, but we were quite happy and would not have minded a much longer journey. Even our meals were brought to us without our having to leave the carriage, and the train ran so smoothly that I was able to have a shave while it was in motion. At Charleroi we stopped for several hours and were able to buy English newspapers—but as they were two days old we did not learn much fresh news from them.

On Monday night we halted again at Huy, between Namur and Leige, and a Canadian Rest-camp in the town gave us a generous free feed and sent us away laden with bread-and-cheese and mess-tins full of tea. We were only just in time, getting back to the train, and for some hectic minutes could not find our own compartment. We lost most of our " buckshee " provisions in a wild scurry up and down the train, tripping over rails and wires in the darkness, and slopping tea over ourselves and each other. We finally tumbled into the right door just as the train started.

Cologne was reached at half-past nine next morning, and with two other men I met in the station, I reported at the Riehl Barracks. Almost the first thing I learned, on rejoining No. 2 Company, was the cheering news that the Guards Division was going back to England shortly ! It was not " official " as yet, but the rumour was everywhere accepted as fact, with every appearance of being true.

.   .   .   .   .   .

Our principal duty in Cologne consisted in mounting guards at certain " strategic " points in and around the city, but as the various units of the Division performed this function in rotation, for two days each, our own turn did not come round very often. Apart from this, on each alternate morning there was a short drill-parade on the Barrack Square, and on other days what we called a " Swank March." This was a ceremonial parade through the streets of the city, with the regimental band and the Colours, the main object of which was to impress the inhabitants and to show off our own military smartness. Civilians had to stand to attention as we passed, and the men were obliged to raise their hats to the Colours; if they refused, they were taken into the ranks and made to march round with us ! (This rule, incidentally, led to a wide-spread fashion of male hatlessness in the city.) But this, so far as I saw, was the only way in which the British acted like a conquering army, and generally speaking the people seemed to enjoy these military displays—as most people do any kind of show, especially when accompanied by the pomp and blare of a brass band. There was no doubt that the troops had become popular with the citizens, among whom we mingled when off duty as freely as in an English town, but there were some I noticed who looked rather dejected as we passed with all the glittering swagger of a victorious army. I could imagine how we should have felt in like circumstances, watching a German army marching down Whitehall.

While at home I had learned that my pal, Arthur Brookes, was still in the Welsh Guards and stationed in Cologne, so at the first opportunity I went in search of him. We were both pleased to renew our companionship, and agreed to make the most of the opportunity for a joint exploration of the city. As we were now free to leave Barracks almost any day after one o'clock we had plenty of time to get about. We went to every place of interest we could hear of, and spent some very enjoyable afternoons. Our usual meeting place was the Dom Platz, the great open space in front of the West Doors of the Cathedral, and from there ranged the city, on foot or by tram. The quaint and narrow Hohestrasse, like a page from the Middle Ages; the Neumarkt; the spacious and beautiful Barbarrossaplatz; the Eigelstein, at the end of which one of the original City Gates contained the remains of a Roman galley; the Rath-haus, the Hohenzollern Bridge, the Neuspannungbrucke; the majestic sweep of the Rhine—Cologne was packed with interest, and our time was too short to see a tithe of it.

One afternoon was devoted to the magnificent Cathedral, under the guidance of a priest who could speak a little English. He took us over the whole building, explaining the points of special interest with so much care and enthusiasm that, when at the end he hinted at the propriety of a " donation to the funds," we felt that our few marks had been well spent. We also climbed the interior of one of the two towers, up hundreds of stone steps which wound in an interminable spiral, until we were dizzy as well as out of breath; but when at last we came out upon the narrow gallery which runs round the base of the spire, we felt that the climb had been well worth while. All Cologne lay spread beneath us, the streets and houses tiny and remote, almost as if viewed from an aeroplane, while beyond the countryside stretched for miles in the clear sunlight, with the river winding like a broad silver ribbon from horizon to horizon. Far away to the east we could just distinguish the faint peaks of the " Seven Mountains," the highest point of Westphalia.

We conscientiously bought picture-postcards of everything that interested us, in the " tourist " tradition, but they were mostly crude, highly-coloured atrocities, quite unworthy of the scenes they claimed to represent. Once or twice we had tea in a German café, but this was more for curiosity than sustenance, for the fare, in those early days after the British blockade, was very " ersatz " and unsatisfying. Our meal consisted of a cup of tea, without milk but with a good supply of rather chalky " sugar," and some queer spongy stuff they called " cake " but which reminded me (as I remarked at the time) of eating luke-warm ice-cream. It cost nearly as much as a full luncheon in pre-war England. But usually we had what refreshments we required at the Variete-Saal in Friesenstrasse, which was the headquarters of the Y.M.C.A., where we could always be sure of entertainment on a wet day.

The Cathedral was our favourite resort, and we never tired of wandering through the sculptured aisles of the wonderful old pile. We would seldom pass a day without entering the building—not for reasons of piety !—and one Sunday afternoon attended a service specially in order to hear the organ. The music was worthy of its magnificent architectural setting.

But, needless to say, enjoyment of the sights and manifold interests of the ancient city did not make up the whole of our life in Cologne, nor did I spend all my time with Arthur Brookes. As we were sometimes reminded, we were there on Garrison duty, not as a party of tourists ! There were various military duties to be performed, the parades and " swank-marches " already mentioned, occasional pickets or fatigues in the Barracks, and the City Guard. For the last, the whole Battalion went on duty together, and the headquarters were in a theatre in Wiedenstrasse, from which detachments were posted in various parts of the city. Guard duty lasted two days at a time, and as the 1st Coldstream had been on guard when I arrived back from Leave, our turn only came round once more before we all returned to England. On this occasion I was on the Headquarters Guard, and did sentry-duty outside the main guard-room; there were so many " reliefs " that we were not all obliged to remain in the guard-room when not actually on sentry. My exploration of the city was, if anything, easier during those two days than at ordinary times. In fact, so " cushy " was the guard that, one evening, Corporal Pritchard, " Peter " (a Frenchman in 6 Platoon) and I were even able to go out to Riehl between spells of sentry-go, and see a performance by the Battalion Concert Party of an original revue called " Tootsie." Peter and I had also been out, souvenir-hunting, in the city during the afternoon and had tea at a café—it was, as we used to say, " some " guard !

Our imminent return to England was now officially announced for March 1st. On February 26th we paraded to receive the Brigadier-General's farewell and an official message of thanks for our war-service from Field-Marshal Sir Douglas Haig. The Brigadier was very fulsome in his praise of the achievements of the Guards during the war, particularly in the final advance, but we took it all with a grain of salt, and went off parade humming " Isn't he a quaint old bird! " (the latest song-hit from " Tootsie").

Preparations for our departure went on apace; there were fatigue-parties every day, packing and loading stores, and, after duty, a last hurried search of the shops for momentos. Early on Saturday morning, March 1st, we marched out of the main gate of Riehl Barracks, and entrained at a small station outside the city. Three bands played us out, and the Brigadier and his Staff were on the platform to give us a send-off. The train left at nine-thirty a.m., and before nightfall we were across the frontier and in Belgium. At Verviers we halted for tea, and at various other stopping-places during the journey we were given generous free meals in addition to our ordinary rations; cigarettes, too, were distributed lavishly and at every halt people gathered to wave and cheer. Altogether, though we were in cattle trucks, it was quite a Triumphal Progress. The route was practically the same as on my return from Leave, except that we ended at Dunkirk instead of Calais.

We stopped at Dunkirk for two days, under canvas in a camp outside the town, during which time we passed through an elaborately-organised " de-lousing " station, where our uniforms were thoroughly fumigated while we had a bath and were issued with a complete new set of underwear—the modern scientific version, I take it, of " shaking the dust of France from our feet! " Then, cleansed and purified, on the morning of Wednesday we marched down to the Harbour and embarked on S.S. "Minominee." The whole of our stay in Dunkirk had been one of incessant rain and leaden skies, but just as we steamed out of the Harbour, to the cheers of a large crowd on the quay and the strains of a band on board, as well as our own vociferous singing, the sun broke through a rift in the clouds and a great double rainbow appeared over the sea, directly ahead of us. It was a fitting farewell to France—the gate, at last, at the end of " the long, long trail! "

The crossing was smooth, although rain fell again at frequent intervals and it was rather cold. We dimly glimpsed the cliffs of Dover through the mist, and skirted the coast past Deal and the Goodwins, rounded the North Foreland and anchored off Southend for the night. Next morning the ship docked at Tilbury, and we disembarked shortly before mid-day. As we filed off the gangway and set foot at last on English soil, each man was handed a bun and a stick of chocolate. To whom we were indebted for this delicate attention I do not know, but it caused great amusement among the troops, and we felt that at last we had received the thanks of a grateful country ! (But, joking apart, it must have cost the unknown donor a " pretty penny.")

The first part of the journey, as the train drew out into the open country, the English fields and hedgerows spread on either hand and we realised that we were indeed back in Blighty for good, was rather silent and emotional. I could see that many of the fellows could not trust themselves to speak and there was much recourse to vigorous nose-blowing; for my own part, although I had been home so recently, it was somehow quite different from coming home on Leave, for this time there was no question of having to go back. We had returned to our own dear native land —never, we swore, to leave it again. England had never meant so much to us as at that moment.

But by the time we reached London the whole train-load was in full song. We went right round the Metropolis without stopping, by way of Hackney, Hampstead, Willesden, Chelsea and Croydon, and as we passed through the various stations they rang to the joyous tune of "Hullo, old London! Hats off to you."

Our destination was Caterham, and when we had alighted from the train we fell-in on the platform in column-of-route, fixed bayonets and sloped arms. Then, with the appropriate ceremonial, the Colours were brought on parade; with a crash of drums and a blare of bugles, the gates were flung open and we swung out into the street. A great crowd lined the pavements, the town was decorated in our honour and all the schools had holiday. The enthusiasm of our welcome was almost overwhelming, and the people could hardly be restrained from breaking into our ranks. Amid tremendous cheering and followed by what seemed to be the entire population of Caterham, we marched through the town and toiled up the long hill to the Guards Depôt.

There, the welcome was no less whole-hearted though more restrained. On the Barrack-square of "Little Sparta," where most of our number had endured the rigours of a Guards training which we ex-H.B.'s had escaped, on ground hallowed by the sweat and consecrated by the curses of generations, under the admiring (or, perhaps, critical) gaze of hundreds of recruits and "old sweats," the returning victorious warriors stood proudly, to receive the praise and thanks of the highest in the land! (At least, that is how we ought to have felt; but I think what we really muttered under our breath was something like: "Get a move on, for Pete's sake, and let me get shut of this bleeding pack! I could scoff a horse!")

The G.O.C., London Area addressed us in the fulsome terms with which we were becoming familiar, and various other important people added their tributes; then a special message from the King was read, and we were dismissed to our quarters in "Tin Town."

At Last!—Active Service was over, and the Guards had come home!

THE LAST PHASE

"'TIN TOWN'" was a large collection of corrugated-iron huts which had been erected outside the walls of the Barracks proper, to accommodate the increased flow of recruits to the Depot during the war. We were not uncomfortably housed, though it was rough compared with the modern barrack-rooms at Cologne, but we knew that we were only to be there for a fortnight, at most.

One of the first events after we arrived was the departure of Captain Frisby. He left very early one morning, and no one in the Company, except, presumably, the officers, was aware of his going until afterwards. It was known that he was to be demobilised soon after we returned to England, and we had planned to give our old Company Officer a big send-off, but probably he got wind of this and slipped away secretly, for he was never a man to court public glory or to " play to the gallery." Of course, we were all very disappointed; he was easily the most popular officer in the Battalion. His winning of the supreme award for gallantry in the field had little to do with this, for we considered his V.C. to be no more that a fitting public recognition of the sterling qualities which we already knew him to possess.

In No. 2 Company, where until recently we had been in daily contact with him and knew him well, he was universally regarded with genuine affection, as well as with admiration and respect. He was an outstanding example of that finest type of officer—one who carried his authority not as a right but as a trust, and who never obtruded his rank "off parade." He won the willing obedience of his men by quite force of character, and their trust by his own confidence in them; we would have followed him any-where. Although a rigid upholder of discipline, he was always even-tempered, imperturbable and accessible to all ranks, and in a hundred small ways he showed his understanding of our point of view and his constant care for our well-being. Any man who was brought before him " on a charge " was sure of a fair hearing and an impartial judgment; the slacker or lead-swinger received short shrift from him, but he was equally ready to give praise where praise was due. At the front he shared, as far as an officer could do, our discomforts and dangers, and never asked us to do what he would not do—and frequently did—himself. No Company could have had a higher sense of morale or " esprit-de-corps " than did No. 2 while under his command, and it was because of his and Corporal Jackson's exploits on September 27th that we were unofficially known as " the V.C. Company "—the only Company in the Guards Division, and perhaps in the British Army, to win two Victoria Crosses simultaneously in a single action! Though we had other fine officers, the Company was never quite the same after he left us, and I for one shall always feel proud to have served under him.

. . . . . .

The Battalion remained at Caterham until the 19th, and then moved to London in readiness for the " March of the Guards," a a great ceremonial Victory parade by the whole Division through the streets of the Capital, to celebrate our return from overseas service. It was to take place on Saturday, March 22nd—whether by accident or by design, the anniversary of the day we were rushed into the line to meet the German offensive. On arrival, the Battalion was divided, two Companies going to Wellington Barracks, and the others, Nos. 2 and 4, being billeted in South Kensington. No. 14, Roland Gardens, in a quiet residential neighbourhood near Brompton Road, was the residence of No. 6 Platoon—a large empty house which made very comfortable billets.

Everything now centred on the preparations for the March, and there was no end to the polishing of brasses and the blancoing of equipment, to the accompaniment, of course, of the usual "wind-up" among the N.C.O.'s and agitation of junior officers. Great excitement prevailed everywhere, and the streets along our route were being decorated. It was the first of the post-war Victory pageants. My parents had secured a window in Fleet Street, and were coming up for the day.

On Saturday morning, we paraded in Roland Gardens and, after the usual inspection, marched to Wellington Barracks, where the 2nd Brigade were to assemble. Here we piled arms and were dismissed, pro tem., and adjourned to the Canteen for light refreshment. The day was cloudy and rather cold, and a few flakes of snow fell at first, but before long the weather cleared, and in consequence we received orders to leave our greatcoats at the Barracks.

At 1.15 the " Fall In " sounded, and the 2nd Guards Brigade formed up on the Square—the 3rd Grenadiers, the 1st Scots, the 2nd Irish and the 1st Coldstream, in that order. On ceremonial parades, the Coldstreams always took the rear of the column, for the reason that, our proud motto being " Nulli Secundus," we refused to follow immediately behind the Grenadiers, who were officially the " senior " regiment. We marched in light order— that is to say, with webbing equipment, rifles and bayonets, but without pack or haversack, and with ground-sheets rolled and strapped to our belts at the back. The Colours, crowned with laurels, were brought on parade amid a rolling of drums and presenting of arms; and after a short interval, the orders to " Slope Arms! "—" Move to the right in column-of-route! "— " Quick March! "—were given. A blare of bugles, a crash of drums, and we swung through the gates into Birdcage Walk—and stopped. For about half-an-hour we were held up, while the head of the immense column got under way, and at last received orders to move forward.

The Division was led by Lord Cavan and the Prince of Wales, on horseback, followed by the three Brigades in order. Many demobilised officers and men followed their respective units in civvies, and disabled men were conveyed in lorries. The Guards Divisional Artillery was also represented, with some of their guns, and those units of the Royal Engineers and the Royal Army Medical Corps which had been attached to the Division in France. The whole column took about two hours to pass a given point.

Entering the gates of Buckingham Palace from Birdcage Walk, we marched to attention, "Eyes Left!" past the dais outside the main entrance, where the King stood to take the salute, accompanied by the Queen, Princess Mary and a number of other members of the Royal Family. The King looked tired and somewhat strained—we were at about half-way along the procession, and he had already been standing at the salute for over an hour, with nearly as long to follow!—but Princess Mary was looking quite animated and seemed to be thoroughly enjoying the show. Queen Mary was seated, and appeared, to judge from her expression, to be "bored stiff!"

As we passed through the opposite gates of the Palace forecourt we encountered the first waves of the cheering, which burst upon us like a hurricane and continued throughout the whole route without intermission. It was a bit difficult to get used to at first, for the vast crowds which choked the pavements on both sides of the road were mad with excitement and communicated a good deal of their enthusiasm to us. They yelled and waved and danced, broke through the cordon and were hustled back by smiling but harassed scouts and policemen; they flung their hats in the air and lost them in the crush; they trod on each other's toes and fainted with the greatest good-humour—in fact, they completely disproved the legend that the British are an unemotional race!

Half-way down the Mall we turned left, past Marlborough House and then into Pall Mall. There we had a surprise that was exclusively ours—for stretched across the road was a large banner, bearing the words, "Good old No. 2 Company, 1st Coldstream!" Of course, this brought vociferous cheers of acknowledgment from us! We never learned definitely who was responsible for this unique tribute to the "V.C. Company," but it was generally attributed to Lady Sybil Grant, who had done a good deal for the Company during the war and who used to print a weekly newssheet, called "The Home Letter," for distribution among all ranks.

Near the end of Pall Mall we halted for a few minutes, and the people in the upper windows started a "bombardment" of cigarettes, which continued all the way. The most intensive phase, however, was in Cannon Street, where they threw down not only cigarettes and cigars, but chocolate, fruit and sweets as well, and the Colonel narrowly escaped becoming a casualty from a well-aimed banana. The excitement was tremendous, and the spectators were so carried away by their own enthusiasm that, having exhausted everything else, they threw their cigarette cases as well, and rained down money upon us. We began to wish we were wearing our steel helmets, and felt somewhat like the bears in the Zoo!

Just after passing Canon Street Station we halted again and fixed bayonets—thus exercising an ancient privilege of the Guards Brigade, to enter the City of London fully armed—and marched past the Mansion House "at attention," where the Lord Mayor took the salute. Back along Cheapside and Holborn, and down Shaftesbury Avenue we went; at many points in Piccadilly the air was filled with confetti and coloured streamers, while from the Berkeley Hotel we were pelted with roses and walked on a carpet of flowers—at considerable cost, I should think, considering the season. And all the way the wild cheering continued. Cæsar's legions could have had no more spectacular a Triumph—even though we had no captive kings or maidens in our train!

From Hyde Park Corner, we turned down Constitution Hill to Wellington Barracks, and the March was at an end. At the Barracks a special "Banquet" was prepared for us, and we each received a printed copy of a special "Message" from the King. Nos. 2 and 4 Companies then returned to Kensington, in high spirits and singing all the way. Before the March, there had been a good deal of grousing about "silly swank" and "——these blinking parades!" (only the word was not "blinking"), but afterwards not a man but admitted that he would not have missed it for a great deal.

Yet, after all, it was not us whom the people should have cheered, but all those thousands of Guardsmen who lay in France —at Ypres and Festubert and Loos; on the Somme, at Arras and Passchendaele; on Bourlon Hill, in Gouzeaucourt, Moeuvres and St. Python, and a hundred other places—the unseen, silent Brigade whose deaths had made our Triumph possible. We were only the lucky survivors, many of whom had done little enough towards winning the war. Did those vast throngs remember that, and was their wild enthusiasm also a homage to those who had earned it with their lives? I like to think so.

And of those who were acclaimed that day, how many, in the years which followed, were doomed to poverty and frustration, to unemployment and misery, their self-respect slowly ground down by the humiliation of the Means Test and the degradations of a soul-less economic system? It was well for some among us that we could not read the future.

.   .   .   .   .   .

We stayed on at Kensington until May 2nd, and as far as military duties were concerned, we had a very easy time. There was usually only one very short parade in the mornings, or sometimes a kit inspection, a rifle inspection, half-an-hour's P.T., or no duties at all. Each morning, Reveille sounded at 6.30, but no one bothered us ; we rolled out of bed when we felt like it, and could always get breakfast until about eight o'clock ! For more than a month it was an unbelievably "cushy" time, for the Army and especially for the Guards. Picket-duty at the billet came round at intervals, and once in a while some of the fellows "clicked" for guard-mounting at Wellington Barracks or "Buck," but I managed to dodge even these intermittent duties, for—after declining an invitation from my Platoon Officer, Mr. Tickle, to become his batman—I was appointed Telephone Orderly at Company H.Q., and was, "ex officio," "struck off the strength" as far as parades, guards and fatigues were concerned.

No. 2 Coy. Office was in another house in Roland Gardens, but it had no telephone, so the instrument in a Salvation Army Hostel opposite was used for official purposes, and this necessitated having a man always in attendance, to take incoming calls and fetch anyone who might be required. I and another man shared this duty alternately, throughout the twenty-four hours, but there was not much to it, for calls were infrequent and we had a well-lighted room, an easy chair, a good fire and all the books and papers we required to pass the time. I rather enjoyed taking duty at night, especially, for then I could read or write undisturbed, and could sleep all next morning instead of hanging about in the billet—for no one was allowed to go out until after one o'clock. For the first time in my life, I was "on speaking terms" with the Nobility, for I often had to "ring up" Lord This or Lady That for one or other of the officers, or take messages for them from their aristocratic lady-friends ! Some of the latter were quite amusing.

My free time (of which I had a good deal) was spent mainly in exploring London and visiting places of interest, usually in company with one of the other chaps, and in going to the theatre or the "pictures." One evening I had the privilege of seeing Ellen Terry in one of her last appearances on the London stage, as the "Nurse" in "Romeo and Juliet"—an unforgettable experience. An afternoon was spent at the Regent's Park Zoo, where there were far fewer animals than before the war and the two remaining elephants were so emaciated that the poor creatures' skin hung in deep folds ! We also went to Westminster Abbey, St. Paul's, the Guildhall, and other free "sights"—for in London we found it necessary to economise our pay. Leave was granted fairly generously, and I managed to get home "from Saturday after duties to Sunday midnight" on several occasions.

But the subject of supreme importance for most of us was the question of "demob." Cushy times were all very well, but it was permanent release from the Army that we wanted. It was now nearly five months since the Armistice and, apart from a few men who had decided to "sign on," the great majority were eager to get back to civvie life as quickly as possible. We felt that we had completed our contract. Now that the war was over, parades and "spit-and-polish" seemed to us a waste of time, and military discipline even more of an irksome irrelevancy. What was the good of trying to become more and more efficient as soldiers, when our future lay—as we hoped and believed—in the paths of peace?

The scheme which the Government had announced immediately after the Armistice, for gradual demobilisation by "classes" and availability of employment, was no doubt excellent in theory, but it was much *too* gradual, it was not operated impartially, and there was no guarantee that the later "classes" would not be seriously handicapped. With the sudden ending of war-contracts, and the cry for "economy," employment was decreasing, and everyone felt that the longer he was kept in the Army the worse became his chances of obtaining a good job in civil life. There was widespread "wangling" of preferential treatment by private influence, and this caused serious dissatisfaction among the troops.

Efforts were continually being made, both on my own part and from home (where I had a job waiting for me to step into), to hasten my release, and I soon accumulated quite a formidable portfolio of documents—records of service, of earlier unsuccessful attempts to enlist, attestation in 1916 and discharge, letters of support for my claim from local magnates, police confirmations, etc. The Battalion Demob. Officer was sympathetic and helpful, but my applications were overruled by "Brigade," and after many periods of alternate hope and despair, they all came to nothing.

In fact, an Order had been issued from higher authorities to the effect that demobilisation in the Guards Division was to proceed as slowly as possible, in order to keep the Division up to full strength until new recruits could be trained to replace us. This, as may be imagined, caused great indignation in the ranks, and our dissatisfaction was intensified by the move, on May 2nd, to Wimbledon.

The new camp, where we arrived soaked to the skin after being kept standing on Putney Bridge for an hour in pouring rain, was in Spartan contrast to the comforts of Kensington. It was in the middle of Wimbledon Common and was composed of Army huts, in which we slept on bed-boards and straw mattresses. The whole of the 2nd Brigade was together again for the first time since Cologne, and there was a corresponding increase in "wind-up" and regimental discipline.

Our accumulated grievances found expression on May 6th, in "the Great Strike."

At Cologne (while I was on leave) the rank-and-file of the Battalion had made a united request to the C.O. that, as a tangible expression of the official recognition of our war-service, so often and so fulsomely made by those in high places, drill-parades should in future be limited to one hour a day, which was the normal peace-time practise. Though this may seem to the uninitiated to be a very easy "working-day," when the time spent in "cleaning up" and the frequent spells of guard, picket, fatigues and other duties were taken into consideration it was not unreasonable for trained men in peace-time, and in any case, the men argued, the war being over their time was being wasted in achieving perfection in spectacular manœuvres which could never be of the slightest use to them in the civilian occupations they were eager to resume. They realised, of course, that demobilisation could not be completed right away, but they felt that, now that the specific reason for their army service had ceased to exist, the delay should be made as easy as possible.

At any rate, reasonable or not, the request was granted without reservation.

Immediately we arrived at Wimbledon, however, it was evident that an attempt was being made to "swing it on us." Daily parades were increased to two hours, orders were issued for a third hour, and in addition—this was the rub!—it was announced that every man was to go through a course of "recruit-training" again, and be "passed-out" in the various stages as if he were a newly-joined rookie! Anything more calculated to exasperate men who had been sufficiently "efficient" to go through a campaign like the late war could hardly be imagined. We determined that this state of things had got to cease.

Accordingly, on May 6th, after performing First Parade as usual, we returned to the huts and called a meeting. A "strike" was immediately and unanimously decided upon, and messengers from No. 2 to the other Companies secured their enthusiastic support. When the bugle for Second Parade sounded, we went in a body to the Square, but not a man moved when the order to "Fall in" was given.

The senior officers had apparently received previous warning of our intention, and did not appear, nor did the R.S.M., but the subalterns, marching up and down the empty space in couples, as they always did before parade, showed by their grins and animated conversation that they were not unsympathetic to our protest. Presently, two of them approached and asked us to state our grievances. After a confused clamour from scores of voices, they suggested that we should return to our lines and appoint representatives to put our case before the Colonel. This, after a short discussion among ourselves, we agreed to do, and selected two delegates from each platoon.

The C.O. received them without delay, and they reiterated our demands. They said (according to their own report) that, while we recognise our obligations as serving soldiers, we had all joined for war-service only, and now that the war was over it was not to be expected that we should submit to the same rigours of discipline as "time-serving" men. We were all fully-trained men who were awaiting our release from the Colours, and it was unreasonable to expect us to undergo recruit-training afresh, when we were expecting almost daily to return to civil life. Our interests were now, naturally, directed to our civilian occupations, and indeed it was to the grave prejudice of our prospects that we were still being kept in the Army while the best jobs were being snapped up. The least that could be done, while endeavouring to speed-up our release, was to restrict parades to the maximum agreed upon at Cologne.

The Colonel's reply was somewhat unexpectedly conciliatory. He said that he understood our point of view and to a certain extent sympathised with us ; he had, however, received orders from higher authorities to give us four hours of "work" a day, and was bound to carry out his instructions. However, he was willing to interpret those instructions in the most liberal way possible, and in future there would be only one hour's drill parade on the Square, and the other three hours of "work" would be spent in organised Battalion sports, cricket, tennis, football, etc.

To this our deputation agreed, and returned to us in good spirits, having, as we all admitted, gained our point completely. A day or so later, the G.O.C. London Area lectured us on parade, and spoke "more in sorrow than in anger," about the deplorable results of refusing to fall-in when ordered ; his remarks were received with scarcely smothered booing. After that the incident was closed.

But the real reason for the very moderate attitude of the authorities in the face of what was, in effect, a mutiny, was not realised until much later. There had been for some time (though it was carefully hidden from us and the general public) a good deal of serious trouble among the troops in various places, both in England and overseas, about the slowness of demob., and there was a very prevalent fear in certain quarters that worse was planned for May 11th. The reason why this date was regarded with apprehension was simple :—The original terms on which all voluntarily-enlisted men had joined the Army during the war were "for the duration of the war and six months after," and May 11th marked six months from the signing of the Armistice, when the surrender of our enemies "ended" the war. The Government claimed that, technically and legally, the state of war would not end until the final ratification of the last Peace Treaty, the first of which was not even signed yet ; but they feared that the men regarded the cessation of hostilities as "the end of the war," and that they intended to claim their discharge "en masse" on May 11th—under the instigation, as any reader of the "Morning Post" knew, of "bolshevist agitators"! Open disaffection in the sacro-sanct Brigade of Guards itself must have semed like a confirmation of their worst fears, and consequently they were afraid of provoking a general outbreak by any hasty "strong" measures to "maintain discipline."

Whatever truth there may have been in the alleged " con-spiracy," there were no outside influences behind our " Strike," which was purely local and spontaneous, and into which the " May 11th" consideration did not enter at all. That fateful day was a Sunday, and passed without incident, at least, as far as Wimbledon was concerned, though the authorities were evidently nervous, for on the previous day those of us who were going on week-end leave were lectured by an officer and warned not to listen to arguments " subversive to discipline."

. . . . . .

Very little that calls for special notice occurred during the next few weeks, outside the regular routine of camp life, which was considerably improved as a result of the " Strike." There was no further attempt to " swing it on us," and (so far as I know) no one was " victimised" for his part in our protest.

Our new quarters, too, when we had settled in and the weather improved, turned out to be much better than we had at first thought. Wimbledon Camp occupied a large area in the middle of the Common, and was built almost entirely of wood; the three Battalions of the 2nd Guards Brigade had each its own lines, complete with dining-halls, recreation rooms, canteens, stores, offices, and all the usual adjuncts of a military camp. The Cold-stream section also contained a well-appointed " Library," furnished with easy chairs and tables, for the use of the " rank-and-file." The huts in which the troops lived, about thirty men in each, were commodious and, although we slept on bed-boards and straw palliasses, not uncomfortable.

The daily routine of Camp, with its guards, pickets, fatigues and parades, was not unlike normal barrack life, and there was considerably more regimentalism and " wind-up" than we had been used to abroad, and especially at South Kensington. But the parades were, in general, not over-strenuous and, unless we were on guard or picket, we were usually finished for the day by twelve o'clock, and were then free to go out if we wished. Our life was governed by the bugle: the Battalion call, followed by Reveille roused us in the morning; " Roll-call," " Cookhouse," " Ten-minutes Warning," " Fall in," " Company Orders," " Letters," " Defaulters," and a score of others punctuated our day, and N.C.O.'s were ready to see that we " jumped to it." We knew all the calls in those days, though I doubt if I could identify many to-day.

After dinner, those of us who were not on duty could leave the Camp, though most, in the lazy Army fashion, would " get down to it " on our beds for an hour or so. The Camp gate was about four hundred yards from the main road and the bus route, but from there we could reach London in about half an hour, via Putney and the Underground. " Trained soldiers," among whom I ranked by reason of my two years' service, were granted " Permanent

Passes" which entitled us to stay out until mid-night ("23.59 hrs.") if we wished, instead of having to be back by "Last Post." Great stress was laid on our smart appearance when "walking-out," and every man had to be approved by the Sergeant of the Camp Guard before being allowed through the gates, but this was largely a matter of form, for most of us were far too conscious of our status as Guardsmen and Coldstreamers to do other than "posh-up" very thoroughly before appearing in public. Nothing sloppy or "grabby-mob" about us! Boots were polished, slacks immaculately creased, buttons and numerals shone like the sun, webbing belt blancoed—the central cross on my cap-star almost disappeared with repeated polishings!

On most mornings we did an hour's drill parade on the "Square," either at Company or Battalion strength, or there would be Physical Training, Musketry, Rifle- or Kit-inspections; sometimes the time would be occupied by "general swabbing," or other fatigues. One morning the whole Brigade paraded together on the Common and rehearsed the ceremony of "Trooping the Colour," with massed bands and an edified audience consisting of one nurse-maid and three dilatory errand-boys!

The hut which housed No. 6 Platoon contained, of course, the usual mixed crowd, but we all got on well together, with very little friction. Many of the men had been on Active Service with the Company during the War, and others had joined us at Maubeuge just before the Armistice and had been with us in the Army of Occupation. It was in "honour" of the latter that we named the hut "Chateau de Maubeuge" and painted the name outside the door.

I shall not easily or willingly forget the little coterie of eight or nine men with whom I occupied the end of the hut nearest the door of the "Chateau," though I have not seen one of them since those days and have no idea how they have fared since demobilisation; they were among the best fellows one could wish to meet. There was Joe Harper, a big, genial ex-policeman from Birmingham; Charlie Harper (no relation of Joe's), dark-eyed, slender and good-looking—he was known, to his own annoyance, as "the Beau of the Batt."; Grissenthwaite ("Griss"), a long, lean, rugged Jerseyite; "Frankie" Frankland, a merry, high-spirited Lancashire lad; "Archie" Weston, who also hailed from "Brummagem"; Langton, somewhat older than most of us (does he remember being chaffed as "Lily Langtry," because of an alleged similarity of name and entire unlikeness of appearance?); "Peter" Dowling, the Frenchman (or part-French) I mentioned earlier, whose home was in Rheims; Clarke, inevitably nicknamed "Nobby." There were many others in the Platoon whom I well remember: Gray, Pounds, Cryer, Dade, Bertolla, Hammond, Foulds—but lists of names convey nothing except to one who knew them. Sgt. Parsons, the platoon-sergeant, Sgt. Davis, Cpls. Spicer and Porter, were " good sorts," efficient and popular.

Those last months of my Army service were, all things considered, a pleasant period—perhaps the best I spent while I was in uniform. Perhaps they seem better in retrospect than they did at the time, for " distance lends enchantment . . . ." and one often remembers chiefly the good and most self-flattering features of the past, but I was certainly not unhappy at Wimbledon. Nevertheless, I no less certainly never ceased to long for my civilian freedom and had no desire to remain in the Army a day longer than I must, still less to " sign on " for permanent service as did one or two of my comrades. In my view, although it offered a measure of economic security and freedom from personal responsibility (like life in a monastry!), military service in the ranks, in peace-time, was a pointless existence, an unmeaning repetition of formal parades and duties which achieved nothing constructive and led nowhere.

There were many things about the Army that I disliked intensely (if " disliked " is a strong enough word!) ; some of these things I have already indicated in the course of this narrative, and there were many others—more-or-less petty exasperations common to a private soldier's life, which became increasingly irksome as time passed and against which I often inwardly rebelled. Chief among them, I think, was the sense of being constantly under orders, of being liable to have one's private plans upset without warning or redress, and the hundred-and-one trivial offences by which one could " lose one's name." (The reason why I seldom lost mine was not, perhaps, because—as I liked to think—I stood well with the authorities, but because I was almost morbidly anxious to avoid trouble!)

But most of my grievances seem now to have been minor ones, real though they were to me then. On the other hand, there were many aspects of service life in the Guards which I felt, even at the time, went far towards compensating for, and to a certain extent cancelled-out, its more uncongenial features. I enjoyed the sense of comradeship in the ranks, among men of my own age and generation, many of whom shared with me memories of the same or of similar experiences in the War ; and, despite my quiet and somewhat reserved nature, I had made a number of good friends among my companions. (I wonder if any of them still remember me !) By this time, too, I had, as it were, " graduated " as a Guardsman : I had served in the Coldstream for nearly a year and a half, and had been a member of the same Company long enough to feel that I was not only " in " it, but " of " it—I had a humble but definite place in its collective entity. I had become familiar with the routine, drill, duties, personnel and traditions of the " V.C. " Company, and was even conscious of enjoying a certain modest measure of " prestige " among my immediate comrades—not, of course, by reason of any individual merit of my own as a soldier, but because my "overseas" chevrons, "wound stripes" and the rest distinguished me as one of the dwindling band of those who had seen active service with the Company. For by now the progress of demobilisation and replacement by post-war recruits had considerably diluted the original Company, and by comparison we of longer service ranked almost as "veterans"!

I was genuinely proud of being a Guardsman and a Coldstreamer, and I felt it to be an honour to be a member of what I believed to be the finest and most renowned troops in the world— The Brigade of Guards; I knew, however much I might grumble or wish myself out of the Army, that there was no other branch of the Service to equal them. Although, in general, I was "fed-up" with ceremonial drill and other formal exercises, there were many occasions when, while on parade or marching in column-of-route behind the Drums, I would thrill with an exultant pride in my Battalion and the knowledge that I was part of it. Even to-day, thankful though I am that my military service lies in the past and little though I have ever wanted to go back to the Army, I still feel an echo of that glow of youthful exaltation when I see a detachment of my old Regiment march by; sometimes I dream, nostalgically, that it would be good if I could parade just once again with No. 2 Company, 1st Coldstream Guards—with all my old comrades. ("The brave music of a *distant* drum," again?)

I cannot claim, of course, to be a typical representative of the "V.C. Company" (in fact, in most ways I was most un-typical), but I think that most of my companions at that time thought much as I did. We never spoke of it, except in half-humorous satire, and groused as loudly as anyone, but I am sure that most of us were very proud of the Company to which we belonged, its achievements and its great reputation; of the Battalion, the Regiment and of "The Brigade." In my own case, this was much more than the ignorant, romantic enthusiasm of my recruit days—a more substantial and enduring "esprit de corps"; in the course of my short experience of them, I had seen the Coldstream in bad times and in good, in disaster and triumph, battle and victory; and, negligible though I was, I rejoiced to feel that I had a share in its corporate life, in common with men so many of whom I admired and liked.

That "esprit de corps" and admiration still remains, and will last, I think, as long as I live. Though I was no more than a "number," and added nothing to the laurels of my Regiment, I shall always remember, with a feeling of real pride, that I—even I!—was once a Guardsman.

.   .   .   .   .

Feeling thus, it may sound inconsistent when I say that I was in a hurry to get out of the Army, or that I grudged every day, now that the War was over and release was in sight, which I still had to spend in uniform. But that was how it was: I do not claim that my sentiments at that time were either logical or consistent.

I was intensely eager to be free from military restrictions, to return to my own home and its comforts, and to be at liberty to order my own life as I wished. My civilian work, uncontrolled by Sergeants and " King's Regulations," although it would probably afford me less leisure than I was at present enjoying, seemed infinitely desirable ! After we returned to England, demobilisation was the supreme objective, the ultimate crown of my ambition.

But demob. seemed as far off as ever. I put in more claims, on " business " and on " compassionate " grounds (my Father's ill-health and over-work, my " indispensability," the danger that " the business would fall into other hands, owing to my absence, and the consequent ruin of my prospects "—every argument I or my parents could think up ; but they were all turned down by Brigade H.Q. as " not strong enough.") The Battalion Demob. Officer, successor to Capt. Frisby, was understanding and co-operative, and I am sure did all he could on my behalf ; he considered that my best card was the record of my early unsuccessful efforts to " join-up," since the War Office was unsympathetic to business claims in my trade at that time. The Corporal in charge of the Demob. Office, also, was a friend of mine, so I was constantly in touch with the latest developments. But apparently my chief handicap was the fact that, during my absence on leave last January, I had been officially " Selected for Retention," and must remain with the Colours for the time being.

Perhaps I ought to have regarded this as a compliment—that I should have been chosen as one of the war-time " amateur " soldiers whom the Authorities were reluctant to release and to whom —as was pointed out to us—were entrusted the honour and responsibility of maintaining the Guards' reputation until new " regular " recruits could be trained to replace us ! But I am afraid that I didn't see it in quite that light ! I and the other " selected " men were paid an extra ten-and-six a week, but we hardly considered that to be an adequate recompense for the loss of our civilian freedom, however easy the conditions of service might be made.

On June 2nd I went with an Advance Party to Purfleet, in Essex, to prepare the camp for the Battalion, which was to commence a three-weeks' Course of Musketry on the 5th. The party consisted of twenty-seven men in all ; but as it included one Drill-Sergeant, six Sergeants and four Corporals, the actual work devolved on the remaining sixteen Guardsmen, and we were kept very busy during the three days of preparation, moving tables, bed-boards and stores of every kind from one place to another, while the N.C.O.'s stood around and " superintended."

With the arrival of the Battalion, firing-practice on the range commenced, and from a military point of view it was badly needed by most of us ; for, strange though it may sound, many of us had not fired a shot for nine or ten months ! In its later stages, the War had become almost entirely a contest of artillery and machine-guns (with the infantry as targets !) and although our rifles had accompanied us everywhere and were religiously cared for, they tended to degenerate more and more into merely "something to drill with." All through the "Big Push" I think that the number of times I had actually fired at an enemy, or had a chance of doing so—apart from blazing-away over the sandbags more or less at random—could be counted on my fingers. The average infantryman seldom caught a glimpse of the enemy in that war of "Blind-man's Buff."

Most of our work on the range was done in the mornings, commencing usually at 6.30 or 7.00 ; two Companies together, one firing while the other "marked," and then changing over. The weather during almost the whole of the course was ideal—so much so, that we got through our firing-schedule more quickly than was anticipated. A considerable allowance had been made for interruption by bad weather, and several times it was necessary to devote days to Field-training or "general swabbing" in order to avoid finishing the programme too soon. Afternoons and evenings were usually free, though there were Camp Guards and Pickets to be done at intervals.

Purfleet itself and the neighbouring village of Grays contained few attractions and the Camp—which was also a demobilisation centre—was lacking in facilities for entertainment when off duty, though there were one or two good concerts at the "Y.M." But it was quite easy to get up to London by rail, from the "halt" which served the Camp, and I went there on several occasions ; a very convenient rendezvous in the West End was "Ciro's," in Leicester Square—once, I believe, a rather notorious "night-club," but then being used as a really excellent restaurant and resort for non-commissioned ranks, where one could get tea or supper in civilised surroundings and there was a comfortable reading-room if the weather was bad. I made good use of it during my stay in and around London.

One evening I went to Euston to see the arrival of Alcock and Brown after their first successful flight across the Atlantic. I had already, three weeks earlier, taken part in the hectic reception at King's Cross of the ill-fated Hawker and Grieve—the men who made the first attempt and failed had a much bigger welcome than they who succeeded ! On another day I met my parents at Southend.

The Battalion returned to Wimbledon on June 27th, and on the following day Germany signed the Peace Treaty. This is not the place to discuss the terms of this "Peace which passeth all understanding"; my own opinion of it is sufficiently indicated by the copy of the full text which I bought shortly afterwards, across the first page of which I scrawled the words : "The Great Betrayal." To my mind, it was a denial of nearly all of the great principles for which we had fought, a vindictive "peace" of revenge such as we had been told the Germans would have imposed had they won, a "peace" utterly unworthy of all the sacrifice and suffering which had bought our victory. The most hopeful thing in the Treaty was the "League of Nations"—if that could be made to work, much might yet be achieved; but, as established by the Covenant, it was as yet little more than a Council of Foreign Ministers, not the democratic World Assembly I had hoped for.

None the less, from a purely personal point of view I, like most of the men still retained in the Army, welcomed the signing of a formal peace-treaty, since it would probably hasten our own release. It had previously been reported, on "good authority," that all "duration-of-war" men with more than two years' service would be demobbed as soon as the Treaty was an accomplished fact, so we joined in the general uncritical rejoicing. But it then transpired that by "accomplished fact" was meant "after ratification by the parliaments of all the Allies."

A few days after I was one of four men detailed from No. 2 Company to assist in lining the route for the March of the London Troops, a similar show to our own March. My position was outside Buckingham Palace, close to the Royal dais, and I had an excellent view both of the parade and of the most notable spectators. There was quite a spate of military displays in London about that time—a sort of "panem et circenses" for the populace, concealing from them for the time being that their victory had still to be paid for. Another was a March of the Australian Troops along the Strand, at which the Prince of Wales took the salute—looking most nervous and miserable !

The greatest and most elaborate of these pageants took place a fortnight later, on the day appointed for the National Victory Celebrations. I received my four-days leave, granted to the troops in commemoration of "Peace," on July 9th, and on returning to Wimbledon on the Sunday night found orders for me to go to Kensington Gardens next day, to join a party which had gone there on Saturday. On arrival, I found that our job was to construct a camp for the detachments of foreign troops which were coming to London for the procession on "Peace Day," July 19th.

All that week we were hard at work, pitching tents and marquees, erecting canteens and recreation tents, digging latrines and constructing all the various offices of a camp, until Kensington Gardens became a city of canvas, and Peter Pan and the fairies had fled completely ! We lived under canvas ourselves, in a part of the Gardens near the Kiosk—about fifty of us in all—and I for one thoroughly enjoyed the time. We were favoured with magnificent weather nearly all the time we were there, and although we worked hard during the day, for considerably longer periods than at Wimbledon, the work was not unpleasant nor uninteresting, and showed more tangible results than any number of drill parades.

The other occupants of my tent—Sharples, " Griss," " Frankie,"
" Tug " Wilson and two or three others whose names I have
forgotten—were all excellent fellows and we got on well together.
Incidentally, we were all paid at a higher rate while engaged as a
working-party (I think it was a pound a week extra), for no
obvious reason, unless to conform to some Trade Union rule !
But, indeed, it was all wrong that soldiers should have been used
for this kind of work at all, for there were thousands of our
unemployed ex-comrades who would have been glad of the job.

The foreign troops arrived on the Friday after we had started
work, by which time the camp was practically complete.   There
were detachments representing all the Allies, as well as a large
contingent from the Navy.   French, Poles, Belgians, Italians,
Serbs, Roumanians, Czechs, Slovaks, Greeks and Americans—to
mention only a few of the nationalities—rubbed shoulders along
the shady walks, and the once-peaceful park became a Garden of
Babel.   Dozens of strange languages and dialects were heard on
every side, but it was remarkable how everyone seemed to make
himself understood—about really important things, at any rate.
I have never heard the identical sentiments expressed in so many
different tongues at the same time, as in the " wet " canteen at
opening-time !

" Peace Day " itself opened in brilliant weather, and soon
after dawn troops could be heard taking up their positions for the
March.   After breakfast we were confronted with the utterly
unexpected order that we, the Construction Party, were confined
to the Camp for the day !   No reason was given, and of course
it was more than we could be expected to take " lying down,"
especially as we felt that we had done a large part of preparing
the show.   So, without waiting to find out if the order was really
official or not, we all got dressed in best " walking-out order "
and marched in a body to the gate.   The military policeman on
duty was powerless to stop us; he made a half-hearted protest,
blushed a deep crimson and stood aside.   Three other men and I,
after trespassing through three private gardens and climbing sundry
walls and fences, found an excellent position from which to view
the procession, sitting on the ten-foot parapet surrounding the
French Embassy and overlooking the " Albert Gate " of Hyde
Park, through which the parade was to issue.

We had half an hour to wait, during which the crowd increased
rapidly, until every available inch of standing room and vantage
point was thronged.   A number of women fainted and were carried
off by the Ambulance people ; even the trees were crowded and one
overloaded branch came down with a crash across the road opposite
us.

On the stroke of ten the March commenced, and for two
hours the troops of the Allied nations defiled through the Gate,
while the spectators kept up a continuous cheer.   The Americans,

led by General Pershing, headed the column, and were followed by the other national contingents in alphabetical order. Marshal Foch, leading the French detachment, was greeted with deafening applause, which he acknowledged by gravely raising his baton, but the culminating point of enthusiasm was reached when Sir Douglas Haig appeared at the head of the British column; the roar that went up was so thunderous that his horse reared and he had great difficulty in controlling it. Every branch of the British Service was represented, the Army, the Navy, the Air Force, the Engineers, A.S.C., R.A.M.C., the Waacs, the Wrens and the Red Cross. Admiral Beatty was there—and his bulldog. Four whippet tanks, a searchlight, a trench-mortar, an anti-aircraft gun and two pontoons were included. There were coloured troops from all parts of the world.

It was an infinitely varied and interesting display. But—and this is, no doubt, a prejudiced view—to my mind it was not to be compared with the March of the Guards. It was a show, a pageant, a symbolic representation of the military might of the Allies, a cavalcade of specimens to illustrate the international variety of the war-effort. Whereas, our March was not merely a parade of carefully-chosen samples, but the real thing. It was the home-coming of a complete Division of the most famous troops in the world, back from the wars after Active Service. And it seemed to me that the people cheered us with a spontaneous, full-throated sincerity which was quite unlike the applause for an elaborately-staged spectacle, however wild the excitement which the occasion aroused. March 22nd was a " Welcome Home; " July 19th a super-" Lord Mayor's Show." But then, as I said, I was not an altogther unbiased witness.

When the crowd began to disperse, we descended from our perch and returned to Kensington Gardens; we avoided our tent-lines at first, for fear of being " nabbed " for some duty or other, but finally went to the dining tent, where, to our surprise, we found that a quite elaborate " Peace Banquet " was provided for us by the N.A.C.B., consisting of six courses; our usually bare tables were covered with white cloths and decorated with flowers and printed menu-cards.

Immediately after dinner—still giving the tents and possible sergeant-majors a wide berth—we went out again, no one attempting to stop us this time, and walked about the crowded excited streets. After a time the three of us found ourselves in Sloane Square, where we had tea in a Y.M., and then, as the weather had turned wet, spent several hours playing billiards. Returning to Hyde Park after dark, we watched the fireworks, a remarkable display although many of the set-pieces had been ruined by the rain, and then set out to view the illuminations in Oxford Street. But after a wild struggle in the dense crowd which filled the road from wall to wall, in the midst of which we progressed about twenty yards in as many minutes, we gave it up at last and fought our way back to camp about midnight.

.   .   .   .   .   .

The foreign troops departed next day, most of them for Paris, where a similar parade was to be held, and we commenced the work of restoring the Gardens to their original state. The dismantling of the Camp was carried out with less urgency than its construction, and occupied us for a further fortnight, though indeed the extra time was needed to clean up after the visitors, some of whom, especially the Italians, had left their tents in a filthy condition. The bulk of the " working party " returned to Wimbledon on August 1st, but a small number, of whom I was one, was left to strike our own tents, and rejoined the Battalion on the following day. Our little community in "Chateau de Maubeuge " was once more complete.

Three days later, however, it was threatened with disruption. The " Powers that be " discovered, somewhat belatedly, that the heights of the men forming the four Companies of the Battalion were not entirely uniform, and with the Army's passion for symetrical grouping, they decided to grade us afresh, and put the tallest of us into Nos. 1 and 4 Coys. and the shortest into 2 and 3. The sole reason for this, so far as anyone could see, was the appearance of the Battalion when on parade, though there was not, in fact, more than two or three inches of difference between any of us. We felt very sore about it, for many of us had served with our present Companies during the war and resented the idea of being shifted about like so many pawns on a chess-board, without regard to the friendships and associations we had formed. When I found that I was marked for transfer to No. 1 Company, while most of my friends remained in No. 2, I at once determined to make a protest. I put in an application to see the C.O., but such Olympian heights were apparently too exalted to be scaled by a mere Guardsman, and I was interviewed by Mr. Clarke, one of our own officers, at " Company Orders."

I put my case with as much eloquence as I could command, and I think created a good impression. I said that I had been in action with the Company, that I had served under Captain Frisby, and was proud to belong to the " V.C." Company; that all my friends were in the Company, and that I hoped to remain a member until I was demobbed.

Mr. Clarke replied that he fully appreciated all my arguments, and he was good enough to say that I was the sort of man they wanted to keep in the Company; if it rested with him, there would be no question of a transfer. Unfortunately, I was slightly taller than the new maximum laid down for No. 2 Company. However, he said he would see the Adjutant, and try to persuade him to make an exception in my case.

He was as good as his word, and next day sent for me and told me that my transfer had been cancelled. I was to remain in No. 2 Company. This was a great relief to me; for, apart from having to leave a Company of which all its members were proud and in which I had served for nearly a year, the transfer would have meant making a new start among men most of whom were strangers to me.

During the next weeks little occurred to warrant special mention. Guards, pickets, "Public Duties," etc., came round in rotation, there was another Brigade rehearsal of "Trooping the Colour," and on most mornings there was a Battalion parade. One of the "snags," I found, of being now one of the tallest men remaining in the Company, was that I was often placed "No. 1 in the front rank," a position of uncomfortable prominence in which one had to keep one's wits very much about one. For example: when fixing bayonets, at the cautionary word, "Fix!" No. 1 must take three very smart and rapid paces forward in front of the platoon (usually being greeted with "As you were. Not nearly smart enough!") and "give the time" to the rest, the cynosure of all eyes. The same applied to the command "Unfix!"; the platoon "dressed" upon No. 1 and took the step from him. On such occasions I often felt nervous and weak at the knees, but I never "lost my name."

About the middle of the month the Camp was inspected by General Matheson, G.O.C. London Area, which was the cause of a universal outbreak of "wind-up" for days beforehand, with endless scrubbing, whitewashing, blackleading, window-cleaning and weeding. But when the General came he just walked through and apparently looked at nothing!

.　　.　　.　　.

One morning I was summoned in a hurry by the Sergeant-Major. Wondering guiltily what I could have done, or omitted to do, this time, I reported at the Company Office and was informed that I had been detailed to join the Guards Detachment of the London Motor Ambulance Column at South Kensington, "forthwith." It seemed that I was not to be allowed to stay with No. 2 Company after all, though at the time I did not expect to be away for long. The L.M.A.C. was in those days the most desired of all "struck-off jobs," and offered a very cushy life to the men lucky enough to get it; when I told my companions in "Chateau de Maubeuge," they were full of envy and congratulation—"Some people get all the luck!" everyone said.

The Detachment was composed of about a dozen men from each battalion in the Guards Division, and was billeted in a large six-storey house, No. 24 Queens Gate Gardens. I can now remember only vaguely three of the four other men who shared with me a top-floor front room, but I was pleased to find that the fourth was an old friend of whom I have already spoken—Ted Barker, who had been with me in the Household Battalion at Windsor, nearly two years earlier, and of whom I had lost sight since we went to France. (Soon after we were both demobbed he came to see me at my home, we corresponded two or three times afterwards, and have always exchanged greetings at Christmas, but did not again meet. Perhaps one day we shall—I hope so !).

The L.M.A.C. proved to be all that rumour had reported—a veritable soldiers' paradise, in fact, and unbelievably easy for the Army. The object of the Detachment was to provide men to meet Red Cross trains at one or other of the London termini and carry the stretcher-cases from the train to the waiting ambulances. For this purpose, the Detachment was divided into two sections, each of which was on duty on alternate days. The men in the duty-section had to remain in the billet to await the possibility of a train being signalled by day or by night, though if there was no expectation of a call by tea-time they were usually dismissed. On off-duty days we were free to follow our own devices after dinner until midnight. Most of the casualties arriving at that time, of course, were sick men from France and the Occupied Areas, but there were occasional train-loads of wounded from Archangel, where Mr. Winston Churchill's " war " was dragging its inglorious course. There were, however, an average of only about two or three trains a week, so we were not overworked. We were conveyed between the billet and the " scene of action " in motor-lorries and rather enjoyed the trips, even when called out in the middle of the night.

Of military formalities there were very few. Every fine morning the whole Detachment (including the section on duty, if they were not away stretcher-bearing) marched to Hyde Park for an hour's parade. The men from each of the five Guards regiments drilled as a separate platoon, and the officers in charge used to make it into a kind of inter-regimental competition for smartness, and roused a spirit of keen rivalry between the " Coldies," the " Bill Browns," the " Jocks," the " Micks " and the " Taffies," into which everyone entered heartily. Apart from this, there were no other parades, except for " Pay," which was even more popular ! The Detachment was commanded by an officer of the Welsh Guards, who was greatly liked by all ranks and was entirely lacking in " side " ; I remember I was impressed by his habit, when we marched "at ease" or travelled by lorry, of passing his cigarette-case to as many of us as he could reach—as I remarked at the time, " you wouldn't find many Guards officers who would do that ! " H.Q. was in another large house at the corner of Queens Gate Place, about a hundred yards from the billet, and there also we took our meals in an ornately-decorated ballroom; the food was the best I had yet encountered in the Army.

With ample leisure at my disposal, I managed to amuse myself pretty well when not on duty and to see a good deal of London. Gloucester-road Tube Station was just across the way, and I could get to any part of the Metropolis quickly and easily. At that time

I had a "craze" for theatre-going, and in one week saw six plays on successive nights. Before the war I had hardly even been inside a London theatre, and in consequence they held for me the fascination of a rare pleasure. But at that time most of the plays running in London were of very indifferent quality, mostly light romantic or sentimental comedies, and I think my "orgy" was largely a disillusionment. I dare say my room-mates thought me unsociable when I disappeared night after night alone, and I don't blame them; I was always something of a "lone wolf," with a preference for my own company.

"Short-week-end" leave was granted to anyone who wanted it once a fortnight, or—for anyone who lived a considerable distance from London—four days every month. And, what added to its value, owing to the regular alternation of "duty" it was possible to plan one's leave well in advance, without risk of disappointment. One had to provide for duty to be taken by someone else during one's leave, but there was never any difficulty in arranging a mutual exchange.

But the great and increasing preoccupation which absorbed my attention was the subject of demobilisation, compared with which the cushiest times in the Army were of no account. At long last, the hour of my return to "civvie life" really seemed to be near at hand, and the fluctuating chances of my early release kept me in a constant state of strained suspense. Early in September a new official order was published which appeared to cover my case, and it was reported from Wimbledon that all "volunteers" would be demobbed before the end of the month. (Although I had finally entered the Army as a conscript, by call-up under the Military Service Act in 1917, I officially ranked as a volunteer for demob. purposes by reason of my earlier rejections in 1914, 1915 and 1916.) Men were leaving the Battalion in drafts of about fifty at a time, and repeatedly I seemed to be on the point of getting my papers through, and as often some unforeseen obstacle cropped up. My letters home became more and more incoherent with excitement.

Then, towards the end of September, things seemed to be moving. On one of my many visits to the Battalion Demob. Office I was told that I would be sent for at once, and would probably hear on Saturday. However, Saturday came, but no news; Sunday and Monday also were silent. The Battalion was expecting to move to Warley, in Essex, and all sorts of alarming rumours were in circulation, stating that demobilisation was to be suspended and the Demob. Office closed until after the move. I was in a fever of impatience to get away before that happened. To my dismay, six men from the Detachment were sent for on Wednesday and my name was not among them! I was off to Wimbledon the same afternoon to know the reason. But, to my relief, it turned out to be due to a "clerical error"; the Corporal in charge, so he said, thought I had been summoned among the earlier batch last week, but by some mistake my name had been omitted ! He promised that the official order for me to report at the Camp would be posted to Kensington without fail that evening, so that it reached the Detachment Officer by the first post next morning. My papers were filled up on the spot and I was measured for a suit of civilian clothes.

In the meantime, I had taken on the post of Detachment Orderly-room Clerk, rendered vacant by the demobilisation of the previous holder, on the assurance that it would not delay my release. The job was an almost complete sinecure, and I held the position for exactly two days ! Next morning, in my official capacity, I opened the Detachment's mail, but to my chagrin the all-important paper was not there. I was once more in despair, and almost ready to descend upon the Wimbledon office with a Mills bomb ! However, about noon the Demob. Officer himself rang-up on the telephone, and I had the exquisite pleasure of taking down my own name and those of two other men, "to return to the Battalion forthwith for demobilisation."

Next morning early, I was away to Wimbledon with all my kit—but not to the "Chateau de Maubeuge"! I found that the authorities had "pulled a fast one" on me in my absence, and that the transfer to No. 1 Company, against which I had previously protested successfully, had been carried out. As I was leaving the Army for ever it was "san fairy ann" and I did not feel in the mood to make a fuss about it, but—I should have liked to have been demobbed from my old Company.

My papers were complete to the last line, and had been despatched to Brigade H.Q. for final signature ; they were expected back next day, and the fifty or sixty of us in that draft were to go to the Crystal Palace for final release at once, without waiting until after the Battalion's move to Warley, arranged for the same day.

. . . . .

But there's many a slip ——! That night, when another twelve hours should have seen me free, the great Railway Strike of 1919 started, and all demobilisation was stopped by order of the Government. That evening I and about sixteen other men had been sent to Wimbledon station, to unload some stores sent there in readiness for the Battalion's coming move, and when the Strike became imminent we were ordered to remain there all night on guard over the "dump." All the evening crowds of people beseiged the platforms and trains in a desperate effort to get home before the stoppage, and right up to midnight ("zero-hour") there were rumours of a settlement of the dispute. Even the railwaymen were not sure, or professed not to be, until the last moment, whether the Strike would take place or not. In ordinary times it would have been an occasion of pleasurable excitement to me, but in my personal circumstances I cannot say that I got all the enjoyment out of it that I might otherwise have done. At twelve o'clock all the men downed-tools and departed, the last stranded would-be travellers drifted gradually away, and the station was left empty, except for us. The rest of the night was spent in alternately tramping the now dark and silent platforms and in trying to sleep on the floor in one of the waiting-rooms. Next morning we helped to unload a milk-train manned by "volunteer" drivers, and afterwards reloaded the Battalion's stores into the lorries and returned to the Camp.

The Strike lasted until October 5th—only nine days, but to the fifty-three of us who were waiting demob. it seemed like nine months. I have probably never followed the progress of an indus-trial dispute so closely as I did on that occasion, but my interest was entirely self-centred and I cannot now remember anything about the pro's and con's of the struggle. Throughout those nine days there was an atmosphere of strained suspense and apprehension in the Camp; no-one knew what turn events would take. In the country generally, the life of the community was slowed down as com-munications were interrupted, and food-rationing—which had been abolished some months earlier—was re-introduced. The troops were kept in a state of permanent "stand-to," we slept partially dressed, with equipment by our beds ready to put on at a moment's notice ; by day, there was practise in street-fighting among the lines of huts, with Lewis-guns, bayonets and smoke-bombs. Not more than twenty-five per cent. of the Battalion was allowed to leave the Camp in the evenings, and then were forbidden to go further than two miles from the gate, so as to be ready for instant recall. The Authorities seem to have "got the jitters"—and, indeed, we our-selves began to be seriously perturbed and to wonder whether, at the very last moment of our military service, we were to be involved in civil war and revolution ! What would have happened if matters had gone to extremes is impossible to say. The Strikers had many sympathisers in the ranks, and to judge from the tone of the talk around it is probable that many of the men would question whether the terms of their enlistment "for war-service" were morally bind-ing in such a contingency. Fortunately, since the Strike was settled peacefully, the case did not arise. The news of the settlement was received in the Camp, especially by us who were waiting to get away, with almost as much enthusiasm as the Armistice itself !

Two days after the end of the Strike the Battalion's delayed move to Warley took place. We "demobilisables" had hoped to be released without having to join in the "trek," but our all-important final papers had not yet been received back from Brigade. We travelled by road on the morning of the 7th, in a fleet of lorries which took us through the heart of the City, past the Mansion House (where there was no Lord Mayor to take the salute this time !) and through the East End to Essex. We found the Barracks at Warley to be well-appointed and comfortable (as such places go), and likely to be a considerable improvement on the Camp at Wimbledon now that winter was approaching, but the surrounding country seemed to be rather dull and flat, and miles from anywhere of interest ; I felt very glad that I was not stopping there for long.

However, I had little time in which to see much, for on the day following our arrival the long-awaited papers turned up. In the evening I handed in my rifle and equipment at the Quartermaster's Store ; I was entitled to keep my "tin hat," as a free gift and souvenir from the Government, but I was so eager to have done with "all that," that I unhesitatingly turned it in as well. I had already sent home by post almost all my personal possessions— including, I must confess, sundry pairs of "scrounged" socks, a webbing belt and a new pair of ammunition boots "sold" to me by the Sergeant-"Snob"! We were all inspected by the M.O., and required to sign a statement that we left the Army in good health and would make no claim on the military authorities in respect of any subsequent disability—a piece of "sharp practice" which we would have been wise to refuse, but which I do not think anyone objected to in the circumstances: we were afraid to risk anything which might delay our release at the last moment. My last evening in the Army was not marked, so far as I can remember, by any special celebration, but I was too excited to sleep much that night.

Next morning, Thursday, October 9th, I gave my buttons and cap-star an extra last polish and said goodbye to my comrades in the barrack-room, with many fervent hand-shakes and promises of remembrance. Then, in response to a shout of "Fall in, the demob. men!," I paraded for the last time on the Barrack-square, with the rest of the draft. I suppose this was the moment, as we were called to attention and the final roll was called, when all the events of the past two years should have flashed through my memory and I ought to have been sentimentally conscious that an important chapter in my life was closing—a chapter to which I should afterwards look back, if not with pleasure, at least with a certain degree of pride—but, in truth, all I remember thinking at the time was "Thank God, that's all over at last!"

We marched to the station, and were taken first to Wellington Barracks. Then, after a short interval, we went on to the Crystal Palace, the final dispersal station, though by what means we got there I have no recollection. My mind during those last few hours was a whirl of suppressed excitement, and very little of what happened at "the Palace" has registered in my memory. But there were only a few last formalities to go through, like the completion of forms relating to Unemployment Insurance and receiving my "Protection Certificate"—an identity document which granted me "twenty-eight days' furlough," after which time I was not entitled to wear military uniform (not that I wanted to !) and would protect me from possible arrest as a deserter. Incidentally, on my "Certificate" the words "Discharge," "Disembodiment" and "Demobilisation" are carefully scored through, and I am shown as being "Transferred to the Reserve"; the "Place of Rejoining in case of

Emergency '' is named as Windsor. As this document has never been officially cancelled, I presume that I am still liable to be recalled to the Colours—but that possibility doesn't worry me !

At the very last—a final '' kick in the pants '' from officialdom —we were each subjected to a very strict search, to make sure that we were not absconding with any Government property other than the uniform we were wearing. It was an ungracious '' farewell '' and a gratuitous insult, I thought, and gave me the feeling that I was a convict being released from prison, rather than a man honourably discharged from His Majesty's Forces after having served my Country !

But that, after all, mattered little, for when I walked out through the gates of '' the Palace,'' conscious that my Army life was at last behind me and that I was at liberty to go where I liked and do what I would, I had thought for nothing but the incredible realisation that once more, and forever, I was FREE !